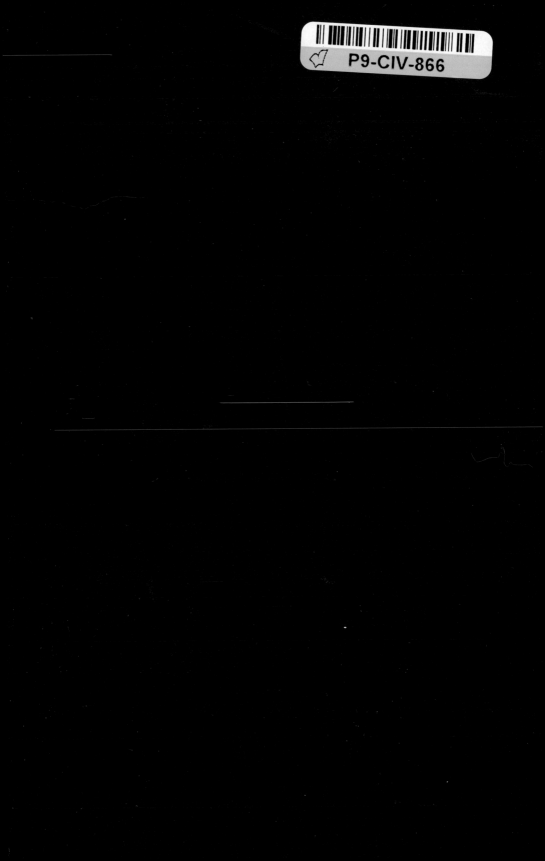

PUNISHMENT WITHOUT TRIAL

PUNISHMENT WITHOUT TRIAL

WHY PLEA BARGAINING IS A **BAD DEAL**

CARISSA BYRNE HESSICK

ABRAMS PRESS, NEW YORK

Library of Congress Control Number: 2021934852

ISBN: 978-1-4197-5029-8
eISBN: 978-1-64700-103-2

Printed and bound in the United States
10 9 8 7 6 5 4 3 2 1

Abrams books are available at special discounts when purchased in quantity for premiums and promotions as well as fundraising or educational use. Special editions can also be created to specification. For details, contact specialsales@abramsbooks. com or the address below.

Abrams Press® is a registered trademark of Harry N. Abrams, Inc.

ABRAMS The Art of Books
195 Broadway, New York, NY 10007
abramsbooks.com

*To Hattie and Dorothy, who have taught me the value
of explaining complicated things in a simple way.
And to Andy, who always does more than his fair share.*

CONTENTS

CHAPTER ONE

DAMIAN'S STORY

When Damian Mills got a call from his cousin telling him that the police were looking for him, he was anxious. Damian knew that the police suspected him of committing some other crimes, but his cousin told him that the police wanted to talk to him about a murder. Damian wasn't always on the right side of the law, but he didn't know anything about a homicide.

When the police caught up to Damian, they accused him of being involved in the murder of a man named Walter Bowman. Walter was at his son Shaun's house on the evening of September 18, 2000, when three men wearing bandanas and gloves burst in. The men shouted for everyone to get down. Walter, who was in the bedroom, was shot when one of the men fired a shotgun through the bedroom door. The masked men fled right after the shooting.

Sitting in an interrogation room weeks after the murder, Damian could see photos and other evidence from the crime scene that the police had hung on the walls. But he knew that he hadn't killed Walter Bowman. He had not been at Shaun Bowman's house, and he had not been involved in the shooting.

Some of the other people who supposedly committed the murder with Damian confessed. The police told Damian to confess too. The police told Damian various details about the murder. And they instructed Damian to tell them that other people in the group had done certain things the night of the shooting. Damian told the police that he couldn't tell them any of those things because they weren't true.

The police arrested him anyway and sent him to jail. They kept Damian in an isolation unit, which separated him from everyone else at the jail, and he was allowed out of his cell for only one hour each day.

After spending two days in isolation, Damian was again interrogated by the police. They questioned him without a lawyer present, and they pressured him to say that he and his friends had been involved in Walter Bowman's murder. Damian knew that he'd had nothing to do with the murder, but he was worried that the police were going to say he had pulled the trigger and killed Bowman. He was also overwhelmed from his time in isolation. So he confessed.

Damian couldn't afford a lawyer, and so the court appointed one for him. The lawyer told Damian that he had lost three cases just like his at trial, and so he recommended that Damian plead guilty.

Damian took his lawyer's advice. He went to court. He told the judge that he wanted to enter an Alford plea, a special type of guilty plea that allows a defendant to be convicted without admitting that he'd actually committed the crime. But the judge wouldn't let him. So Damian said he helped kill Walter Bowman and pleaded guilty to a murder he didn't commit. He served more than ten years in prison.

* * * * *

When I met Damian in his hometown in western North Carolina, I never would have guessed that he had been in prison. I was late to our meeting, and so I was a bit flustered. I apologized and explained that I was late because I had been dealing with my two strong-willed daughters. Damian was very kind. He had a daughter the same age as my oldest, and he was quick to relate. He smiled and laughed a bit as he told me about his daughter.

I could have had a similar conversation with any number of parents at my daughters' school. Damian even looked like a few of the fathers I'd met at school events. He wore glasses and a black T-shirt. Damian's voice was soft and tinged with the Southern accent that I've learned to love since moving to North Carolina a few years ago. And his face communicated that same mix of adoration and frustration that I see on other parents' faces when we talk about our kids.

But Damian's face soon lost that look as our conversation turned to his case. Any trace of a smile disappeared, and his answers became shorter and more halting as he spoke about pleading guilty to the murder of Walter Bowman.

After Walter Bowman was shot, police received tips about two different groups of people who supposedly committed the murder. The first group included a man whom police mistakenly thought was in jail, so they discounted that tip and focused on the second group. The tip about the second group didn't mention Damian, but it included people that he knew. When the police interviewed the people in the second group, they all denied any involvement in the death of Walter Bowman.

One of those people, Larry Williams, was only sixteen years old. Police interviewed him twice, and he denied any involvement in the shooting. When police interviewed Larry a third time, he again denied having anything to do with Walter Bowman's death. Then the Buncombe County sheriff, Bobby Medford, showed up. Everyone except Sheriff Medford left the interrogation room, and then Medford proceeded to scream at Larry—who didn't have a lawyer or an adult with him in the room—telling him that he would spend the rest of his life in prison if he didn't confess to the murder and implicate others. Sheriff Medford then got Larry to agree that he was involved in the murder. The sheriff used a series of leading questions to feed Larry details about the murder, including that Damian was involved.

Right after his confession, Larry told other police officers that he'd lied: everything he'd said about the murder was just because Sheriff Medford had terrified him. But by then it was too late. Police had one false confession, and they used that confession to get false statements from eyewitnesses and confessions from the other men in the group.

But the truth was that the other group of men about which police had gotten a tip—the group that the police did not focus on—had committed the murder.

If the police had not mistakenly believed that one of those men was in jail when Walter Bowman was killed, then they might have solved the case. They had collected physical evidence that would have proven this other group of men had committed the crime. Police had obtained video surveillance footage of the men leaving a nearby gas station just minutes before the shooting. But whether through incompetence or malevolence, between the time when police got the tape from the gas station and the time they officially logged it into the police evidence room, someone taped a soap opera over the portion of the videotape that actually showed the men at the gas station.

Police also recovered bandanas and gloves by the side of the road right near the crime scene. The bandanas and gloves had been discovered by a postal worker the morning after the murder. Police had the clothing tested for DNA, but they tested only to see whether the DNA matched Damian or the other people that they suspected in the murder. The results came back negative. Years later, when police finally tested the bandana and gloves to see whether they matched the men in the other group, the test results came back positive.

One of the men from the other group even confessed to Walter Bowman's murder in 2003. He told an FBI agent about the crime in an attempt to get his sentence in a federal drug case reduced.

No one told Damian or his lawyer about the confession even though he was sitting in jail for that crime. They didn't tell him about the negative DNA results, either, even though police and prosecutors knew about those negative results before Damian and his friends formally pleaded guilty.

Only after his release in 2010 was Damian able to use this other evidence to prove his innocence. In 2015 a judge declared that Damian and all of his codefendants were innocent of the murder of Walter Bowman. The judge vacated their convictions and dismissed all of the charges against them.

Damian's story is not unique. There are countless others who have pleaded guilty to crimes that they have not committed.

In Massachusetts, thousands of drug convictions were thrown into doubt when Annie Dookhan, a chemist with the Massachusetts state drug lab, admitted that she had contaminated samples and faked test results. Innocent people pleaded guilty when they were faced with false test results saying that they had possessed drugs. Only after years of court battles did people get their convictions reversed, but many served time in jail and prison before that happened. Massachusetts is not the only place with a crime lab scandal: San Francisco, Houston, Oklahoma City, and St. Paul all had serious scandals too. Those scandals also revealed that false test results had led innocent people to plead guilty.

False drug tests aren't just the result of a few bad apples in state labs. In-depth reporting from ProPublica has shown that drug field tests are incredibly unreliable. Police departments across the country use these tests so that officers can quickly determine whether to arrest someone for possessing drugs. For example, one test turns blue if the material being tested is cocaine. But it also turns blue for more than eighty other substances, including some acne medications and common household cleaning materials.

In addition to the unreliable nature of these kits, police departments often fail to train their officers to use them correctly, and so officers end up incorrectly interpreting the results and arresting people. Desperate to get out of jail and terrified of the mandatory minimum penalties for many drug crimes, some of those innocent people plead guilty.

* * * * *

Damian's story—as well as the stories of innocent people in Massachusetts and elsewhere—raise an extremely important question: Why does our system pressure innocent people to plead guilty?

The answer is simple: innocent people are pressured into pleading guilty because *everyone* is pressured into pleading guilty. Ours is a system of pressure and pleas, not truth and trials.

Trials are supposed to tell us whether a person that police suspect of committing a crime actually did something wrong. Only if a jury believes law enforcement and convicts the defendant is a person supposed to be punished. But we have gotten rid of trials and replaced them with a system that hands out punishment based only on what police and prosecutors suspect. Maybe that seems like a good idea for the people who actually did commit a crime. But it's obviously a disaster for the people who did nothing wrong.

Innocent people plead guilty because anyone who goes to trial and is convicted will get a much longer punishment than someone who pleads guilty. When there is evidence that suggests an innocent person is guilty—like the false confessions about Damian or the incorrect drug tests in Massachusetts—the risk of being convicted after trial can't be ignored.

The difference in punishment for those who plead guilty is by design. Those longer punishments after trial exist so that people will feel pressure to plead guilty.

The possibility of more punishment isn't the only pressure people feel. Our system of pretrial detention places a lot of pressure on people to plead guilty too. For those people who are accused of low-level crimes, agreeing to plead guilty can mean walking out of jail that same day rather than sitting in jail for weeks, if not months, waiting for their trial to take place. Even if a jury eventually acquits them, they don't get that time in jail back. We've managed to punish them *before* we convict them, so they might as well make that punishment as short as possible.

Keeping people in jail before trial isn't the only way that we punish people before we convict them. We also let police officers take their money and property based just on the suspicion that the money is profit from a crime or the property was used to commit a crime. We also let court systems charge people fees for staying in jail, posting bail, or even empaneling a jury. When those fees are due before conviction, then they punish both the guilty and the innocent. And when they apply only after conviction, then they are another way to pressure people into pleading guilty.

Even the court process itself can feel like punishment. People have to sit in dingy courtrooms for hours, waiting for their cases to be called. They have to miss work and lose wages to appear in front of a judge. Most often those appearances are just going to result in yet another court date being set, which will require another trip to the courthouse and another day off from work. The process wears people down, making them willing to accept a plea bargain just to avoid more and more trips to the courthouse, where nothing happens.

Our system of pressure and pleas doesn't just lead to the punishment of innocent people. It also damages the very foundation of our criminal justice system. Instead of providing a process that is supposed to sort out the truth of what happened, our system just lets lawyers negotiate an outcome. Lawyers negotiate about what the defendants' sentences will be, and they sometimes negotiate about what crimes the defendants will admit to committing. The specific crimes the lawyers pick may have nothing to do with what the police think the defendants actually did; it's just what the lawyers were able to agree on, usually because it has a punishment that both sides find acceptable.

By abandoning trials and embracing negotiation as the process for our criminal justice system, we have given up on the search for truth itself. As a result, we can't rely on a defendant's conviction to tell us what actually happened: the defendant may have committed a much more serious crime, or he may have committed no crime at all.

It is hard to overstate the extent to which the modern system has circumvented most every constitutional and political protection against punishment. Whether a person faces time in jail or loses property is, in many instances, dictated by hastily made decisions by police or prosecutors. Plea bargaining ensures that those hasty decisions remain hidden from view and are never subject to judicial review or public scrutiny. What is worse, the current system creates a feedback loop that all but guarantees that the problems with the current system will only get worse.

In recent years the conversation in this country has moved toward the idea of criminal justice reform, but very slowly. Congress and some state legislatures have modestly decreased sentences. A few states have decriminalized marijuana possession. And some cities have elected prosecutors that ran on progressive platforms of change.

But these modest reforms and reformers are unlikely to make much of a difference unless we address the dysfunction at the core of our criminal justice system. Our system is now designed to impose punishment without trial—and that is a fundamental change to the very foundations of the criminal justice system. Minor sentencing reforms and a handful of new prosecutors can't undo those structural changes; they are like Band-Aids on the gaping wound that is mass incarceration. More important, those small changes can be undone at any time: Even when they talk about criminal justice reform, lawmakers continue to increase sentences, and a progressive prosecutor could be voted out of office if the political winds change.

Only when we realize that the entire premise of the criminal justice system has been undermined can we start to focus on reforms that could have a real and lasting impact. We need more than slightly less harsh laws and prosecutors who take a less punitive approach to their jobs. We need to make it more difficult for the government to punish people without trials.

* * * * *

This is a book about the criminal justice system. But there is no single "system" of criminal justice in our country. Each state has its own criminal laws, as does the federal government. Within the states, counties elect their own local prosecutors and sheriffs, while mayors and city councils appoint police chiefs. Each courthouse and sometimes each courtroom has its own practices and procedures too.

Despite all of these different rules and cultures, I still use the words "criminal justice system" in this book because the book is about something that all of these people and places have in common. All of them have, to varying degrees, chosen a certain approach to criminal justice. Specifically, they have all chosen efficiency as an overriding goal.

Efficiency may look different in your state or in your town than it does in the stories you will read in this book. But that doesn't mean this book isn't about where you live. Efficiency looks different in different places, but it has displaced truth everywhere. Efficiency has warped the criminal process so that it no longer looks like something that an ordinary American would recognize as the system we learned about in school—a system in which you are innocent until proven guilty beyond a reasonable doubt.

But at the end of the day, this isn't just a book about abstract ideas like truth and efficiency. It's also a book about people. The lawyers, judges, defendants, and victims and how the prioritization of efficiency and the rejection of truth has affected them. These people live in different cities and states across the country. But all of their stories are about the same problem.

If you are a lawyer, you may not agree with everything you read in this book. Criminal justice looks different in different places and in different cases and when it involves different people. As a result, the stories that I tell may be different from the stories that you would tell about plea bargaining. But even if your stories are different, you will recognize the truth behind all of the stories—the truth that we live in a system that not only succeeds in punishing people without trial but also is designed to do precisely that.

Some people will want to defend the practices that I talk about in this book. Some people who work in the criminal justice system think that these practices are good—or as good as they can be, given the resources and the laws that we have. They may be right. Maybe we can't do better than what we have now.

But I don't think so. I think we can change the system so long as we are willing to reject the idea that our system is supposed to be built on pressure and pleas rather than truth and trials.

As you read these pages, I hope that you will keep an open mind about the stories that I tell. Don't just dismiss the emphasis on efficiency and the neglect of justice as "the way things are" but instead ask yourself if this is the way things *should be.* Can we defend a system that chooses speed over truth? A system that is so hidden from view that we often don't have all of the information about how it works, let alone the ability to assess whether it works well?

* * * * *

"You cannot write a book about criminal justice in American that isn't about race. Certainly you can't write a book that talks about criminal justice in cities that *doesn't* talk about race." This was the advice that I got from Sarah Staudt, a senior policy analyst and staff attorney for Chicago Appleseed Center for Fair Courts, a nonpartisan research and advocacy organization that seeks to study and reform the legal system.

Sarah is right. The people who spoke to me for this book invariably talked about the fact that so many of the people who get swept up in our criminal justice system are Black or Brown. They are often—though not always—prosecuted by attorneys who are White and sentenced by judges who are White. The laws that they are punished for breaking have been written by people who are overwhelmingly White.

The impression that this creates is one of racial oppression. And anyone who cares about racial equality in this country should be disturbed by the mountain of studies that show how Black and Brown Americans are disproportionately affected by the criminal justice system.

So, because this is a book about the criminal justice system, it is inevitably a book about race. Damian Mills is a Black man. He was swept into the system by a White sheriff and sent to prison by a White district attorney.

Even though race plays an undeniable role in the criminal justice system, the deep structural problems of the current system cut across race and class lines. The ability to punish without trial is a key feature not only of prosecutions involving poor people of color but also of cases involving white-collar professionals accused of corporate wrongdoing. Given that powerful individuals are at risk and that wealthy defendants have sometimes been pressured into pleading guilty, one might think that they would have the clout to change the plea bargaining system. Instead, they have largely tried to change the laws that regulate their businesses, ignoring the structure of the system.

It is far from obvious why we have allowed the current system to proceed unchecked. Jury trials should appeal to liberals and conservatives. Liberals should like them because they help protect poor and disenfranchised groups. Jurors in the Bronx, for example, have developed a national reputation for refusing to convict defendants, even in the face of overwhelming evidence. For their part, conservatives should like juries because they act as a check on government power and thus protect liberty. Indeed, conservative Supreme Court justice Antonin Scalia voted to invalidate federal and state laws that encroached on the power of the jury, writing powerful opinions about how the jury is the "circuitbreaker" of democracy "in the State's machinery of justice."

But instead of liberals and conservatives working together to restore the jury, both groups have reinforced the structure of the current system. They have focused on those cases where they want to ensure convictions. For liberals, those cases include sexual assault cases and white-collar offenses. For conservatives, those cases include drug cases and other street crimes. In focusing on cases where they want convictions, both sides have painted jury trials as a hurdle to overcome rather than the foundation of our criminal justice system. And while Justice Scalia was willing to use a robust version of the jury trial right to strike down certain criminal laws that gave power to judges, he accepted plea bargaining "as a necessary evil" because "without it our long and expensive process of criminal trial could not sustain the burden imposed on it, and our system of criminal justice would grind to a halt."

* * * * *

When I was a kid, my teachers taught me that, in America, you are innocent until proven guilty. That's what's fair, and it's what we should expect from a country that calls itself "the land of the free and the home of the brave."

But that's not what we have in this country. As the next two hundred or so pages will explain, we have a system that is designed to punish people without trial. It forces innocent men and women to say they've committed crimes. And it deprives everyone of their constitutional right to a jury of their peers.

As you read the stories of the men and women swept up in the criminal justice system, remember that all of this is being done in your name. And so you have the power to insist that things change.

CHAPTER TWO

THE RISE OF PLEA BARGAINING

John Peter Zenger was born in Germany. He immigrated to the colony of New York with his family in 1710, while he was still a boy. After his father died, John served as an apprentice to William Bradford, the first printer in New York. Eventually, after he grew up, John opened up his own printshop on Smith Street in Manhattan.

One of the items John printed was a newspaper called the *New-York Weekly Journal*. The *Journal* was the colony's first independent newspaper, and it often criticized the royal governor, William Cosby. Cosby had a reputation for corruption and removing officials who didn't give him his way. The *New-York Weekly Journal* reported on these stories, accusing Cosby of tyranny and violating the colonists' rights. That criticism often took the form of satire and lampoons; basically, the paper made fun of Cosby.

As you might imagine, this criticism made Governor Cosby angry. So he decided to shut down the *Journal* by arresting John. Apparently, Cosby thought that if John was in jail, then the *Journal* couldn't get published. John was one of the few skilled printers in New York at the time, and the other printers would probably have been too scared by John's arrest to agree to begin publishing the *Journal*.

In 1734, John was arrested and charged with seditious libel—a crime that basically forbade saying things that criticized or provoked dissatisfaction with the king, the government, or other public officials. Because there was no real dispute that John had published the *Journal* and that the *Journal* had criticized Governor Cosby, it looked like John was going to be convicted.

But John's lawyer—a famous attorney named Andrew Hamilton (no relation to Alexander)—convinced the jury that they should acquit John. Hamilton didn't dispute that John had published the newspaper. Instead, he told the jury that they should consider whether the statements in the newspaper were true. Hamilton concluded his argument to the jury—a jury made up of other New York colonists, at least some of whom probably disapproved of Governor Cosby's actions—by saying that the case wasn't just about "one poor printer." It was a case that "may in its consequence affect every free man that lives under a British government on the main of America. It is the best cause. It is the cause of liberty." After a brief deliberation, the jury returned a verdict of not guilty.

Students of American history may know the John Peter Zenger case as a key moment in First Amendment history. People often point to the Zenger case as convincing the public about the necessity of a free press.

But the Zenger case is also a famous example of colonial juries refusing to enforce unfair laws. In the decades before the American Revolution, colonial juries routinely refused to convict their peers of violating unfair laws, like the Stamp Act. The British government responded by allowing these cases to be tried by judges without any juries.

These unfair laws led the colonies to demand their independence. One of the specific complaints against King George III in the Declaration of Independence was that he deprived the colonists of trial by jury. More generally, the colonists rebelled against England because they thought the English government made it too easy to restrict their liberty, take their property, and throw them in jail.

After winning their independence, Americans formed their own government and wrote a constitution. A big portion of that constitution is devoted to protecting the rights of people accused of crimes. The U.S. Constitution protects against abusive police investigations, prohibits cruel and unusual punishments, and sets out a number of protections and procedures for criminal trials. The protections and procedures include the right to a lawyer, the right to be notified of the charges against you, the right to have witnesses testify in your favor, the right to confront the witnesses against you, the right to refuse to incriminate yourself, and the right to a speedy and public trial by a jury.

These procedures and protections are designed to protect innocent people. That is why, as a general matter, they make it difficult for the government to punish people. It would be much easier to convict people if we didn't let them have a lawyer or didn't let them call witnesses who would testify to the defendants' innocence. Some of these protections—especially the right not to incriminate yourself—might also benefit guilty people. But the people who wrote the Constitution were more concerned about protecting the innocent than convicting the guilty. Their commitment to this principle was embodied by one of the most famous legal sayings of all time: "It is better that ten guilty persons escape than that one innocent suffer."

Of all these protections, the jury trial is arguably the most important. It was a major hurdle that the government had to clear before convicting anyone. Trials require the government to present witnesses and other evidence supporting a defendant's guilt, which in some cases can take a lot of time and effort. In addition, the government has to persuade ordinary citizens—the defendant's "peers"—that the defendant did something wrong and should be punished. If those other citizens aren't convinced, then the defendant goes free.

Because the jury trial is so important, it actually shows up twice in the Constitution. The original text of the Constitution says "The Trial of all Crimes, except in Cases of Impeachment, shall be by Jury . . ." The right to a jury trial was also included in the Bill of Rights—the first ten amendments that were adopted just a couple of years after the Constitution first took effect. The Sixth Amendment says, "In all criminal prosecutions, the accused shall enjoy the right to a speedy and public trial, by an impartial jury . . ." All of the state constitutions also protect the right to a jury trial in criminal cases.

But while the people who created this country wanted to make it difficult to punish people, the people in charge today want the opposite. They want to make it easy to punish people. They don't want to have to give someone a trial or all of those other rights before putting them in jail.

And they have succeeded. It is relatively easy to punish people in modern America. As a result, our prisons are overflowing. Even innocent people end up in jail.

How did this happen? How did the states and the federal government make it so easy to punish people?

The simple answer is that governments have circumvented many of the constitutional hurdles that were supposed to make punishment difficult.

They did this by creating a system that can impose punishment without ever holding a trial. The centerpiece of that system is plea bargaining. As the Supreme Court said a few years ago, "Criminal justice today is for the most part a system of pleas, not a system of trials."

How, exactly, that system was created and why it continues today is a complicated story.

* * * * *

American colonists thought the British efforts to deprive the colonists of their right to jury trials was part of a conspiracy to deprive the colonists of their liberty. The Revolutionary War was fought, in large part, as a resistance to this conspiracy. But even in the earliest years of our country, people were sometimes convicted without trials. Specifically, some defendants would enter a plea of guilty, admitting to the judge that they had broken the law and waiving their right to a trial. Historians have found evidence of guilty pleas dating back at least to the late sixteenth century. But the historical evidence suggests that guilty pleas were relatively rare; most defendants pleaded not guilty and went to trial. Indeed, there are historical records showing that, when some defendants tried to plead guilty, trial judges would resist accepting the plea and encourage the defendant to go to trial.

If you think about it, it makes sense that at least some guilty defendants would have no interest in exercising their right to a trial. Trials exist so that we can figure out whether something happened. If a defendant knows that he committed a crime, and if he knows the evidence against him is overwhelming, then he may not want to have a trial. The trial is not going to help him, and he will have to sit and listen to witnesses talking about something embarrassing or shameful that he did. He might simply want to acknowledge that he did something wrong and then accept whatever punishment is coming. In fact, he might hope to regain some dignity or respect from his neighbors by acknowledging that he did something wrong; after all, we tend to think more highly of those people who take responsibility for their actions than those who try to avoid consequences.

Even though some places had a lot of guilty pleas, punishment in early America was still largely meted out by a system of criminal trials. One study of New York City criminal cases found that only 15 percent of people convicted of felonies pleaded guilty in 1839. Even in Boston, which some say was an early adopter of plea bargaining, only 35 percent of convictions were the result of guilty pleas at that time.

It was because trials were such an important part of early American society that some judges were hesitant to accept guilty pleas. If a defendant appeared in front of a judge and entered a plea of guilty, the judge would try to talk him out of it. Judges would refuse to accept guilty pleas until defendants had time to reconsider, and judges would sometimes appoint lawyers to advise defendants or make sure that the defendants weren't suffering from mental illness. Judges would also make sure that the defendants were independently making the decision to plead guilty—asking the defendants and even prison officials questions to make sure that no promises or threats had been made.

Eventually—it isn't quite clear when—judges started treating defendants who pleaded guilty better than defendants who went to trial. Treating defendants differently wasn't possible when judges had no choice about what sentences to impose. But even before judges gained the power to tailor punishment to individual defendants, they had some limited ability to recommend mercy.

As judges gained the power to give different sentences to different defendants, it appears that some judges were swayed by the idea that taking responsibility for your illegal actions is good. Defendants who took responsibility for their crimes and appealed to the mercy of the court could hope for a lighter punishment, and they sometimes got it. Once it became common for judges to treat those defendants who pleaded guilty more leniently, then defendants had to consider whether to give up the chance of a lighter sentence by deciding to go to trial. Some defendants who might have otherwise preferred a trial may have pleaded guilty in the hope of more lenient sentences. But because those defendants weren't actually being promised something in return for their guilty pleas, it was hard for defendants to make a strategic decision about pleading guilty: they didn't know in advance whether the judges would show mercy or how merciful they would be.

As this began to occur, guilty pleas became more common. And as they became more common, some evidence can be found that defendants weren't just independently choosing to waive their right to a jury trial by pleading guilty. Instead, the government—mostly prosecutors but also sometimes judges—began to actively incentivize or pressure defendants into giving up the right to a trial. Once a prosecutor explicitly agrees to give something up in return for a defendant pleading guilty, then we have a plea bargain. And when judges pressure defendants into pleading guilty by threatening to impose longer sentences on those who insist on their right to a jury, then we have something quite similar to plea bargaining called a "trial penalty."

The history of this shift from guilty pleas to plea bargains and trial penalties is murky. Because plea bargaining was frowned upon, it mostly occurred in secret. But scholars have identified some early examples of explicit plea bargains. For example, in his book *Plea Bargaining's Triumph: A History of Plea Bargaining in America*, Professor George Fisher describes two early explicit plea bargains that he discovered in his search of court records in Massachusetts. Both cases involved prosecutions for unlicensed liquor sales during the early 1800s. Each of those cases involved four distinct criminal charges; the prosecutor agreed to drop three of the charges in return for no contest pleas on the remaining charge. (A no contest plea is a way for a defendant to plead guilty without having to admit that he is, in fact, guilty.)

These sorts of plea bargains—in which prosecutors agree to drop some charges or accept a plea to a lesser crime—are quite common today. But in the early 1800s they were not widely accepted. When one Massachusetts prosecutor, Asahel Huntington, began routinely dismissing liquor charges as part of plea bargains in the 1830s, he found himself hauled before the state legislature to explain himself. One of the lawmakers accused Huntington of "malpractice," because every time he dismissed a charge in a plea bargain, the state received smaller fines as punishment than if the defendant had been convicted on all charges. Huntington defended his practices to the legislature, saying his plea bargains were justified by his heavy caseload and insisting that plea bargaining actually served the "public interest." Huntington's explanation won over the state lawmakers, who praised his hard work and ingenuity. They concluded that plea bargaining in liquor cases was the best method to "attain the just end of all punishment"—namely, preventing crime and reforming defendants. Subsequent prosecutors took the legislature at its word and plea bargained even more cases than Huntington.

Appellate judges were also hostile to plea bargaining when they first learned of it. In the decades following the Civil War, many state courts refused to uphold guilty pleas when the defendants had pleaded guilty because of pressure from prosecutors or trial judges. For example, in 1879 the supreme court of Michigan reversed a defendant's conviction because the trial judge had told the defendant that he would receive "a severe sentence" if he did not plead guilty. The Michigan court called this behavior by the trial judge a "great impropriety," adding that that "no sort of pressure can be permitted to bring the party to forego any right or advantage however slight."

Early U.S. Supreme Court cases suggest that the justices were hostile to plea bargaining as well. An 1878 case, for example, involved an agreement between prosecutors and defendants in which the defendants agreed to plead guilty and testify against others in exchange for the government dismissing other charges and agreeing not to seize their property. When the government later tried to seize the defendants' property, the defendants sued on the grounds that the seizure was forbidden by the plea agreements with the prosecutors. But the Supreme Court said that federal prosecutors had no authority to enter into that agreement with the defendants, and so the seizure could go forward.

Despite resistance in the appeals courts, plea bargaining increased. Once lawyers and trial court judges realized that they could dispose of their cases quickly, without trials, the practice became popular. In New York, for example, guilty plea rates increased steadily during the mid- and late nineteenth century. Similarly, Professor Fisher's study of Massachusetts courts found that plea bargaining increased significantly beginning in the 1870s.

These plea bargains occurred largely in secret. Prosecutors and defense attorneys did not usually publicize their agreements—presumably because of the negative reactions that plea bargaining had received. Nonetheless, evidence of plea bargaining can be found in the large number of cases where the defendant pleaded guilty, but only to less serious crime than what was originally charged. One or two such cases might be shrugged off as instances in which the prosecutor made a mistake in his initial charging decision. But as the number of those cases grew significantly, it is fair to assume at least some of those guilty pleas were the result of under-the-table bargaining between prosecutors and defense attorneys.

* * * * *

Although it became routine, plea bargaining was largely unknown outside of the criminal courthouse. People knew that defendants pleaded guilty, but they did not know about the bargains that were being struck with prosecutors. While it was generally accepted that defendants were free to plead guilty, many thought that the Constitution did not allow prosecutors to incentivize (or to pressure) defendants to give up their right to trial. And when rumors of the practice reached the public, it was condemned as corrupt. But despite the fact that it was arguably illegal and clearly disfavored, plea bargains continued to occur. And when bar associations and academics set out to study the criminal courts in the 1920s, they were surprised and shocked to discover that plea bargaining wasn't just a one-off occurrence: it was pervasive.

Professor William Ortman has documented the "discovery" of plea bargaining in the first half of the twentieth century. As he explains, plea bargaining's discovery was a result of the crime commission movement of the early twentieth century—a series of criminal justice surveys conducted in the 1920s and 1930s by public bodies, universities, and private civic associations in different cities and states. Those surveys found extensive plea bargaining in the criminal courts.

The first of those surveys, "Criminal Justice in Cleveland," was prompted by two issues: rising crime in the city and the dramatic acquittal of a local judge for murder based on perjured testimony. These events convinced a local philanthropic foundation to fund a study of the Cleveland criminal courts. The study was led to two very prominent men: Roscoe Pound, who was the dean of Harvard Law School, and Felix Frankfurter, who was also on the faculty at Harvard and who would later go on to serve as a justice on the U.S. Supreme Court.

"Criminal Justice in Cleveland" was quite critical of what it found—namely, that most felony cases did not result in defendants receiving sentences of jail or prison. Some of the cases were rejected by grand juries or by judges who conducted preliminary hearings. Prosecutors also dismissed some cases, and some cases resulted in acquittals after trial. But even those defendants who were convicted often received only suspended sentences—a sort of informal probation. The Cleveland report authors expressed deep concern over these findings. "With all these avenues of escape open," the report said, "it is not surprising that Cleveland has had extreme difficulty in punishing its criminals or in restraining crime by swift and certain justice."

In their statistical analysis of criminal cases, the Cleveland report authors found a large number of guilty pleas. Of those defendants who changed their original pleas from guilty to not guilty, 26 percent pleaded guilty to less serious crimes. The Cleveland report did not thoroughly investigate the reason for these sorts of guilty pleas, but later crime commissions did. Reports from studies in Missouri, Illinois, New York, Georgia, and elsewhere not only found a very large number of guilty pleas; they also discovered that those guilty pleas were the result of compromises between prosecutors and defendants. Sometimes those compromises resulted in the defendants pleading guilty to lesser crimes; other times the pleas were to the original charges, but the defendants would receive either suspended sentences or sentences of probation.

Once they had identified plea bargaining, the commissions were quick to condemn it. Some called plea bargaining corrupt, pointing to the political connections of defendants or defense attorneys who got lenient deals. Others criticized prosecutors for using plea bargaining to inflate their conviction statistics to help them during reelection. But the most pervasive criticism echoed the criticism from the Cleveland report: that defendants were not being held responsible for their crimes and they were getting less punishment than they deserved. The study authors thought that it was entirely inappropriate for defendants to escape the serious punishment that the law imposed for their crimes. Allowing defendants to escape the serious punishment and instead receive lesser convictions or lesser sentences, according to the commissions, caused distrust and disrespect for the law.

The president of the Chicago Crime Commission was so outraged that he demanded the immediate removal of three judges from the bench. He believed the judges should be removed because they had allowed defendants to plead guilty in exchange for a reduction of felony charges to misdemeanors. The trial judges were allowed to keep their jobs only after a committee of appellate judges conducted an inquiry and concluded that prosecutors rather than the judges were responsible for the plea bargains.

The New York commission complained that plea bargaining resulted in the legislature's laws having "no binding force." It pointed to the state's repeat offender law, which carried a mandatory life sentence for people convicted of a fourth felony. Of defendants who were initially charged under this law and eventually convicted, one half of them were allowed to plead guilty to a lesser crime and escape the life sentence.

So when people outside of the criminal courts found out that plea bargaining was happening, the dominant reaction was to condemn it as either bad policy or flat-out illegal. But, remarkably, plea bargaining not only didn't stop; it got worse. Guilty pleas and plea bargaining continued to increase. And eventually those within the legal community began to accept it.

* * * * *

It's hard to say why, exactly, lawyers outside of the criminal courts began to accept plea bargaining. It may be because plea bargaining was efficient. Despite their distaste for plea bargaining, those on the crime commissions wanted to create a more efficient criminal justice system. If efficiency is your goal, I suppose it doesn't make sense to throw out the one feature of the existing system that is already efficient. Or maybe the acceptance of plea bargaining was, as Professor Ortman argues, one example of a larger shift in legal theory.

Whatever the reason, even as plea bargaining drew heavy criticism, more plea bargains took place. In the federal courts, for example, plea bargaining increased dramatically over the course of the twentieth century. In the year 1910, 65 percent of federal cases that resulted in either a conviction or an acquittal—that is to say, all of the cases that prosecutors decided not to dismiss—were resolved by a guilty plea. By 1930 that number had risen to more than 85 percent. And since 1995 the guilty plea rate has remained above 90 percent.

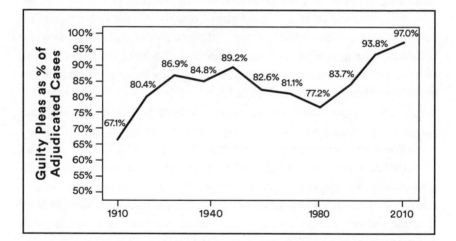

During most of the twentieth century, it wasn't clear whether the Supreme Court thought plea bargaining was legal. Early cases suggested maybe not. Only in the 1970s, after the practice was well established across the country, did the U.S. Supreme Court make clear that plea bargaining was, in fact, constitutional. By that time plea bargaining was so common—more than 80 percent of cases in the federal system were resolved by guilty pleas—that it was difficult to imagine our criminal justice system without it. In fact, the widespread nature of plea bargaining seems to have played a significant role in the Supreme Court's decision to permit plea bargaining.

In 1970 the Supreme Court decided a case called *Brady v. United States*. That case involved a defendant who had pleaded guilty to kidnapping in federal court. When the defendant in a kidnapping case pleaded guilty, he could avoid both a trial and the death penalty; federal law allowed a defendant convicted of kidnapping to be sentenced to death only if the jury recommended the death penalty. Therefore, as a practical matter, only kidnapping defendants who insisted on going to trial could be sentenced to death; defendants who pleaded guilty would never have a jury that could recommend death. The Supreme Court eventually decided that the kidnapping law was unconstitutional because it "made the risk of death the price of a jury trial." But that decision wasn't made until after the defendant in *Brady* pleaded guilty.

Mr. Brady appealed to the Supreme Court, arguing that the risk of the death penalty made his guilty plea "involuntary." Previous court decisions made clear that guilty pleas have to be "voluntary and intelligent" in order to be valid. If the justices agreed with Brady that his plea was involuntary, then he would have been allowed to withdraw his guilty plea and proceed to trial—a decision that was much more attractive, since the Supreme Court decided that the death penalty portion of the kidnapping law was unconstitutional.

But the justices didn't agree with Mr. Brady. They said it was totally fine if Mr. Brady had pleaded guilty in order to avoid the death penalty; that decision was voluntary.

It's hard to argue that a decision to avoid a risk of death is voluntary. If someone attacks me when I am walking down the street and says that they will kill me if I don't give them my wallet, we would never say that I was "voluntarily" giving that person my wallet.

But that's not how the Justices saw it. Mr. Brady's case seems very dramatic: he was pleading guilty to literally save his own life, not just to shave a couple of years off his prison sentence. But, as a legal matter, his decision was no different than that of any defendant who pleaded guilty to reduce prison sentence by a year or two. The Supreme Court said this quite explicitly—that "there is little to differentiate Brady" from a defendant who pleaded guilty because his lawyer told him that "the judge is normally more lenient with defendants who plead guilty than with those who go to trial." The justices were obviously were worried that, if they said Mr. Brady's guilty plea was involuntary, then it would cast doubt on the thousands of guilty pleas that were entered every year.

Brady v. United States rejected the argument that appellate courts had embraced in the nineteenth century—that pressure to plead guilty because of the threat of a greater sentence is a "great impropriety." While those earlier judges had said, "No sort of pressure can be permitted to bring the party to forego any right or advantage however slight," the *Brady* justices took for granted the idea that judges would be more lenient with defendants who pleaded guilty. They also assumed the judges' leniency would be widely known and understood by defendants and their lawyers.

Still, *Brady* was not a case about plea bargaining. It was a case about what is called the trial penalty—the substantial increase in punishment that a defendant will receive if she goes to trial, rather than pleading guilty. Trial penalties can be enforced by judges. Plea bargains, on the other hand, require prosecutors. Specifically, a prosecutor has to offer a defendant something in return for pleading guilty. That something can be a promise to do something, like drop other charges or argue for a lower sentence. It can also be a promise to *not* do something, like not bringing more serious charges or not arguing for a higher sentence.

The Supreme Court put its stamp of approval on plea bargaining the year after *Brady*, in a case called *Santobello v. New York*. *Santobello* involved a defendant who agreed to plead guilty to a lesser crime in exchange for the government dropping more serious charges and agreeing not to argue for a harsh sentence in front of the judge. But when it came time to sentence the defendant, a new prosecutor had been assigned to the case. The new prosecutor argued for the maximum sentence, and that's what the defendant received.

The justices in *Santobello* said that the prosecutor wasn't allowed to violate the plea agreement. And in the course of saying that, the Supreme Court said that plea bargaining was legally allowed. In fact, the justices didn't just say that plea bargaining was allowed; they said plea bargaining "is to be encouraged." They even went so far as to say that plea bargaining was "highly desirable" and "an essential component of the administration of justice."

Why did the Supreme Court not only accept plea bargaining but also praise it? Why would the justices want to encourage a system where people get more punishment for exercising their constitutional right to a trial? One reason was that plea bargaining was so widespread. The *Brady* opinion explained "that at present well over three-fourths of the criminal convictions in this country rest on pleas of guilty, a great many of them no doubt motivated at least in part by the hope or assurance of a lesser penalty than might be imposed if there were a guilty verdict after a trial to judge or jury." I imagine that the Supreme Court didn't want to say that something that most courts appeared to be doing is unconstitutional. That might make it seem as though the Court was out of touch with what happened in regular courtrooms.

Another reason—maybe the most important reason—was a lack of resources. The Supreme Court didn't think that the criminal justice system could handle more trials. Without plea bargaining, the *Santobello* opinion said, "the States and the Federal Government would need to multiply by many times the number of judges and court facilities." Chief Justice Warren Burger, who wrote the opinion in *Santobello*, had given a speech the year before in which he explained that the justice system absolutely depended on defendants pleading guilty. He said, "Systems of courts—the number of judges, prosecutors and courtrooms—have been based on the premise that approximately 90 percent of all defendants will plead guilty, leaving only 10 percent, more or less, to be tried." Chief Justice Burger did not believe that the system could handle more trials, warning that if only 80 percent of defendants pleaded guilty, then they would have to double the number of "judges, court reporters, bailiffs, clerks, jurors and courtrooms." Eager to hammer his point home, he added that the number would have to triple if only 70 percent of defendants pleaded guilty.

Reading Chief Justice Burger's gloomy predictions, it is no wonder that he wanted not only to allow plea bargaining but also to encourage it. Because he believed that even a modest increase in the number of trials would overwhelm the justice system, he wanted to avoid a ruling that would prevent judges and prosecutors from pressuring defendants into pleading guilty. If defendants didn't face that pressure, more of them might insist on their right to a trial.

Indeed, the story of "the vanishing trial" (as lawyers often call it) is partially a story about resources. Courts do not have the time or the money to hold trials. Throughout the second half of the twentieth century, American governments devoted more money to law enforcement. But that money went almost entirely to hiring more police and prosecutors and to building new jails. While law enforcement has gotten more funding, the budgets for court staff and for public defense have not kept up. For example, as prosecutions increased almost 70 percent in the final decades of the twentieth century, judicial staffing increased by only 11 percent and public defense lawyer staffing increased by only 4 percent. Put simply, we increased the number of people coming into the criminal justice system, but we did not increase the ability of the system to give those new people trials.

Some historians think that the formal procedures of modern trials contributed to the rise of guilty pleas and plea bargaining. When trials were less formal, they could be conducted relatively quickly—a single judge could hold multiple trials in a single day. For example, Professor John Langbein's study of late seventeenth and early eighteenth century records from the Old Bailey court in London revealed that juries heard an average of twelve to twenty cases a day. Those trials were conducted without lawyers and without formal rules of evidence. More recently, when the Supreme Court began to recognize more procedural rights in the mid-twentieth century, the length of trials increased. The average jury trial in Los Angeles, for instance, increased from three and a half days to more than seven days during the 1960s.

The courts could not keep up with all of the new cases and new procedural requirements, and so plea bargaining had to increase. Since the Supreme Court confirmed the constitutionality of plea bargaining, we have seen the plea bargaining rate increase even further. In 1970, 81 percent of convictions in federal court were the result of guilty pleas. By 2000 the rate was nearly 94 percent. A 2018 analysis of federal court cases by the National Association of Criminal Defense Lawyers concluded that the rate is now more than 97 percent.

Of course, we shouldn't just look at federal courts. The states actually play a much larger role in the criminal justice system: more than 90 percent of people charged with crimes in this country are charged in state courts. But people often use federal data to talk about the criminal justice system because it is difficult to obtain reliable data about what happens in state courts. The limited data we have suggests that plea bargaining dominates the entire country, but the extent of that domination varies from state to state. One study of twenty-two states found that the rate of criminal trials dropped from 8.5 percent in 1976 to 3.3 percent in 2002.

More recent data suggests that, as in the federal courts, the trial rate continues to fall in the states. Data collected by the National Center for State Courts shows that, in 2017, New York had 2.91 percent of criminal cases proceed to trial, Michigan had 2.12 percent of cases go to trial, and

Texas had fewer than 1 percent of cases go to trial. None of the twenty-two states for which the NCSC has data had more than a 3 percent trial rate.

Statistics alone, however, do not paint a full picture. It is important to understand not only how often plea bargaining occurs but also how it has changed the very fabric of our system. For example, the idea that defendants will—and should—plead guilty is so pervasive that some states have even passed laws charging defendants fees if they require the state to seat a jury and hold a trial.

It is hard to understand how these fees don't violate the Constitution. What if we charged people a fee to exercise their right to free speech? Or their right to vote? There is little doubt that judges would declare those fees unconstitutional. In fact, the Supreme Court has said that charging people fees to vote *is* unconstitutional. And yet, when it comes to the jury trial, arguments about unconstitutionality routinely take a back seat to arguments about efficiency and cost.

In any event, resources alone can't explain what has happened to trials in this country. It is certainly true that our courts could not possibly hold trials for all of the criminal cases that come through the justice system. But this lack of capacity does not explain the incredibly small number of trials we have now. In fact, in both the state and federal systems, the number of trials has gone down even as the capacity to hold trials has increased. In 1990 there were more than 7,800 criminal trials in federal court. By 2016 that number fell to less than 1,900. One judge gathered these statistics and

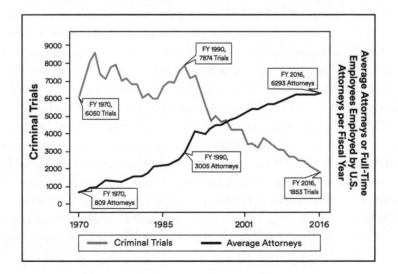

put them in an opinion. He showed that not only did we used to have more trials, but the number of trials has fallen even as the number of people employed in federal prosecutors' offices has increased.

The same thing is true for the number of federal judges. As the number of trials has gone down, the number of federal judges has gone up. As a result, judges now have far fewer trials than they used to. In 1973, a federal judge had an average of 21.65 criminal trials per year. By 2016 that number plummeted to 2.79 trials per year.

There is a similar problem with the assumption that plea bargaining was caused by more formal trial procedures. Formal rules of evidence and the ability of a defendant to hire a defense lawyer predate the rise of plea bargaining by more than a hundred years. Nor does there appear to be an obvious relationship between the modern rise in plea bargains and the length of trials. For example, although the plea bargaining rate increased significantly between 1965 and 2002, a prominent study found "no noticeable increase in the length of federal criminal trials" during that time period.

So while it is true that our system could not handle *every* criminal case going to trial, the system *could* handle—and *has* handled in the past—far more trials than it does now. So there must be other reasons that help explain why we have so few trials.

* * * * *

The number of jury trials may also have decreased because the very idea of juries became inconsistent with our ideas about modern government, progress, and expertise. The Progressive movement of the late nineteenth and early twentieth century ushered in a new attitude toward government— an attitude that government could do more to improve modern life. Old institutions, like Congress, were seen as impediments to progress. New institutions, like administrative agencies, were needed to govern a modern society. Those new institutions combined expertise and efficiency.

The criminal justice system generally, and juries in particular, were not exempt from this new attitude toward government. Juries were seen not only as outdated but also as unsophisticated and unpredictable. As law professor Andrew Kent has documented, many prominent lawyers and government officials began to criticize the jury trial as an institution. One of those prominent critics was William Howard Taft, who served as both president of the United States and chief justice of the U.S. Supreme Court.

Taft called the criminal justice system "a disgrace to our civilization" because skilled lawyers could confuse juries with irrelevant information and trick them into acquitting a guilty person. And while he acknowledged that the jury was too entrenched in American culture to abolish, Taft successfully argued against expanding the jury trial right to new American territories. Taft's criticism of the jury was part of his larger argument that criminal law was outdated and overly focused on the liberty of the individual. Taft thought that the "science" of modern law should focus more on preventing crime and protecting the community.

Taft was hardly alone in his criticism of the criminal justice system. Many other prominent legal figures criticized the criminal justice system as too protective of individual rights and not concerned enough with convicting guilty people and protecting the community. According to these critics, juries were too softhearted and willing to acquit.

During this period the specialized journals written for lawyers were full of articles that criticized juries. The jury trial was criticized as "an intolerable burden" that was "destroying the certainty of punishment." The verdicts that juries delivered were characterized as "lawlessness." Some people even went so far as to argue that the right to a jury trial was unnecessary in the United States. Unlike the English, who were ruled by tyrannical monarchs, Americans had "no reason to fear oppression of the people by those in authority." Because the American people wielded the power of the government through voting, they argued, the jury trials were no longer necessary to protect individual liberty.

Calls for abolishing jury trials were not limited to criminal cases. Elite lawyers complained about having to rely on the uninformed judgments of jurors and antiquated trial procedures in civil cases involving business interests too. Reformers suggested that judges should conduct civil trials either without any jurors or with "expert jurors" who possessed business experience.

Disdain for juries was not limited to private discussions between lawyers. Major newspapers and magazines published criticism of juries too. The magazine the *Nation* ran an essay in 1895 that said, "The evils of our jury system are so glaring, and so promotive of crime, that it is surprising that neither the judiciary nor the bar have before now made any effort to reform it." The Boston magazine the *Arena* published an article a few years later characterizing jurors as either corrupt or ignorant.

As these examples show, around the same time that plea bargaining was becoming entrenched in the trial courts, many—though certainly not all—people stopped seeing juries as something that protected the rights and liberty of individuals. Instead, they saw juries as an antiquated institution that were too quick to acquit defendants. Because they were inefficient and because they were made up of amateurs, people believed that juries stood in the way of progress. By eliminating juries, they argued, the criminal justice system could be more efficient and important decisions could be made by experts.

At the same time that some in the Progressive movement were criticizing jurors, the criminal justice system was becoming more professional. Lawrence Friedman and Robert Percival point to the professionalization of the criminal justice system as a potential reason that plea bargaining increased in the late nineteenth and early twentieth century. During that time police became more professional, district attorneys became full-time public employees, and the system grew to include other experts, such as probation officers and parole boards. Friedman and Percival argue that amateur juries were no longer the best way to sort the innocent than the guilty; instead we could rely on prosecutors and police, as well as "police science"—think fingerprints—rather than the jury to "try" the defendant. "Plea bargaining," they explain, "was part of the new system; it was part of a more 'rational,' 'professional' process."

These ideas of efficiency and expertise have had a lingered effect on the criminal justice system. For example, judges have sometimes justified their deference to prosecutors' decisions because prosecutors are in a much better position to make decisions about policy priorities and resources. Prosecutors have been empowered to dispose of cases using streamlined procedures like plea bargaining or diversion programs. And some policy decisions have been delegated to "expert" agencies, like sentencing commissions.

But the Progressive ideals never fully transformed the criminal justice system. For one thing, the image of the jury has improved. Even as it was willing to recognize the constitutionality of plea bargaining, the Supreme Court declared that the jury trial is a "fundamental right" and no state can punish a defendant for more than six months in jail without giving him the right to a jury. Perhaps because plea bargaining is so widespread, the legal community no longer criticizes juries as unsophisticated or inefficient. Instead, in recent decades, state and federal judges have often given speeches and written opinions talking about the importance of the jury.

Although plea bargaining has given a lot of powers to supposedly expert officials, those decisions are hardly a model of "scientific" expertise. For example, prosecutors' most important decisions—what charges to bring and what plea bargains to offer—are generally made on a case-by-case basis by lawyers who don't have any scientific training. When some prosecutors have standardized those decisions by adopting charging or bargaining policies, those policies are just orders that come down from on high; they are not based on rigorous empirical study.

Even the expert criminal justice agencies do not look like the experts that we see in other fields. For example, when Congress created the U.S. Sentencing Commission and told it to create sentencing guidelines for judges, the commission's process for developing those guidelines was far from scientific, and it has been roundly criticized. And unlike other expert agencies, which face judicial review for arbitrary or capricious decisions, the Sentencing Commission hasn't been required to justify its decisions, which are shielded from judicial review.

To be clear, there is no doubt that the modern system is more efficient at processing cases than a system of juries and trials. But it is far from clear that the gains in efficiency and expertise are worth the sacrifice of individual rights that they required.

* * * * *

Resource limitations and a new emphasis on efficiency and expertise may explain how we arrived at our current system. But they do not tell us why the system remains. They do not explain, for example, why the number of federal criminal trials has continued to shrink even as the number of prosecutors and judges has increased. Nor do they explain why expertise and science do not play a larger role in setting criminal justice policy.

I cannot pretend to have a definitive answer here. In fact, I'm not sure that anyone can *prove* why we have the system that we do. But there is a theory that seems to make more sense than others: culture. As Milton Heumann has shown, even those lawyers who come into the criminal justice system thinking that they will try a lot of cases before a jury eventually change their tune; they adapt to the system and start plea bargaining like everyone else. I think this same explanation holds true for the system as a whole: at some point everyone started to expect cases to plea bargain. And because everyone expected it, that's what happened the vast majority of the time. That is how plea bargaining became, as Professor Ortman put it, "normal."

It's kind of like what happened with hats. For decades, men were expected to wear hats when they were outside. They didn't necessarily think about it; they just wore a hat because that's what everyone else was doing. But that changed in the 1960s. Once they were no longer expected to wear hats, most men stopped—again, not because they necessarily had strong feelings about hats one way or another. The cultural expectations shifted, and so did most people's behavior.

This idea of a plea bargaining culture first occurred to me when I read a statement by Arlen Specter about plea bargaining. (Specter eventually went on to serve in the U.S. Senate, but at the time he made the statement he was the district attorney in Philadelphia.) Specter said that he thought plea bargaining was an especially good idea in murder cases because those cases often involved questions of intent, self-defense, or provocation. If a defendant acted unintentionally or after being provoked, then he was guilty of only manslaughter rather than murder. And if a defendant acted in self-defense, then he was not guilty of a crime at all. Specter thought plea bargaining was a good idea in those cases because the lawyers could not predict whether a jury would return a verdict of murder, manslaughter, or not guilty. Avoiding a jury and instead negotiating, he explained, "enables the assistant district attorney and the defense lawyer to bargain on the middle ground of what experience has shown to be 'justice' without the defense running the risk of the occasional [murder] conviction which carries a mandatory minimum of life imprisonment and without the Commonwealth tying up a jury room for 3 to 5 days and running the risk of acquittal."

When I read this, I was horrified. When I teach criminal law to my first-year law students, we spend weeks and weeks talking about intent, self-defense, and provocation. We spend so much time discussing these subjects because the difference between a conviction for murder, a conviction for manslaughter, and an acquittal are incredibly important. A murder conviction could result in a death sentence, while an acquittal means that the defendant literally walks free. There are ancient legal rules that distinguish between these things—rules which are supposed to be applied by a jury.

But Specter assumed the precise opposite. He thought that, because different juries might make different decisions, these cases should be resolved by negotiation rather than trials. That sort of attitude only makes sense if you think that juries aren't supposed to make the decisions about difficult facts or if you think that the criminal justice system isn't about arriving at a single answer about what happened (or both).

Specter didn't make this comment in a back room somewhere. He wrote it down and published it in one of the top legal journals in the country. And the statement wasn't made defensively; he made it in a matter-of-fact way, which made me think that a lot of other prosecutors probably agreed with him. In fact, Specter bragged about the fact that his office was less likely to plea bargain than others. And so, if this is how someone who doesn't see himself as a champion of plea bargaining thinks, then a lot of lawyers probably assume that criminal cases aren't supposed to be decided by juries at all.

The idea of a plea bargaining culture—a background assumption that juries shouldn't decide cases—became more and more plausible to me as I spoke to people across the country for this book. Some of those stories are included in the chapters that follow—stories about judges threatening lawyers in their courtrooms if they dared to bring their cases to trial, and stories about prosecutors who told defendants that they couldn't get a plea deal if they invoked their right to see the evidence against them.

Not all of the stories I heard are included in this book. Some of the stories were told to me in confidence. Many of the people I spoke to for this book still work in the criminal justice system, and they don't want to upset the judges or their supervisors by publicly explaining how they have been pressured not to bring cases to trial. They told me the stories because they *knew* the stories were shocking—that they revealed something wrong with the culture in which they work.

To be clear, these stories would not shock people who work inside of the criminal justice system. They know that most cases will never go to trial; that is simply the reality in which they do their jobs. But while plea bargaining is now the culture within the criminal justice system, that does not mean that it has changed the culture in the rest of the country. People outside of the system—ordinary Americans who don't know much about criminal law—may be shocked. Many people have no idea that we live in a system that is designed to pressure them into giving up their right to a trial if they are accused of a crime.

It's fair to ask why people do not realize that we live in a system of plea bargains rather than a system of trials. One explanation is that there have been a number of very high-profile trials in recent decades—the OJ

Simpson trial in the 1990s, the Martha Stewart trial in the early 2000s, more recently the trials of Donald Trump's associates Paul Manafort and Roger Stone, just to name a few. Those trials, when they occur, have dominated the news. For people who don't pay much attention to the criminal justice system, they may see coverage of these trials and assume that criminal trials are the rule rather than the rare exception.

And even if people know that a lot of defendants plead guilty, the average person may not realize *why* they plead guilty. They likely do not know, as the next chapter explains, that prosecutors have so much power that they can essentially force people to plead guilty or that judges will routinely impose longer sentences as a penalty on those people who go to trial. Instead, people just assume that everyone who pleads guilty actually *is* guilty and that those people didn't think that it was worth invoking their right to a trial.

* * * * *

Why should average Americans care that we have largely eliminated criminal trials? Jury trials were important to the people who wrote the Constitution. But there are many who think the ideas of those people who wrote the Constitution should not continue to shape our decisions today. After all, the Framers of the Constitution had no problem with slavery or with limiting votes to White men who owned property, so maybe we shouldn't assume that all of their ideas were good ones.

But the authors of the Constitution had a very good reason for wanting to protect jury trials: They saw what could happen if it was too easy to punish people. They saw that the power could be—and was—abused.

We seem to have forgotten that lesson. In eliminating the major safeguards of our criminal justice system—in eliminating trials—we have made it too easy to punish people. And that is how we ended up with mass incarceration.

The United States has the highest incarceration rate in the Western world. We have increased our prison populations even as crime has been falling. In fact, both plea bargaining and incarceration rates increased dramatically at the very end of the twentieth century. Guilty pleas were common throughout the century. In the federal system, for example, although the percentage of pleas would rise and fall, they never fell below 50 percent. And since the 1990s, guilty pleas have climbed above 90 percent, where they have remained. At the same time that very high plea bargaining rates

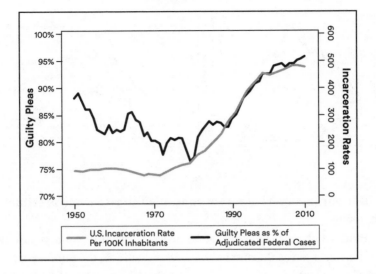

were stabilizing, the number of people in prison increased dramatically across the country.

It's always hard to know why, exactly, things happen in the criminal justice system. There are thousands of people who work in the system, and they operate under different laws and in different courthouses. And so I can't say for sure that plea bargaining caused mass incarceration. But logic tells us that eliminating trials would result in more people going to prison. After all, trials are expensive and unpredictable, which makes them worth the cost only if a serious crime has been committed. By eliminating trials, our current system makes punishment cheap, simple, and predictable. So it should not be a surprise that we punish more and more people; we've made it very easy to do so.

There is also some data to support a link between plea bargains and mass incarceration. If a prosecutor doesn't have to try cases, and if she can pressure people into giving up other rights—like the right to view the evidence against them—then she can prosecute a lot more people. As John Pfaff argues in his recent book *Locked In: The True Causes of Mass Incarceration—and How to Achieve Real Reform,* modern mass incarceration has been caused, in significant part, by prosecutors pursuing more cases.

Pfaff explains that there are several reasons why the American imprisonment rate increased during the twentieth century. One reason is that the crime rate went up. If more people are committing crimes, then we should expect to see more people go to prison.

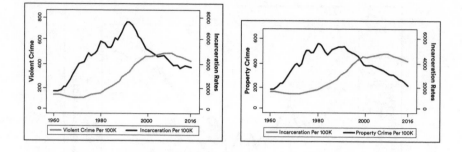

But our incarceration rate continued to rise even as crime rate went down.

Pfaff attributes the increase to prosecutors filing charges in more cases, saying "even as the number of arrests declined, the number of felony cases filed in state courts rose sharply." By the time that the increase in incarceration per crime began to level out—or at least not increase as dramatically—"the probability that a prosecutor would file felony charges against an arrestee basically doubled . . ."

The spike in new case filings that appears to have driven mass incarceration happened at the same time that trials all but disappeared. It's possible that this is a coincidence, but I would be surprised if the two things were unrelated to one another.

What's more likely is that the system we have built—a system that is designed to punish people as efficiently as possible—is working as it is intended. Plea bargaining allows us to punish people quickly and easily, and so it should come as no surprise that we have punished more and more people.

CHAPTER THREE

"IT'S A BUSINESS DECISION"

Harry owned a small business that depended on investments.* When the bottom fell out of the U.S. economy in 2009, some of his investors lost money. One of those investors was friendly with an official at the Securities and Exchange Commission, the federal agency that regulates the stock market and other investment activities. After that investor complained to his friend, the SEC raided Harry's company over a holiday weekend, taking all of the company's computers and records. Those computers and records still haven't been returned.

In addition to the SEC investigation, Harry and his partners were charged with fraud. Federal prosecutors threatened Harry and his partners with more than two hundred years in prison. All of Harry's money had been seized by the government, and so he had to borrow money to hire a lawyer. Harry explained to his lawyer that he didn't do anything wrong. He didn't defraud any of his investors; it was just bad luck. Harry's lawyer talked to the prosecutors, but they were only willing to offer a plea deal of twenty years in prison. So Harry and his partners decided to go to trial.

As the trial date got closer, the prosecution started to offer better plea deals. Harry and his partners kept insisting they hadn't done anything wrong—they'd followed all of the SEC's rules and they hadn't defrauded

---

* Harry is not his real name.

anyone—so they wanted to tell the jury what happened. But their lawyer said that might not matter. He said that the jury was not going to understand the SEC rules. He'd seen juries who thought that defendants were probably innocent, but then they convicted on one count just in case.

The lawyer explained to Harry that, if the jury convicted on even one small count, he was still in big trouble. Even if you are acquitted of one crime, federal law allows judges to give you a higher sentence if they think you probably committed other crimes. For example, imagine a prosecutor charges you with burglary and murder; the jury acquits you of murder but finds you guilty of burglary. If the prosecutor convinces the judge that most of the evidence suggests you are guilty of the murder, then the judge will give you a very high sentence—probably the highest allowed by law—on the burglary charge. Even though you won at trial, you'd lose at sentencing.

Harry knew that, if the jury acquitted him of most charges, the judge would probably give him the maximum punishment—or close to it—on any charges for which he was convicted. But he and his partners still wanted to go to trial. He knew that he was innocent. And as he put it, "Lawyers spend their lives convincing people to plead guilty."

Harry's lawyer understood that his clients thought they were innocent. But he couldn't understand why they were insisting on going to trial rather than just trying to negotiate the best plea deal possible. "At some point the lawyer was yelling at us, telling us we were ruining our lives," Harry recounted. "'This isn't about guilt or innocence,' he said. 'It's a business decision.'"

Finally, the prosecutors offered a deal that Harry felt he couldn't refuse. Although they had initially insisted that Harry serve fifteen or twenty years in prison, when it became clear that Harry was willing to go to trial, prosecutors offered him a much better deal: only two years.

Harry's resolve to take his case to trial began to waiver. "You dream of going to trial and winning," Harry said, "but what do you really win? You win your innocence. But in a lot of ways you still lose. And if you lose at trial, then you leave your family with nothing."

Even though he still adamantly believed that he was innocent of any wrongdoing, Harry accepted the plea deal. He had a good lawyer. He had a good case. His lawyer didn't even think that the things Harry had done were actually illegal. But Harry realized the inevitable: the deal was too good to pass up.

Talking to Harry, I can't say that he made the wrong decision. Based on the charges that prosecutors brought, Harry was facing up to two hundred years in prison if convicted at trial. It is doubtful that a federal judge would have imposed a sentence that high. But it was quite plausible that the judge would have imposed a sentence of twenty or thirty years if Harry had been convicted after a trial. So it actually would have been irrational for Harry to have turned down the plea offer of only two years.

When I say that it would have been irrational for Harry to turn down the plea offer, I literally mean that no rational person would have turned down that offer. The math just doesn't add up. It might sound strange, but we can actually use math to assess whether a defendant's decision to plead guilty is rational. We can do this by calculating what economists call the "expected punishment."

You can calculate a person's expected punishment by multiplying the punishment that the person would receive if they are convicted at trial by the probability that they would actually be convicted. For example, if I have been charged with a crime that carries a ten-year sentence, and there is a 50 percent chance that I will be convicted at trial, then my expected punishment is five years. If a prosecutor offers me a plea bargain that would require me to serve less than five years in prison, then I should take the deal.

The idea of calculating expected punishment might seem crazy. After all, if I am acquitted at trial, then I will spend zero time in prison. In accepting a plea deal, I give up my chance at acquittal. But at the same time that I have given up my chance at acquittal, I have also limited my risk of spending more time in prison if I am convicted at trial.

The idea of expected punishment treats going to trial as a gamble: you might win big or you might lose big. The plea bargain allows you to hedge your bet. And calculating expected punishment lets us evaluate whether that plea deal is a better bet than the gamble of going to trial.

An expected value calculation tells us that Harry would have been irrational to turn down the plea deal. Let's assume Harry was facing a twenty-year sentence if convicted at trial—and he may have been facing even more than that. The plea deal required Harry to spend only two years in prison. Two years is only 10 percent of twenty years. So even if Harry thought that there was an 89 percent chance that he would be acquitted at trial, it was still rational of him to take the plea deal. The deal allowed him to hedge his bet, and it was less than the expected punishment.

Everyone in the criminal justice system knows that plea bargains are about defendants hedging their bets. If a prosecutor offers a good enough deal—a plea bargain with a sentence that is significantly less than the expected punishment—then a defendant would have to be crazy to turn it down.

That's actually what everyone thought about Joseph Tigano: they literally thought he was crazy because he turned down a plea deal and insisted on going to trial.

Joseph Tigano and his father were arrested for growing more than a thousand marijuana plants. Joseph's father pleaded guilty to a lesser crime—manufacturing fifty or more marijuana plants—but Joseph refused to plead. He sat in jail for more than nine months waiting for a trial. When his lawyer postponed a court date without telling him, Joseph went on a hunger strike. The defense attorney responded by asking the judge to order a competency evaluation—that is, a mental health screening to see whether Joseph was mentally capably of standing trial. The lawyer's request to the judge and the judge's decision to order the competency evaluation were based, in part, on Joseph's insistence that he receive a trial and his complaints that the trial hadn't taken place yet. The competency evaluation came back: Joseph was competent to stand trial.

Because his lawyer was not respecting his wishes about scheduling the trial right away, Joseph asked the judge to let him serve as his own lawyer. The judge eventually granted Joseph's request but insisted on appointing a new lawyer to serve as Joseph's standby counsel—that is, someone who would come to all of the court dates and help Joseph if necessary. This second lawyer also thought Joseph's continued insistence that he wanted his trial to take place right away was incredibly strange. And so she suggested *another* competency hearing, which also found that there was nothing wrong with Joseph's mental abilities.

Despite his repeated pleas to hold his trial, Joseph sat in jail for years after that second competency evaluation. One reason for the delay was that the lawyers tried to negotiate a plea bargain. Another reason for the delay was that the government failed to hand over some documents to Joseph and his standby lawyer. Crowded court dockets also contributed to the delay.

Through this long delay, Joseph kept telling the attorney who was helping him that he wanted to go to trial right away. That attorney responded by filing a confidential motion with the judge recommending a *third* competency evaluation, saying that, in refusing to plead guilty and insisting on his right to a trial, Joseph was acting "imprudent[ly]" and "not in his best interest." The prosecutor agreed that Joseph should have another competency evaluation—not because he thought that Joseph was actually incompetent to stand trial, but because he thought there might be "some other psychological problem that's going to prevent him from understanding the difference between what he potentially looks at as far as a conviction as well as what's being offered by way of this plea." In other words, the prosecutor thought that something must be mentally wrong with Joseph because he didn't seem to understand that the plea deal he was being offered was much better than what would happen if he went to trial.

After sitting in jail for nearly seven years, Joseph finally got his trial. He was convicted. But he later got that conviction reversed because forcing him to wait more than six years for the trial violated his constitutional right to a speedy trial.

Like Harry, Joseph was facing a much lower sentence by pleading guilty rather than going to trial. After he was convicted at trial, Joseph was sentenced to twenty years in prison. Joseph's father—who was arrested with Joseph for the exact same crime—pleaded guilty in return for a sentence of time served. At that point, both he and Joseph had sat in jail for four years.

It's no wonder that his lawyer, the prosecutor, and the judge all thought Joseph was crazy. If he had pleaded guilty, Joseph would have spent only four years in jail. By going to trial, Joseph risked another sixteen years in prison. Like the two-hundred-year maximum sentence that Harry was facing, the twenty-year sentence that Joseph was facing allowed prosecutors to place a lot of pressure on him.

The higher the sentence prosecutors can threaten, the more it changes the expected punishment calculation in their favor. If I'm facing one hundred years in prison if convicted, then I'm going to jump at a plea deal of only one year. But if I'm facing only three years if convicted, then I'm more likely to go to trial. In other words, the longer the sentences, the more leverage prosecutors have in plea bargaining.

How did prosecutors get this sort of leverage? Well, they got a lot of help from legislators.

* * * * *

It is no accident that we have very harsh criminal laws—laws that authorize extremely high penalties, even for nonviolent crimes like fraud and growing marijuana. Many politicians have campaigned on law-and-order platforms. And then, once elected, they have consistently voted in favor of harsh criminal laws. To do otherwise would open them up to charges that they are "soft on crime." As a result, the two major political parties have sometimes tried to outdo each other to see who can be the harshest when it comes to crime.

For example, when Congress decided to pass a law aimed at the crack cocaine epidemic in the 1980s, the legislative process quickly turned into a bidding war to see who could propose the harshest approach. Ronald Reagan's administration proposed applying the same mandatory minimum sentences for crack crimes as for crimes involving 20 times the amount of powder cocaine. Democrats controlled the House, and they proposed treating crack crimes the same as crimes involving 50 times the amount of cocaine. In the Senate, the number got inflated again: suddenly dealing 5 grams of crack cocaine would get the same harsh mandatory minimum sentence as someone who dealt 500 grams of powder cocaine. There was no scientific evidence offered in support of this 100-to-1 ratio. Instead it was arrived at through the political bidding war between Republicans and Democrats, who were both trying to win the votes of people who were afraid of America's growing drug problem.

Prosecutors have greatly benefited from this political dynamic. And they have even helped to fuel it. Prosecutors routinely testify in front of Congress and state legislatures about the need for new, harsher criminal laws. When legislation is introduced that might roll back some of the harshest sentences or otherwise make it more difficult to prosecute cases, prosecutors' associations will often send representatives to lobby against those reform efforts.

Shon Hopwood, a law professor at Georgetown, has collected numerous examples of the Department of Justice and the National Association of Assistant U.S. Attorneys, a lobbying group of federal prosecutors, opposing federal criminal justice reform. Those groups and others are especially hostile to any efforts to eliminate or reduce mandatory minimum sentences. For example, in 2017, the NAAUSA sent a letter to Congress opposing a federal law that would have reduced mandatory minimum sentences for certain nonviolent drug defendants, claiming that this law would "make it even more difficult for investigators and prosecutors to pursue the most culpable drug dealers and secure their cooperation to pursue others . . ." In other words, they said prosecutors need those sentences to pressure defendants into pleading guilty and cooperating against other people.

My own research on state prosecutors has revealed similar behavior. To pick just one example, during the years 2015–2018, prosecutors in California supported 127 bills that would have created new crimes or lengthened criminal sentences. During that same session they vocally opposed a law that would have allowed the release of elderly prisoners who were more than sixty years old and had served at least twenty-five years in prison, a law that would have allowed "community-based punishment" for certain misdemeanors rather than jail, and a law that would have limited the ability of prosecutors to lengthen prison sentences by stacking multiple criminal charges.

Although they have often been successful lobbyists on their own behalf, prosecutors do not deserve all of the blame for harsh sentences and other laws that pressure people to plead guilty. Legislators have been active and willing partners. They pass these harsh laws—and refuse to change them—precisely because they *want* to give prosecutors this sort of leverage. It allows them to say they are "tough on crime" when they run for reelection.

The crack cocaine laws and mandatory minimum sentences show just how difficult it can be to reduce prosecutors' leverage. As crime rates began to fall in the 1990s and 2000s, public support for repealing those harsh laws began to grow. In the Senate, a bipartisan group of lawmakers began to push for drug sentencing reform.

These lawmakers introduced legislation that would reduce mandatory minimums for drug crimes. But they were only partially successful. Reformers were able to push through legislation that decreased the crack-cocaine ratio from 100 to 1 to 18 to 1. So now a person who sells 28 grams of crack cocaine (instead of just 5 grams) will receive the same five-year mandatory minimum sentence as a person who sells 500 grams of powder cocaine. But legislation to change the mandatory minimum sentences themselves didn't pass.

Senator Chuck Grassley of Iowa was a major opponent of the effort to reduce mandatory minimum sentences for drug laws. He seemed to acknowledge that the mandatory minimum sentences could sweep up people who didn't deserve those punishments, like drug mules—people who are paid small amounts of money to transport large quantities of drugs. But Senator Grassley nonetheless insisted that Congress shouldn't reduce mandatory minimum sentences because it would reduce prosecutors' leverage. He said this leverage was one of the goals of these harsh sentences: "That is an intended goal of current Federal sentencing policy, to put pressure on defendants to cooperate in exchange for a lower sentence so evidence against more responsible criminals can be attained."

Grassley also pointed to the fact that most defendants ended up serving a sentence below the mandatory minimum as proof that the system was working. He noted that "the average sentence" for drug mules was actually significantly below the mandatory minimum sentence, and he added: "That seems to be an appropriate level." That's pretty remarkable if you think about it: a senator said that the system is working as "intended" when the law he supports is being avoided through plea bargaining.

In recent years, Grassley's stance toward drug sentences has softened. Some say this change of heart is due to the toll that the opioid epidemic has taken in his home state of Iowa: as more of his constituents have been swept up in drug prosecutions, their families have attended town halls and other events to tell him about the effect that harsh drug sentences were having on them. In 2017, Grassley sponsored the Sentencing Reform and Corrections Act, which would have reduced mandatory minimum sentences for nonviolent drug crimes. But that legislation never passed. The mandatory minimum sentences for drug crimes are still on the books, and they continue to give prosecutors enormous leverage to pressure defendants to plead guilty.

It is important to understand why mandatory minimum sentences are such a helpful plea bargaining tool for prosecutors. The defendant knows that if she doesn't agree to plead guilty, then she will have to go to jail for as at least as long as the mandatory minimum sentence. For example, right now the mandatory minimum sentence for selling 28 grams of crack cocaine is five years in prison. A defendant who is caught selling that much crack knows that she will spend at least five years in jail. So if a prosecutor offers her a plea deal—a deal that will allow her to plead guilty to selling only 14 grams—she will likely take that deal. There is no mandatory minimum for selling that amount of cocaine, and so she will likely spend far less time in prison. If the defendant accepts the deal, then the prosecutor will allow the defendant to plead to this lesser crime, and he will dismiss the more serious charge of selling 28 grams or more.

This practice—allowing a defendant to plead to a lesser crime—is so common that it has its own name: charge bargaining. Charge bargaining also occurs when a prosecutor agrees to dismiss some charges in a multi-count indictment. It's pretty easy for a prosecutor to bring multiple charges against a defendant who committed what we might ordinarily think of as one crime. For example, a defendant who robs a convenience store wouldn't just be charged with robbery. He would also be charged with assault, theft, reckless endangerment, a weapons charge, and several other crimes that are probably less familiar to people. By stacking these charges on top of one another, the prosecutor gives herself more leverage in plea negotiations. The prosecutor can offer to dismiss one or more of those charges in return for a guilty plea on others. And depending on the local rules about running sentences consecutively or concurrently, the defendant might even be willing to plead guilty to the most serious charge, robbery, in order to keep the less serious charges from increasing his maximum possible sentence.

Legislatures have enabled this charge stacking as well by passing new criminal laws that overlap with existing criminal laws. Indeed, many times when a legislator introduces a bill for a new criminal law, that law covers behavior that is already illegal. For example, long ago Congress passed a law making it a crime to make false statements to federal officials. This law is incredibly broad, and yet Congress has also decided to pass many other laws aimed at false statements to government officials in various specific contexts. A 1998 study found that there were 642 separate sections in the federal criminal code about crimes involving false statements to government officials. Because of these laws, a person who lies to FBI agents can be charged with multiple crimes for that single lie. The fact that prosecutors can pile on multiple charges gives them more leverage at plea bargaining.

Finally, legislatures create additional leverage when they attach other, noncriminal consequences to convictions for certain crimes. Common consequences include licensing restrictions, losing government benefits like public housing, and deportation. These consequences, which lawyers often call "collateral consequences," aren't technically considered part of a defendant's criminal sentence; they are just applied automatically after conviction, and so prosecutors may not be able to put them in the formal plea bargain with the defendant. But the prosecutor can still use collateral consequences as leverage by offering a charge bargain to a crime that does not carry those same collateral consequences. For example, if a doctor will lose her medical license if she is convicted of a felony, then the prosecutor may allow her to plead guilty to a misdemeanor instead.

This sort of leverage can be very effective when it comes to sex offenses. People convicted of sex offenses are often subject to a number of noncriminal penalties, such as being placed on sex offender registries and being subject to restrictions about where they can work or live.

These collateral consequences can be devastating, which makes a charge bargain—specifically, pleading guilty to lesser crimes that don't require registration or restrictions—even more attractive to defendants.

What's striking to me about all of these harsh laws is that neither lawmakers nor prosecutors really believe that these laws strike the right balance of punishment. No one would argue, for example, that a person like Harry actually deserves two hundred years in prison for fraud. And the prosecutors in Joseph's case clearly thought that four years was a long enough sentence for growing marijuana, since that's the deal they gave to his father.

Rather than arguing that long punishments are necessary to punish or to discourage people from committing crimes, lawmakers and prosecutors argue that these punishments are necessary to make defendants cooperate with law enforcement and to plead guilty. They openly say that they need these harsh laws to punish people like Joseph who *won't* agree to plead guilty. If people like Joseph *don't* get a much harsher punishment for refusing to plead guilty, then more defendants might go to trial. And our system tries very hard to avoid that.

* * * * *

You might think that judges would step in to stop this collusion between legislators and prosecutors. After all, judges are an independent branch of government, and we are all taught that separating power into the three branches is supposed to make those branches check and balance each other's power. Even more important, judges are part of the branch of government that is supposed to protect the rights of individuals and uphold the Constitution against abuses by the political branches. After all, what is the leverage that these harsh laws give to prosecutors if not a threat to individual rights and an abuse of the Constitution's guarantee of a jury trial?

But judges are not the heroes in this story. Judges were actually pressuring defendants to plead guilty long before legislatures got in the game by enacting a lot of mandatory minimum sentences. For decades, judges have routinely imposed harsher sentences on those defendants who insist on going to trial rather than pleading guilty, and they have done so in order to discourage people from going to trial.

The judges have not been doing this in secret. They have been quite open about it.

For example, in his famous 1974 study of the New Haven courts, Professor Malcolm Feeley documented a "two-tiered sentencing policy"—more lenient sentences that are proposed during plea negotiations, and then more harsh sentences that are imposed if the defendant insists on a trial. The defense attorneys that Feeley interviewed told him that they viewed the harsher sentences "as an unwritten but nevertheless strictly enforced threat by judges to intimidate defendants" into pleading guilty.

Judges have even been known to explicitly threaten defendants or defense attorneys to discourage them from going to trial. Albert Alshuler tells the story of a young law professor who was representing an indigent client accused of selling drugs. The prosecutor was offering an attractive deal: he would dismiss the charges that carried a ten-year mandatory sentence and recommend a sentence of two to five years if the defendant pleaded guilty. But the defense attorney was reluctant to have his client accept a plea bargain because the client kept insisting that he was innocent. When the judge realized that the defense attorney didn't seem inclined to accept the prosecutor's offer, he jumped in, saying: "I'm not going to tell you what to do, young man, but I can tell you what *I'll* do. If your client goes to trial and is convicted, the minimum term will not just be the ten years required by the statute. The minimum term will be twenty years in the penitentiary."

Think about that for a second. A judge told a lawyer that if his client didn't plead guilty, then he would send him to jail for an extra ten years. Judges resent these defendants for making everyone—including the judges themselves—go through the time and effort of a trial. And apparently this judge thought that the defendant should lose an extra decade of freedom as punishment for that inconvenience—never mind that the "inconvenience" is guaranteed by the Constitution.

This practice is so widespread that it even has a name: the "trial penalty." Studies of plea bargaining routinely find that judges impose longer sentences after trial in order to punish defendants who didn't plead guilty. And the difference between sentences after trial and sentences after guilty pleas can be quite severe.

One recent study of the trial penalty found that people who went to trial received sentences that were, on average, three times longer than people who pleaded guilty. In other words, the trial penalty tripled people's sentences. For some crimes, the trial penalty was even larger. Defendants convicted of antitrust crimes served on average less than one and a half years in prison if they pleaded guilty. But if they insisted on a trial, then their average sentence was more than twelve years.

The trial penalty has been around for decades. The federal agency responsible for the administration of the courts used to keep track of it in federal cases. That's how we know, for example, that even back in the 1970s the average defendant who insisted on a jury trial received a sentence that was three times longer than those of the defendants who pleaded guilty.

How can judges justify this? If governments tried to put people in jail because they exercised other rights—like the right to free speech, the right to belong to a church, or the right to vote—judges would quickly step in and stop it. Yet the Supreme Court has decided to allow the government to imprison people longer based on the mere fact that they insisted on their right to a trial.

Some people say that the trial penalty doesn't punish people for exercising their right to a trial; it just grants a benefit (a shorter sentence) to those who are willing to plead guilty. Personally, I don't see how a judge's explicit threat to put someone in jail for an extra decade can be recharacterized as a benefit to some other defendant who pleaded guilty. But even if it were, that shouldn't make a difference as a constitutional matter. The courts don't usually let government officials force you to waive your constitutional rights even if they give you something in return. If, for example, the federal government told you that you have to give up your right to vote in order to get social security benefits, judges would say that was an "unconstitutional condition" and tell the government it couldn't do that.

But judges haven't extended their unconstitutional conditions cases to plea bargaining. Instead, they allow government officials to send people to jail for longer just for exercising the right to a jury trial. It doesn't even matter that officials are doing this in the open—threatening people with longer sentences or more serious criminal charges unless they agree to plead guilty. The Supreme Court and other judges have said this is perfectly okay.

How do judges defend their decision to allow the trial penalty and all of the threats and extra punishment associated with plea bargaining? Sometimes they muddy the water by talking about how they shouldn't second-guess the power of prosecutors to make charging and bargaining decisions. Or they explain that the judge who was giving a longer sentence after a trial did so only because the defendant didn't "accept responsibility" and therefore might pose a greater risk of committing crimes in the future. But the real answer is that the Supreme Court concluded that plea bargaining was necessary, and then it had to ignore its ordinary constitutional law rules in order to preserve the practice.

The Supreme Court admitted as much in a 1978 case, *Bordenkircher v. Hayes*. The opinion in *Bordenkircher* was written not too long after the Supreme Court decided that it had to allow plea bargaining because the courts couldn't accommodate bringing every criminal case to trial. The prosecutor in the *Bordenkircher* case wanted Paul Lewis Hayes to plead guilty to forgery in return for a sentencing recommendation of five years in prison. The prosecutor told Hayes that if he did not plead guilty, then he would bring new charges against him under the state's habitual offender statute, which carried a mandatory life sentence for anyone convicted of three felonies. (Hayes had two previous convictions.) Hayes refused the plea bargain and was convicted and sentenced to life in prison.

Hayes appealed, relying on Supreme Court cases that said punishing a person for exercising his constitutional rights is unconstitutional. The Supreme Court reaffirmed that it is "patently unconstitutional" for a government official to penalize people for exercising their "legal rights." But then the Supreme Court said that plea bargaining does not punish people for exercising their right to a jury trial, but it is instead a "give-and-take negotiation" that occurs "between the prosecution and defense, which arguably possess relatively equal bargaining power."

I don't know how the Supreme Court could say that Paul Hayes and the prosecutor have "equal bargaining power." All Hayes had was the right to require the prosecutor to prove his case to a jury beyond a reasonable doubt—something that was probably inconvenient but otherwise didn't really affect the prosecutor. The prosecutor, on the other hand, had Hayes's freedom *for the rest of his life* as leverage.

Perhaps because the bargaining power between Hayes and the prosecutor was so obviously unequal, the Supreme Court admitted that it had to allow Hayes to be threatened with life in prison because otherwise it would have to declare plea bargaining unconstitutional. And when I say the Supreme Court "admitted" this, I mean that literally. The Court said "by tolerating and encouraging the negotiation of pleas, this Court has necessarily accepted as constitutionally legitimate the simple reality that the prosecutor's interest at the bargaining table is to persuade the defendant to forgo his right to plead not guilty." It also said "acceptance of the basic legitimacy of plea bargaining necessarily implies rejection of any notion that a guilty plea is involuntary in a constitutional sense . . ." In other words, the Court said that, because it had already accepted the constitutional-ity plea bargaining, it also had to allow government officials to pressure defendants to plead guilty and to impose longer punishments on them if they insist on a trial.

* * * * *

The idea that plea bargaining is just a "negotiation" and not punishment for exercising constitutional rights isn't just something the Supreme Court says. A number of very smart people have said something similar when they have attempted to defend the institution of plea bargaining.

Those attempts to justify plea bargaining describe a plea bargain as a contract between the prosecution and the defendant. As one well-known defense puts it: "The defendant will trade the right to plead not guilty and force a trial for the prosecutor's right to seek the maximum sentence." In these contract-based descriptions of plea bargaining, defendants have some leverage: the ability to force a prosecutor to spend the time and effort to take the case to trial. Because prosecutors have lots of cases, the assumption is that they do not have the ability to try more than just a few cases, and so any threat by a defendant to take a case to trial has to be taken seriously.

Contract-based descriptions of plea bargaining also assume that the bargains reflect the strength of the evidence against the defendant. Just as we expect people to negotiate prices in other contracts to reflect what they get in return, a criminal defendant should be able to demand a shorter sentence in return for giving up a higher likelihood of acquittal at trial. In contrast, a defendant who is more likely to get convicted should get less of a sentence reduction in his plea bargain. People who defend plea bargains speak about these different plea bargains as "different prices."

Defenders of plea bargains are quick to discount many of plea bargain-ing's problems. Any problems with innocent people who plead guilty as part of a plea bargain are recast as problems with trials, not plea bargains; after all, it is the risk that innocent defendants will lose and be convicted at trial that causes them to plead guilty. Similarly, plea bargaining's defenders dismiss arguments about how the trial penalty and harsh sentences create too much pressure on defendants to plead guilty as criticisms of sentenc-ing laws rather than plea bargaining. But these arguments ignore how plea bargaining creates or exacerbates those other problems. For example, many of our harsh sentencing laws exist to make it easier for prosecutors to pressure defendants into pleading guilty. And by encouraging the law-yers involved in plea bargaining to calculate "expected punishments," plea bargaining makes the risk of convicting innocent people at trial seem like just a number to calculate, instead of a horrifying injustice.

Nonetheless, characterizing plea bargains as contracts and negotia-tions carries a lot of rhetorical force. It taps into strong American feelings about freedom of contract and the virtues of a free-market economy. As Professor Darryl Brown explains in his book *Free Market Criminal Justice: How Democracy and Laissez Faire Undermine the Rule of Law*, courts have embraced the idea of plea bargaining as "free markets," and this idea has made the criminal justice system much, much worse. It has caused judges to shirk any oversight of the plea bargaining process on the theory that it is a private negotiation between the parties.

* * * * *

"Do you think that plea bargaining is like a contract, where the two parties negotiate over the terms in order to reach an outcome that benefits both sides?" I asked Katie Gipson-McLean, a young public defender in Phoenix. Known as KGM by her colleagues in the Maricopa County Office of the Public Defender, she had worked as a social worker after graduating from college and was inspired to go to law school when she saw a public defender get some criminal charges dismissed for one of her teenaged clients. The client, whom KGM referred to as one of her "kiddos," had gotten into trouble at school, which the school officials decided to deal with by calling the police and having him arrested.

To me, KGM seemed like the perfect person to ask about the "free-market" theory of plea bargaining. She brought five cases to trial in her first year as a defense attorney. Other defense attorneys practice for years before trying five cases. Since she is so quick to bring cases to trial, I thought KGM would be the sort of defense attorney who saw the threat of going to trial as something she could use for her clients.

But when I asked her about plea bargains as contracts, KGM's first reaction was to laugh. After she stopped laughing, her face became serious. "I think that—" she said, pausing. "I think that maybe—" She stopped again.

"No," KGM said after thinking for a minute. "I don't think that anyone in the system thinks of it in that way. I can't remember what word we would have used to describe this in my law school contracts class, but I think it's 'coercive.'" (A coercive contract is a contract entered into under conditions that involve harm or threats of harm. And as a matter of contract law, coercive contracts aren't enforceable.)

"One side," KGM explained, "has the upper hand. They have all of the power in the situation. There's no way to overcome that no matter what kind of negotiation you do. They can always say no, and there is nothing that you can do. You can't change your part of the negotiation. I mean, what are you going to do? You don't have anything to offer. There's nothing really that you have as a bargaining chip, and so there's nothing you can take away."

"But don't you have one big bargaining chip?" I pressed. "You can bring a case to trial. You've had a lot of trials. Don't you feel like threatening to take a case to trial is a bargaining chip that you have with the prosecutors?"

KGM paused again before answering. "You know, I think it probably depends on the prosecutor, to be honest. Some prosecutors are lazy, and so that would work with them. But a lot of them aren't lazy. And they've had enough trials themselves that they are, like, 'Whatever' if I say I'll go to trial."

KGM also didn't think much of the idea that weaknesses in a prosecutor's case get "priced into" the plea bargain deal—that defendants get better plea offers when there is a legal problem with a prosecutor's case. She sometimes had success getting a better offer if she could convince prosecutors that they had a problem with their case, such as a legal or a factual problem that would make it difficult for them to prove their case at trial. But those arguments weren't always successful. "Even on cases where they have horrible legal issues," she explained, "they have so many blind spots that they are super-arrogant about their case and about the strength of their case. They just say, 'Okay, we'll see,' and they are willing to take it to a jury."

It's not surprising that someone in the system thinks the idea of plea bargains as free-market contracts is laughable. Free-market principles obviously don't apply to plea bargaining. A free market depends on the idea of competition. But there is no competition in the criminal justice system. A defendant can't approach a different prosecutor to get a better deal if he doesn't like what the first prosecutor is offering. Prosecutors have a monopoly, and the harsh criminal laws make sure that the only alternative—going to trial—is too expensive.

Of course, prosecutors aren't the only actors involved: judges are ultimately responsible for imposing sentences on defendants. But the involvement of judges doesn't change the prosecutors' monopoly. As a practical matter, many judges impose whatever sentence the prosecutor recommends. One study of felony courts in Houston found that five of the six judges in the court "followed the prosecutor's sentence recommendation in almost every guilty-plea case that came before them." The one judge who didn't always follow the prosecutor's recommendation—a judge who was "considered a maverick by prosecutors and defense attorneys alike"—followed the prosecutor's recommendation in approximately 90 percent of cases. It says an awful lot about the power of prosecutors that a judge who follows their advice in only nine out of ten cases is considered a maverick.

Not only are judges uninterested in breaking the prosecutors' monopoly and creating competition, but sometimes judges have no choice: they are required to impose the sentence that the prosecutor wants. If the plea bargain is framed in terms of a defendant pleading guilty in return for a specific sentence, then a judge's options are limited to either imposing that sentence or rejecting the plea bargain altogether. Mandatory minimums also tie judges' hands: if the prosecutor insists that the defendant plead guilty to a crime that carries a mandatory minimum sentence, then the judge cannot impose a sentence below that minimum.

Ironically, to the extent that judges do not follow the recommendations of prosecutors, it may make the criminal justice system seem less fair. A defendant who negotiates with a prosecutor—such as a defendant who agrees to plead guilty and cooperate against other defendants—does so in order to get the benefit of a reduced sentence. If a judge then ignores the prosecutor's sentencing recommendation and imposes a higher sentence, then it seems like the defendant got a raw deal; after all, he gave up his right to a trial and testified in other cases in order to get a lower sentence.

This is an intractable problem. If judges simply defer to prosecutors' sentencing recommendations, that gives prosecutors more leverage in the plea bargaining process. But if judges ignore the prosecutors' recommendations and instead impose the sentences that they think are appropriate, then the defendants could lose any benefits from the bargains they made.

The source of this problem is plea bargaining itself. Judge are *supposed to* impose the sentences that they think are appropriate; that's why judges have the sentencing power. While prosecutors are supposed to be advocates, judges are supposed to be neutral. Sentencing is one of the traditional powers of judges: they consider all of the evidence and listen to arguments from both sides before imposing sentence. Giving the sentencing power to prosecutors would be inappropriate.

Allowing prosecutors to choose the sentence of a criminal defendant is like allowing the plaintiff in a civil lawsuit to declare what money damages she should receive from the person that she sued. In other words, plea bargaining turns the justice system on its head. It allows prosecutors to circumvent the judge and the jury by negotiating with the defendant over her guilt and her sentence. And when a prosecutor can't get what she wants from that negotiation, then she can turn to charge stacking, charge bargaining, and mandatory minimums to pressure the defendant into a better deal.

For some reason, society has been able to see the potential for abuse in that arrangement when it comes to civil lawsuits. When it became clear that unscrupulous civil plaintiffs who probably would have lost their civil lawsuits could nonetheless get big-dollar settlements out of businesses and other wealthy civil defendants, the country responded by reducing their leverage. In addition, states across the country have enacted laws that cap money damages or make it easy for companies to avoid courtrooms and send civil claims to arbitration. But we've done the opposite for criminal cases—handing prosecutors more and more leverage that allows them to squeeze criminal defendants into giving up their rights.

* * * * *

The misguided free-market idea of plea bargains has other consequences. Because judges have given prosecutors (and themselves) a free pass to pressure defendants into giving up their constitutional right to a trial, they've also removed any real check on what else prosecutors can demand as part of a plea bargain's "contract." As a result, prosecutors having increasingly demanded that defendants waive a number of other constitutional rights, in addition to their right to a jury trial, in order to get a plea deal. Because of their "free-market" approach to plea bargaining, some judges see this additional bargaining as a positive development: they say it gives defendants more to bargain with in their negotiations with prosecutors. But in reality it just means that defendants usually have to give up even more rights in order to get a reasonable plea bargain.

Prosecutors now routinely require defendants to waive all sorts of other constitutional rights, in addition to their right to a jury trial, as part of the plea bargaining process. Prosecutors will often insist that a defendant waive her right to see the evidence against her, the right to a preliminary hearing in front of a judge, and the right to an appeal as part of the plea bargain. Because courts do not like to "interfere" in the "negotiations," prosecutors are free to tell defendants that they must waive these additional rights even without giving them a better deal in the plea offer.

These other waivers leave defendants plea bargaining in the dark and unable to get any errors corrected on appeal. As you might imagine, the result is a system in which prosecutors have enormous power—power that they use against the guilty and the innocent.

* * * * *

On November 30, 2001, at approximately 6:30 in the morning, a man broke into the house of an eighty-three-year-old woman in Clarksburg, West Virginia. The man robbed the woman and then raped her. After the man left, the woman called the police. The police took her statement and also took her to the hospital for medical attention. The woman wasn't able to provide a very good description of the man because he had worn a white bandana to cover his face. But medical personnel were able to obtain a DNA sample because the rapist hadn't worn a condom.

About a week after this assault, Joseph Buffey was arrested for breaking and entering three businesses in downtown Clarksburg. Police questioned Joseph about the rape. While he readily admitted that he had broken into the businesses, Joseph denied any involvement in the robbery and rape of the elderly woman. After nine hours of questioning, officers got Joseph to say that he had broken into the woman's house, but the details Joseph provided were inconsistent, and he said he could not remember any rape. When pressed some more by police, Joseph said that he had nothing to do with the break-in or assault of the elderly woman; he had only said otherwise because the police were pressuring him.

Despite these denials, prosecutors decided to charge Joseph with robbery and rape in addition to the three business break-ins. Joseph couldn't afford an attorney, and so one was appointed to help him. Joseph admitted to his lawyer that he had broken into the three businesses, but he insisted that he had nothing to do with the rape or robbery. In fact, he had an alibi the night the rape occurred.

Joseph's lawyer asked the state to turn over any evidence of the crime, including any DNA evidence. But instead of turning over evidence, the prosecutors gave Joseph's lawyer something else: an offer to plea bargain. They were willing to dismiss the breaking and entering charges against Joseph if he would plead guilty to the robbery and rape.

The plea bargain presented Joseph with a difficult choice: if he wanted to plead guilty and have a better chance at a reduced sentence, he had to plead guilty right away. The prosecutors had put a time limit on the plea bargain that wouldn't let Joseph and his lawyer wait for the DNA results. There was no guarantee that those results would exonerate Joseph—DNA tests are sometimes inconclusive—and so Joseph's lawyer strongly recommended that Joseph take the plea deal.

Joseph eventually agreed. He went to court and said that he had broken into the elderly woman's house and raped her. But Joseph knew he had done no such thing. And so, six months after his guilty plea, Joseph filed a petition with the court to overturn his conviction. The court appointed Joseph a new lawyer for his appeal. That new lawyer contacted prosecutors to follow up on the DNA testing.

That is when something astonishing came to light: at the time that the state had offered Joseph the plea deal, they had already received the results of the DNA test. Those results proved that Joseph hadn't raped the victim. By offering him the time-limited plea deal, the prosecutors had pressured Joseph into pleading guilty to a crime that he hadn't committed.

It took multiple lawsuits and a number of appeals before a judge was willing to say that Joseph's guilty plea was invalid. In the meantime, Joseph served more than thirteen years in prison for a crime he didn't commit.

Prosecutors routinely require defendants to give up their right to see the evidence against them—evidence that is sometimes called discovery or *Brady* material (after the famous Supreme Court case *Brady v. Maryland*, which established the right). And the Supreme Court has said that is okay.

When a defendant complained that requiring her to give up some of her discovery rights in order to get a guilty plea was unconstitutional, the Supreme Court dismissed this argument in a unanimous decision. Allowing defendants to insist on those discovery materials, the Supreme Court said, would require prosecutors to spend more time and effort on a case before plea bargaining, "thereby depriving the plea-bargaining process of its main resource-saving advantages." The justices were concerned that, if plea bargaining became less efficient, then the government might "abandon [its] heavy reliance upon plea bargaining." The justices even went so far as to say that, if prosecutors did not continue to plea bargain "in a vast number" of cases, that would be a "radical" change—a change that they didn't think was justified "in order to achieve so comparatively small a constitutional benefit" as discovery for the defendant.

It is hard to read that opinion without thinking that the Supreme Court wanted to make sure that plea bargaining continued to be the main source of convictions in America. Even though denying defendants discovery might result in the conviction of innocent people, the Supreme Court didn't want to make plea bargaining less convenient for prosecutors. In fact, the Supreme Court's reasoning tells us that it was totally fine for prosecutors to force Joseph to plead guilty before knowing the results of the DNA test. The only reason his conviction got reversed was because prosecutors lied to Joseph and his attorney about having the DNA test results. If not for that lie, Joseph probably wouldn't have gotten his conviction reversed. He might still be in jail for a crime he never committed.

* * * * *

In Phoenix, requiring defendants to waive their right to discovery is not just routine; an entire formal court system has been created to facilitate that waiver. Arizona actually has pretty good discovery laws. Unlike some places, which make defendants wait until just before trial to see the evidence against them, Arizona gives defendants their discovery right after the charges are formally filed. But rather than giving defendants their discovery, as the law requires, Phoenix has created an entire court system—the regional court centers (RCCs for short)—to avoid those obligations and to pressure defendants into taking a plea bargain right away.

When I spoke to KGM, she explained that the RCCs initially began as an alternative to trials—a way for people who were charged with low-level felonies to avoid the harsh consequences associated with the regular trial courts. People would go to the RCCs in order to get treatment rather than just punishment. But in the years after they were created, the RCCs morphed into something else. Rather than being safety valves for low-level felonies, they became sort of clearinghouses for all but the most serious crimes, like homicides and sex offenses. KGM estimates that anywhere from 80 to 90 percent of felony cases in Phoenix start out in the RCCs.

Right now, the point of RCCs isn't to get a defendant treatment. It's to get a guilty plea as quickly as possible. When a defense attorney shows up in an RCC, all she has is a file she received the night before. That file includes a police report, a list of the client's prior convictions—a list that is often riddled with errors, according to KGM—and a plea offer from the prosecutor's office. The defense attorney and her client have thirty days to accept, reject, or renegotiate the plea offer. But the message from the prosecutor is clear: once the case leaves the RCC and the defendant either has a preliminary hearing or gets indicted—which is to say, once the charges have become formal and the defendant is entitled to discovery—the plea offer goes away. The Phoenix prosecutor's office official policy is that the RCC plea offer will be the best offer. If the defendant turns down the offer, any subsequent offer she gets will be much harsher, and she may not even get another plea offer at all.

This process deprives defendants of discovery: their opportunity to see the evidence against them. Without that, defendants and their attorneys can't make an educated decision about whether to plead guilty or whether to proceed to trial. KGM says that only in very rare circumstances is she able to get prosecutors to give her more information about a case in an RCC. If, for example, there is video evidence of what happened and if her client insists that the video will show that the defendant is innocent or that the crime was not as serious as what was charged, she will ask the prosecutor to either send her the video or to at least check the video themselves. In those limited circumstances, she said some prosecutors "will try to be flexible. But generally you are just going to get a police report. And for a lot of the police reports, there's not a lot of information in there."

Why would a prosecutor's office have a policy of withdrawing the "best" plea offer once the defendant is actually entitled to see those videos and the other evidence against them?

"Well, then the prosecutors don't have to do very much work," KGM said with a wry smile. "They're not going to have to worry about sending out any subpoenas. They're not going to have to worry about setting up any interviews with their witnesses or police officers. They're not going to have to worry about actually *proving* anything." She added that she thought some prosecutors do not conduct any independent investigation on a case at all, but instead rely only on the police report to decide what charges to bring and what plea offer to give.

The practice of prosecutors withdrawing a plea offer because a defendant is invoking some other right—like the right to discovery or the right to file a suppression motion—is hardly limited to Phoenix. But what *is* unusual about Phoenix is that they have set up a whole court system that helps prosecutors formalize that practice. There are judges in the RCC, called commissioners, who reinforce the practice by explaining to the defendant what the difference is between the plea offer and the expected sentence after trial.

To be clear, there is a good reason why the RCC judges give that explanation. The Arizona Supreme Court has said that a defendant can have her conviction reversed if a defense attorney fails to accurately explain the relative merits of the plea offer as compared to the expected sentence after trial and then the defendant goes to trial based on that bad legal advice. The Constitution guarantees defendants effective lawyers to defend them, and a lawyer who doesn't explain to his client the difference between the plea offer and what will happen at trial hasn't been effective.

Having judges explain the difference between the plea offer and the expected sentence after trial ensures that defendants will have the information necessary to decide whether to plead or go to trial. It also ensures that any conviction after a trial can't be challenged as unconstitutional because the defense lawyer was ineffective. But it also legitimizes the prosecutor's decision to circumvent the discovery rules. It suggests that the prosecutor's decision to deprive the defendant of the right to discovery has the blessing of the judge.

Even without the apparent blessing of the judge, we should still be deeply concerned about making defendants give up their right to discovery in order to get a better plea offer. The whole idea behind plea bargaining is that defendants are able to estimate their chances of winning at trial and then use that information to negotiate a plea offer that is less than their expected punishment. But it is impossible for defendants to do that if they don't know what evidence the prosecutor has. This lack of information is probably most damaging for people like Joseph Buffey—defendants who are actually innocent of a crime. Some of them may have no idea why police even suspect them of the crime in the first place.

The right to discovery may be the most important right that defendants are asked to waive in plea bargaining. But it isn't the only constitutional right that is up for grabs.

* * * * *

Years after it happened, Josh Vaughn remembers the woman in the courtroom. Josh was at the courthouse in Franklin County, Pennsylvania. At the time, Josh was a reporter for the *Sentinel,* a newspaper in central Pennsylvania that served the area near Harrisburg and Carlisle. Josh was at the courthouse to report on the preliminary hearing of a prison guard who had been charged with sexual assault.

Josh noticed that the courtroom was very full. Franklin County schedules all of its preliminary hearings for the same day, and so there were about fifty or sixty people sitting on the benches. As Josh sat in the general seating area of the courtroom, waiting for the prison guard's case to be called, he saw a woman sitting just a couple of rows away from him. Because he had been covering court proceedings for a while, he was able to figure out that this woman was a defendant in a case that was also scheduled for a preliminary hearing. She must have been released on bail after her arrest because she was sitting in the same part of the courtroom as Josh, rather than in a holding cell outside of the courtroom.

While other cases were being called, an assistant district attorney approached the woman to talk to her about pleading guilty. That was a common practice in Franklin County. Even though the court rules didn't allow the judge to take a plea at this type of hearing, the prosecutors used the hearing as an opportunity to meet with defendants and get them to agree to a plea deal. Then, at the next court date, when defendants would be formally arraigned, they could plead guilty right away.

The prosecutor had given the woman a folder that had the relevant documents in it and they started talking. Josh didn't hear what the plea offer was, but he did hear the woman tell the prosecutor: "I think I might ask the judge to give me a lawyer."

The woman had a constitutional right to a lawyer, and if she couldn't afford one, then she could ask the judge to appoint a lawyer for her. The first time she could make that request was at the preliminary hearing—the hearing that was going to happen in the courtroom that day.

But the prosecutor was annoyed that the woman was going to ask for a lawyer. "At that point, the assistant district attorney took the file out of her hand, looked at her, and said, 'You're welcome to do that. But if you do that, this deal is off the table,'" Josh recalled.

I couldn't imagine how the woman must have felt when the prosecutor told her that her plea deal would go away if she asked for a lawyer. Josh continued: "The woman looked upset and said, 'Well, am I going to get a deal if I ask for a public defender?' But the prosecutor's response was basically 'I'll give you a deal, but it's not going to be the same one.'"

"And did 'not the same deal' mean a worse deal?" I asked Josh.

"Oh, yeah," he said. "Yeah. I mean, again, the prosecutor literally took the folder out of her hand and told her, 'If you get a public defender, if you apply for one, this deal is off the table. And we'll think about something else to offer you whenever you get your lawyer.'"

Josh couldn't understand the prosecutor's behavior. "What difference does it make to public safety to let her get a lawyer and have the lawyer look over the plea agreement?" he asked rhetorically. "It just seems asinine."

You might think that prosecutors shouldn't be allowed to pressure a defendant into waiving their right to have a lawyer represent them. And you'd be right: they aren't allowed to do it. It's actually a violation of the legal ethics rules, which specifically tell prosecutors not to ask people who don't have a lawyer for a "waiver of important pretrial rights." (The right to a lawyer is obviously an important pretrial right.)

Even though it might be unethical for a prosecutor to do this, that doesn't mean they can't or that they face any real consequences if they do. Ethics complaints against prosecutors almost never result in any discipline or other consequences. And because prosecutors know that, some don't even bother to hide the unethical pressure that they bring to bear in plea bargaining. "It was stark," Josh emphasized to me again at the end of our interview, "literally just taking the file out of her hand and walking out the door. And to do that in the middle of the courtroom—just the brazenness of it. It was like the prosecutor thought, 'I really don't care if people see that I am doing this.'"

In addition to not having a lawyer, the woman also didn't have any discovery. In Franklin County, defendants don't get their right to discovery until after the formal arraignment. So she had to decide whether to plead guilty without the help of a lawyer *and* without being able to see the evidence against her.

Playing fast and loose with the right to a lawyer doesn't just happen in Franklin County, Pennsylvania. For several years, some federal prosecutors required defendants to waive their constitutional right to effective assistance of counsel as part of plea negotiations. As I mentioned earlier, a defendant can have her conviction overturned if her attorney gave her incorrect information about the consequences of pleading guilty. So, for example, a defendant might have pleaded guilty because his lawyer told him that the judge could sentence him to probation, but then he ended up in prison because there was actually a mandatory minimum sentencing law. Ordinarily, the defendant could ask the appellate court to throw out the conviction based on ineffective assistance of counsel, and then the defendant is free to either negotiate a new plea offer or go to trial. But if prosecutors made him waive his right to effective assistance of counsel, then the defendant would have to go to prison despite the fact that his attorney made a terrible error.

In 2014 the Department of Justice adopted a new policy, telling federal prosecutors that they "should no longer seek in plea agreements to have a defendant waive claims of ineffective assistance of counsel . . ." Notably the memo explaining that policy said that the department was "confident" that those waivers were "both legal and ethical." As with all internal policies, the department has the ability to change that policy at any time. And even though the policy tells prosecutors not to ask for those waivers, it doesn't give a defendant any rights if a prosecutor decides to violate the policy. In other words, as with most everything associated with plea bargaining, the choice and the power remain with the prosecutor.

* * * * *

Plea bargaining doesn't just mean that we don't have trials. It dramatically changes the entire criminal justice system. It leads to incredibly harsh punishments for those people who *do* want to have a trial. It also deprives people of other constitutional rights, like the right to discovery or the right to an attorney. Perhaps most important, it changes the expectations and assumptions of everyone within the criminal justice system. A person like Joseph Tigano who insists on his right to a trial is seen as literally crazy.

That attitude—that plea bargains are normal and trials are crazy—warps the very fabric of our criminal justice system. In Phoenix it led to the creation of a whole new court system—a system that exists only to pressure defendants into pleading guilty. I said that to KGM during our interview, asking her, "Isn't this almost like a structure that has been set up just to facilitate plea bargaining."

"Exactly. One hundred percent," she responded. And then she added that every time a new attorney joins her office, they all say, "Isn't this unconstitutional? Why do we have this?"

There is a simple answer to that question—one that the Supreme Court gave in *Bordenkircher*: Once we decide to accept plea bargaining, we can't try to enforce constitutional rights. It's a whole new ball game. And basically anything goes.

CHAPTER FOUR

THE DESIRE TO BE FREE

"As a public defender for over 7 years, I have yet to have a single client turn down a plea offer that gets them out of jail. The chance to go home overwhelms the question of whether they are innocent or guilty. Innocent people plead guilty all the time."

I saw this statement as I was scrolling through Twitter one afternoon. I checked the account. The person who posted it was a public defender in the Bronx named Michael Bloch. On a whim, I reached out to Michael and asked if he'd be willing to talk to me.

We ended up speaking by telephone a few days later. When I asked him to give me an example of a client who prompted his tweet, Michael told me about his client, José.* José had been arrested in the Bronx for a very minor offense. It was the sort of minor crime for which Michael and his colleagues were often able to get charges reduced or even dismissed. José was on supervised release—which is similar to probation or parole—for having committed a federal crime, and so it was absolutely imperative that he not get convicted of a new crime.

Michael met with José, who was being held in jail after his arrest. José explained his situation. Michael told José that he would try to negotiate a plea to a reduced charge. And so Michael approached the prosecutor who

---

* José is not his real name.

was on duty in the courtroom that day to handle cases. Michael asked the prosecutor whether she would be willing to offer José a plea to a noncriminal violation on his misdemeanor charge. A violation is essentially a ticket, and so it wouldn't cause any problems for José on his federal charge.

Although prosecutors routinely made such deals with defense attorneys, this prosecutor was reluctant to do so. She explained that the case actually belonged to another prosecutor. She was only covering for that prosecutor, and she didn't feel as though she could offer a plea to a reduced charge, since it wasn't her case. All she had been authorized to do was accept a guilty plea to a misdemeanor, but the sentence would be time served. She told Michael that the other prosecutor would be back in court two days later and he could talk to that prosecutor about offering a reduced charge then. So Michael went to tell José that he'd have to wait two extra days for the better plea bargain.

José said no. He told Michael he would plead guilty to the misdemeanor charge so long as it meant he could leave right then. Michael was concerned. He explained to José that if he was convicted of a misdemeanor, then federal prosecutors would say he violated the terms of his supervised release and they would send him to prison—and not just for two days. Michael told José that if he just waited two more days in the New York jail, he was confident he could get the prosecutor to give him a better deal. He assured José that he got deals like that from prosecutors all the time.

But José had made up his mind. He insisted on taking the plea deal so that he could get out of jail that day. He took the deal against Michael's advice. And once the federal prosecutors found out about his new conviction in the Bronx, they sent him to federal prison for a year.

I was surprised by Michael's story. It was clear that José would have been much better off if he'd waited the two extra days. I told Michael that I couldn't understand why José acted so irrationally. He knew that he would spend a lot more than two days in prison if he took the deal, and so it didn't make any sense for him to plead guilty right away.

"It's hard for me to say," Michael responded. "From an outside perspective it may seem irrational. One year is obviously longer than two days. But I've never been in jail. I can't say that I wouldn't make the same choice. The desire to be free is just that strong."

* * * * *

Even if an innocent person doesn't plead guilty in order to be released from jail, there is still a very big problem: an innocent person is sitting in jail.

Jail is a terrible place. Jails are full of people who are desperate and who have already demonstrated that they are unwilling to follow the law. Some of those people prey on the others, inflicting horrific violence or acts of sexual abuse. Many jails are also understaffed and unable to provide basic medical care to their prisoners. More than half of incarcerated prisoners suffer from mental illness, which being incarcerated doubtlessly exacerbates. The lack of adequate medical care, the violence in jails, and the despair that accompanies an arrest and incarceration can be so overwhelming that people in jail sometimes take their own lives. The suicide rate in jail is much higher than the rate for people who are not incarcerated.

When innocent people are in jail, they are desperate to get out. But there is very little that they can do. They can try to convince prosecutors that they should drop the charges against them, negotiate plea deals, or just wait for their trials. If that doesn't work, those innocent people sometimes stay in jail for a very long time.

That's what happened to Jerome Hayes.

Police arrested Jerome for a series of robberies. Each robbery followed a similar pattern: A person would respond to an ad on Craigslist selling electronic equipment, like a phone or headphones. When the would-be-buyer arrived, he would pull a gun and steal the equipment rather than paying for it.

Three separate robberies following this pattern were reported to police. The police followed up on the phone numbers that were used to text responses to the Craigslist ads. That investigation led them to some email addresses associated with the phone numbers. Two of those email addresses—*jermauriceh97@gmail.com* and *Jermauricehayes17@gmail.com*—looked like they included combinations of the names Jerome and Maurice. Using this information and IP addresses, police began to suspect Jerome Hayes, whose middle name was Maurice. They showed Jerome's photo to the robbery victims, who identified him.

Soon after, police arrested Jerome. He insisted that he hadn't committed any robberies. When police told him about the photo identification and the email addresses, Jerome asked the officers whether they had talked to his younger brother. As Jerome explained to the officers, he and his brother look a lot alike, and they even have similar names: His brother is named Jermaurice.

But the officers didn't listen. Instead they sent Jerome to jail to wait for a trial on robbery charges.

Jerome didn't give up. He let the prosecutor on his case know that his brother Jermaurice had been seen with new electronics equipment, including new headphones. He had his girlfriend go to the two restaurants where he worked and get records showing that Jerome was at work when two of the three robberies were committed. Jerome had his lawyer send those records to the prosecutor just a few weeks after his arrest, but the prosecutor wouldn't dismiss the charges.

Jerome's lawyer took this information to the judge along with the results of a lie detector test that Jerome had passed. The lawyer presented the information to the judge and argued that the judge should release Jerome from jail while he waited for the robbery trial. But the judge refused.

It's shocking that a judge would keep Jerome in jail under these circumstances. There was strong evidence suggesting that Jerome was innocent and that his brother had committed these crimes. When a newspaper reporter, Topher Sanders, wrote a story about Jerome's case, he reached out to the judge to ask about why he denied bail, keeping Jerome in jail. But the judge didn't respond to Sanders's request for a comment.

Sanders wasn't surprised by the judge's decision to deny bail. "My experience covering the criminal justice system in the South has taught me that there's an almost symbiotic relationship between judges and prosecutors," he said when the two of us spoke by phone about Jerome's case. Sanders is a reporter for ProPublica who has written about innocent people who plead guilty. He reported extensively about Jerome's case when he was a reporter at the *Florida Times-Union*.

"Many judges are former prosecutors, and they still think like prosecutors," he explained. "The judges, they come into the job with that perspective, and they lean on that experience when they have to make decisions like whether to set bail."

Jerome sat in jail for months. His case changed hands: a new prosecutor was appointed, and the public defender's office switched his defense attorney multiple times. All the while, Jerome kept wondering why he was still sitting in jail for a crime he didn't commit. After Jerome had spent more than four months in jail, police finally interviewed Jerome's brother, Jermaurice. But Jermaurice just denied having committed the robberies, and police never even told Jerome's lawyer about the interview.

While Jerome waited to prove his innocence at trial, months turned into a year, and his life outside of prison fell apart. His girlfriend had given birth to their daughter after Jerome was arrested, and the strain of jail fractured their relationship. Jerome lost his two restaurant jobs, and his now ex-girlfriend began raising his child without him.

Finally, as the date for Jerome's trial approached, things started to fall apart for the prosecution. Jerome's new defense attorney had been requesting information from the prosecution about the eyewitness identifications and about any investigation that the police had done of Jermaurice's involvement. The prosecutor falsely told Jerome's attorney that police had never interviewed Jermaurice and that he didn't have some of the paperwork from the eyewitness identifications. The prosecutor also missed a court deadline to turn evidence over to Jerome's attorney. In the days leading up to trial, Jerome's attorney finally got his hands on important evidence: proof that police had interviewed Jermaurice, proof that law enforcement had detailed employment records showing Jerome could not have committed two of the three robberies, and even statements from the restaurant supervisors saying that Jerome was definitely at work that day. This information had been sitting in the prosecutors' files for months!

Prosecutors have a legal obligation to turn over evidence to defendants before trial—especially evidence that is helpful to a defendant's case. And they are not allowed to lie about what evidence they do have. Jerome's attorney took all of this evidence and his complaints about the prosecutor's misconduct to the judge. The judge still didn't release Jerome, but the evidence convinced him to issue an ultimatum: law enforcement had to conduct a physical lineup for the robbery victims that included both Jerome and Jermaurice or else the judge would release Jerome from jail. When the lineup was held a week later, one victim positively identified Jermaurice. Another said she couldn't tell if Jerome or Jermaurice had robbed her. No one positively identified Jerome.

Prosecutors had no choice. They released Jerome and dismissed the charges against him. By the time that Jerome was released, he had served one year, seven months, and nine days in jail.

Unfortunately, Jerome's case doesn't appear to have made much of an impact on the police officers or the prosecutors who kept him in jail. The police officers told Topher Sanders that they arrested the right person. "They still believed that Jerome was the guy," Sanders said. "They think this was a fish who got away, not the wrong fish. So they aren't concerned about the time he spent in jail."

As for the prosecutor, he was investigated by the Florida state bar for withholding evidence in Jerome's case. But he escaped any punishment by assuring the state bar that he had made changes in how he worked "to avoid similar occurrences." Yet his name popped up just a couple of years later as the prosecutor in another case in which an innocent man was kept in jail for more than three years on murder and arson charges before prosecutors dismissed the charges.

* * * * **

You might wonder why Jerome's story is in this book. After all, he didn't plead guilty. Police eventually realized their mistake and dismissed the charges against him. But the thing is, Jerome still got punished: he spent nineteen months in jail before the charges against him were dropped. And the reason he was in jail is a major way in which modern governments are able to punish people without ever having a trial.

Like José, Jerome had been arrested. Neither José nor Jerome had been found guilty of committing a crime. Yet they were being held in jail along with people who had already been convicted and were serving their sentences.

For José, the prosecutor was offering a plea bargain where the court would recognize that the time José had already spent in jail was punishment enough for what he had done. These sorts of sentences are so common that they have a nickname: "time served." Prosecutors were not offering Jerome a plea to time served; the crime he was accused of was too serious. But if Jerome had been found guilty at trial, the time he spent in jail before the trial would have been subtracted from any prison sentence that he received. This is also a common sentencing practice called "credit for time served." As these common practices recognize, *the government had already begun to punish José and Jerome even though they hadn't been convicted.*

It is hard to understand why we allow the government to keep people in jail when they haven't been convicted of a crime. After all, Jerome's case teaches us that at least some of the people in jail are innocent. If the state hadn't dismissed the charges against him, Jerome would have been acquitted at trial. That's why we have trials: to sort out who is guilty and who is not. And before that trial happens or before a person pleads guilty, we have to assume that they are innocent. Lawyers call this idea the "presumption of innocence." It is the same idea behind the common expression "innocent until proven guilty."

So why do we allow the state to punish an innocent man like Jerome? Why do we let them keep José in jail before proving that he is guilty? Why do we let them punish the hundreds of thousands of people who sit in jail every year and who haven't yet been convicted?

Well, the people in criminal justice system don't say that they are punishing people before trial. They say that they are merely *detaining* these people, not punishing them. But that seems like little more than wordplay: people like José and Jerome are being treated no differently than the people in jail who have been convicted. That's why, if they are actually convicted, their sentencing judges will say that the time they spent in jail counts as punishment. Of course, the time a person spends sitting in jail doesn't magically transform into punishment just because she is later convicted. Yet that's what judges say the law does: they say sitting in jail isn't punishment before someone is convicted; it isn't punishment if the charges are dropped or the person is acquitted; but it *retroactively becomes punishment* if the person pleads guilty or is convicted at trial.

Why do we let our government officials use wordplay and legal fictions to punish people before they have been proven guilty? And how could this happen in a country where we say that everyone is innocent until proven guilty?

The truth is that we didn't used to let the government detain so many people before trial. When our constitution was written, the assumption was that someone like José, who was accused of a minor crime, could not have been detained before trial. And for the first century after the Constitution was adopted, someone like Jerome also would have been released. Because Jerome's crime was more serious, a judge probably would have required him or someone close to him to provide a financial guarantee that Jerome would show up in court for his trial. For example, Jerome might have had to pledge the deed to his house, which would have been forfeited to the court if he had failed to show up for trial. Or if Jerome didn't own a house, then a wealthier relative would have had to agree to forfeit some property or money if Jerome didn't show. But unless there was some reason to believe that Jerome would not come back to court, the judge could not have just refused to let Jerome out of jail before his trial.

José's case was so minor that he probably would not even have been arrested. And even if he had been arrested, he would have been released as a matter of course. He certainly would not have had to plea bargain with the prosecution in order to get out of jail.

To be clear, there were exceptions to the rule that people had to be released. People who were charged with capital crimes were denied the right to bail. The theory was that a person facing the possibility of the death penalty was more likely to run away; they would run because losing their property or the property of their friends and family is better than the risk of being executed. Historically, a number of crimes—not just murder—were capital crimes. But until the middle of the twentieth century, making someone stay in jail until her trial was still the exception rather than the rule.

The right to be released from custody and remain free before trial was considered an important right by the people who wrote our constitution. They were familiar with what happened in England, where people had to fight to make sure that prisoners could be released. That right not to be detained before trial was included in the Magna Carta, and Parliament passed a famous law to stop court officials from setting the financial guarantees so high that people couldn't meet them. To avoid these problems and abuses in America, Congress passed a law when it first met in 1789 that ensured all defendants were entitled to release pretrial except for those facing the death penalty. Two years later, when the Bill of Rights was adopted, it included the directive that "excessive bail shall not be required."

The right of defendants to be released before trial grew weaker in the mid-twentieth century. In the 1940s the federal criminal justice system adopted a series of procedural rules. Those rules did not frame the question of pretrial release just in terms of whether the defendant was likely to appear at trial. Instead, the rule told judges to consider the crime the defendant was charged with, the strength of the evidence against him, the defendant's financial situation, and his character in setting the financial guarantee. These new factors didn't make sense in a system that presumed everyone innocent until proven guilty.

At the same time, judges started setting high bail amounts that people couldn't possibly pay, presumably because the judges didn't want to release the people at all. Congress intervened in 1966. It passed a law trying to make sure that judges didn't set bail amounts too high and that judges didn't use pretrial detention to keep defendants from committing new crimes while awaiting trial.

But the 1966 law also validated the criminal procedure rules, telling judges to consider what crimes defendants were accused of committing and to weigh the evidence against them when setting the conditions of release on bail. The 1966 law also gave judges the authority to deny bail altogether in noncapital cases if they decided that the defendants were unlikely to appear for future court dates. Although it endorsed the idea that judges should weigh evidence and could deny bail even in noncapital cases, all told, the 1966 law still favored releasing defendants before trial.

That changed in the 1980s. In 1984, Congress passed a new bail law that told judges to consider whether it was safe to release a defendant before trial. If the judge thought that a defendant posed a danger to the community, then the judge was instructed to keep the defendant in jail rather than set any conditions for bail. The law also said that judges should assume defendants accused of many different types of noncapital crimes could not be safely released pending trial. This flipped the presumption of innocence on its head by *presuming* that a person accused of a crime should be detained and shifting the burden to justify release onto the defendant.

This new bail law was part of a larger set of federal laws aimed at cracking down on crime, which had surged in the 1960s and 1970s. Importantly, the Supreme Court signed off on these new bail laws and validated using bail to restore "law and order." It decided that the Constitution's rule against excessive bail didn't prevent the courts from refusing to set any bail whatsoever and just keep defendants in jail before trial. And it also blessed Congress's decision to make "dangerousness" part of the bail decision. In short, the justices allowed the government to dramatically change the balance of power before trial. Prosecutors could keep defendants in jail for extended periods of time without having to convince juries of anything; all they had to do was convince the judge that the defendants probably committed the crimes or that they were likely to commit more crimes if they were released back into their communities while awaiting trial.

The people who wrote the Constitution expected that most people accused of a crime would be set free rather than held in jail pending trial. But two hundred years later Congress and the courts had largely abandoned the view of pretrial detention as an exception rather than the rule. Jail was presumed for a lot of crimes, and judges were explicitly invited to short-circuit the presumption of innocence and weigh evidence themselves.

Then—remarkably—things got even worse. In recent decades more and more people have been held in jail before being convicted. This increase in pretrial detention has a few different causes. First, more people are getting brought to jail in the first place. In 1984, the year that Congress passed its second bail reform law, just over 50 percent of all arrests ended in someone being brought to jail. Everyone else was simply given a summons to appear in court and remained free until that date. By 2012, 95 percent of arrests resulted in the suspect being brought to jail. Those numbers are remarkable not only because of the large increase but also because crime rates dropped significantly from 1984 to 2012. Even though there was less crime, police brought more people to jail.

Another reason that pretrial detention has increased is because it is now more difficult for people to get out of jail while waiting for trial. In 1990, only one-half of defendants had to provide a financial guarantee to be released from jail. The rest were "released on their own recognizance"—that is, the courts trusted them to come back without having to give a financial guarantee. By 2004, nearly two-thirds of defendants were required to provide a financial guarantee. Bail amounts have also increased. From 1990 to 2004, the average amount of bail in a felony case increased more than 40 percent—from $38,000 to $55,400. Even misdemeanor defendants are sometimes required to pay bail amounts of up to $20,000 to be released before trial.

The result of these changes has been devastating. Nearly half a million people sit in jail every day in the United States because they cannot make bail. Many of those cases involve poor people accused of misdemeanor crimes who simply do not have the financial resources to pay even relatively modest financial guarantees. In New York City, one study found that more than 80 percent of defendants charged with low-level crimes were unable to make bail that was set at less than $500. Those people—people who were presumed innocent and accused only of a minor crime—were stuck in jail because they were poor.

* * * * *

It might not seem like a bad idea to keep people who have committed crimes or people who are likely to commit crimes in jail. After all, people should be punished when they commit crimes, and one reason to punish them is to keep the rest of us safe.

But even it if is a good idea to keep *some* people in jail before trial, our system is very unfair in how it decides who stays in jail and who is let out. The decisions are made quickly—sometimes without a defense lawyer and sometimes without a real judge. And we also treat rich people and poor people differently, allowing rich people to buy their release and forcing poor people to stay in jail. It's hard to say that what happens at bail hearings qualifies as "due process of law," which the Constitution guarantees before anyone is deprived of their liberty. It's also hard to say that rich and poor people are getting the "equal protection of the laws," which the Constitution also guarantees. Because of this, legal advocacy groups have been challenging bail practices across the country. One of those groups—Civil Rights Corps, an organization devoted to challenging systemic injustice in the American legal system—had a big win in Houston, Texas.

* * * * *

In March of 2016, Elizabeth Rossi traveled to Houston. She went to the Harris County Criminal Justice Center, a large building in downtown Houston that houses much of the county's criminal justice system. She entered the building, went through the metal detector, and asked for directions to the courtroom where bail hearings take place. It wasn't at all obvious where the courtroom was—she had to walk through people's offices to get there—but eventually she found it and took a seat in the back of the courtroom.

At the front of the courtroom was a hearing officer—not a judge, but a person who had been selected by the judges in the county—a prosecutor, and a representative from pretrial services, the agency responsible for helping the courts with the logistics of detaining and releasing defendants who are awaiting trial. There was also a big television screen in the courtroom. Every couple of hours, the television would be turned on, and Elizabeth could see a couple of sheriff's deputies and anywhere from twenty to forty-five people. Some of those people were wearing orange jumpsuits; others were still in their street clothes. All of them had been arrested within the past day or so.

Elizabeth watched as those people were called, one by one, to stand in a red square that had been painted on the floor. None of the people had a lawyer. They were in the county jail, and rather than take the time and effort to bring these people to the courtroom, county officials decided to conduct their bail hearings from the jail itself via a video link.

The idea that officials wanted to avoid time and effort was evident from more than just the fact that these hearings were held on a television rather than in person. The hearings themselves were incredibly perfunctory. "They lasted anywhere from twenty seconds to maybe a minute and a half—three minutes at the outside," Elizabeth calculated. "The hearing officer would make a finding of probable cause, basically confirm the bail amount that was printed on the court's bail schedule, and ask the person if they wanted a lawyer to be appointed for their case. And then they would move on to the next person. It was basically a cattle call, one person after the next."

Elizabeth sat in the back of the courtroom for several days watching these bail hearings. She also spent some time in the courtrooms of judges who handle misdemeanor cases—low-level crimes that carry punishments of less than a year in jail. She noticed that the people she saw on television in their bail hearings would end up in the misdemeanor courtrooms a day or two later. "I would see the exact same people coming through the court-rooms," she remembered. "They were shackled together in orange jumpsuits to enter guilty pleas. And the sentences they received were almost always to time served."

Elizabeth took detailed notes of what she saw in these courtrooms. She saw hearing officers deny personal bonds to people because they were homeless and to people who had committed crimes of poverty, like sleeping at a bus stop or asking for change outside of a gas station. She saw the officers treat the people appearing before them very rudely, telling them to "shut up" and "stop talking" And doubling people's bail if they thought the person was being disrespectful.

Elizabeth took all of these notes back with her to Washington, D.C. She used to be a public defender, but she had left that job to join a new civil rights organization. Civil Rights Corps had been filing civil rights lawsuits against small towns primarily in the South. Those towns were keeping poor people in jail for weeks on low-level offenses just because they couldn't afford the bail amounts that had been set by the judges.

Judges don't necessarily agree whether it's constitutional to keep people in jail just because they can't afford bail. The Supreme Court has said that poor people can't be sent to jail as punishment simply because they are unable to pay their fines, but the justices haven't addressed whether people can be *detained* before trial because they are too poor to pay bail. State courts and lower federal courts are split on the issue. Nonetheless, when Elizabeth's colleagues brought their early bail lawsuits, they would win because these towns' practices were incredibly difficult to defend: it just doesn't seems wrong to keep poor people in jail for weeks at a time for nuisance crimes like jaywalking and public intoxication when people with access to a few hundred dollars can go home.

Having racked up some wins in these small towns, Civil Rights Corps was looking for someplace to test their litigation strategy on a larger scale. Elizabeth spent months doing research online and speaking to grassroots organizations. She made the trip to Houston to see whether it might be the right place for their lawsuit. Her investigation convinced them that it was, and so they filed a lawsuit against the sheriff, the county, and the hearing officers. The lawsuit claimed that these officials were violating the civil rights of misdemeanor defendants who were too poor to pay the bail amounts that the hearing officers were setting.

The hearing officers in Houston were following something called a bail schedule—a list of suggested dollar amounts for each crime that defendants must pay before a judge will agree to release them. Bail schedules are quite common. The idea behind them is that judges shouldn't be setting different bail amounts for people accused of the same crime because that wouldn't seem fair. But bail schedules themselves aren't particularly fair. For one thing, bail schedules often set bail amounts incredibly high, even for crimes that don't pose any danger to the public. For example, the 2021 bail schedule in Los Angeles suggests that judges set bail at $25,000 for bribery and $50,000 for campaign finance violations. Bail schedules are also unfair because they set the same amount for everyone rather than different amounts based on a defendant's ability to pay or the likelihood that they would come to court without paying bail.

Elizabeth found that the hearing officers in Houston were blindly following the bail schedule instead of asking defendants about their ability to pay. In fact, during her investigation, Elizabeth interviewed several hearing officers and discovered that they weren't even allowed to deviate from the bail schedule at these bail hearings.

When Elizabeth spoke with me about the lawsuit in Houston, she emphasized both the systemic and the individual impact of the bail practices. She explained that Civil Rights Corps chose to litigate in Harris County (where Houston is located) because it is a huge system. It has a population of more than 4.5 million people, making it the third largest county in the country. Around 45,000 people are arrested every year in the county on misdemeanor charges, many of them too poor to pay bail. Elizabeth also stressed the very human problems faced by their clients: Maranda ODonnell, who had been arrested for driving with a suspended license, was told that she could return home immediately, but only if she paid money bail of $2,500. Loetha McGruder was arrested for drug possession and told she had to pay $5,000 or she would be detained. Robert Ryan Ford was arrested for shoplifting from Walmart and was also told that he had to pay $5,000 in order to be released from jail.

All of Elizabeth's clients were poor. Even those who had jobs had no hope of being able to come up with that sort of money. Yet none of them were ever asked if they could afford to pay these bail amounts. And there were hundreds of other people in the Harris County jails just like them—people who had been arrested for low-level crimes and who could have been released immediately only if they could pay the amount on the bail schedule. Because Elizabeth's clients couldn't pay, they ended up back in the courtroom a day or two later, pleading guilty. If they didn't plead guilty, they'd have to sit in jail for weeks or even months, waiting for their trials to be scheduled. The desire to be free—to go home to their families and their jobs—overwhelmed any desire to invoke their right to a trial.

Elizabeth and her colleagues at Civil Rights Corps are not the only people to file a bail lawsuit. Nor were they the only organization drawing attention to pretrial detention in Houston. But their lawsuit had a lasting impact.

The federal judge in the lawsuit held a hearing at which Elizabeth and her colleagues presented mountains of evidence about the unconstitutionality of the Houston bail practices. "The hearing was hugely cathartic. Community members packed the courtroom. It was the first time that the money bail system had been tested in open court—the first time that the rationality of it, the effectiveness of it, and the harms that it causes had been aired in any forum even approximating this and with such a significant level of time, investment, and attention," Elizabeth said. She explained that the data analysis, court testimony, and the bail hearing videos that were presented at the hearing "changed the way people thought about what the system is doing."

It was, as Elizabeth put it, an opportunity to "put money bail on trial." While she was at the hearing, she kept thinking about all of the people whom she saw standing in a red square during their bail hearings and who then got sent to jail for days or weeks: "It felt like we were putting the judges, the other defendants, and the whole system sort of in that red square in a way—holding them up to scrutiny."

After the hearing, the federal judge granted them something called a preliminary injunction—a ruling that allows a judge to require or prohibit certain actions before a trial takes place. In order to grant a preliminary injunction, a judge has to find that a plaintiff (the person who brought the lawsuit) is likely to win at trial and that there will be irreparable damage or injury if the judge waits until trial to address the conduct underlying the lawsuit. The preliminary injunction required county officials to determine whether every person arrested for a misdemeanor was able to pay bail, and it ordered them to release everyone who could not pay and who would have been released if they had been able to.

Harris County officials fought hard against the judge's decision to grant the preliminary injunction. They appealed and managed to get some of the important parts of the judge's decision overruled. The case was scheduled to go to trial in December 2018 when something momentous happened.

The November 2018 elections gave Democrats a majority of county commissioners, and all of the Republican judges lost their reelection campaigns—a result that some saw as a "reckoning" for what they had done in the bail system. These new officials entered into settlement negotiations with Elizabeth and her colleagues at Civil Rights Corps. Those negotiations resulted in a consent decree—basically a contract that the parties could enforce through the federal courts. That consent decree made sweeping changes to the misdemeanor bail system in Houston.

The Houston bail litigation received a lot of national media attention. It also created an important precedent that people can't be detained pretrial simply because they are too poor to pay their bail. But despite the attention and the precedent, Elizabeth was very cognizant of the limitations of their win. The federal court had criticized specific legal aspects of the Houston system—the rigid bail schedule and the failure to ask defendants about their financial ability to pay bail. "But if you take away the bail schedule, without other reforms and significant culture change, there is a risk that the system will revert to the same levels of pretrial detention," she noted. For that reason, the consent decree includes strict limitations on the use of money bail, which can no longer be used as a condition of release in most misdemeanor cases, as well as other provisions that are intended to change the way that the courts operate. She emphasized that money bail is not the fundamental problem. "You know, pretrial detention is the problem—just the number of people we have in jail and the fact that they are overwhelmingly Black or Brown."

I asked Elizabeth if she had seen a change in other cities and counties after the Civil Rights Corps win in Houston. I was curious about this because I'd heard defense attorneys here in North Carolina warn judges and prosecutors that local bail practices could draw a civil rights lawsuit from Elizabeth and her colleagues. "Yeah, you do see jurisdictions trying to differentiate themselves from Houston and Harris County. But the fact is that they're all—or at least most places across the country are—doing exactly the same thing. They are doing it in one way or another, but the result is that way too many people are detained pretrial."

* * * * *

"You can't understand the criminal justice system and how we arrived at mass incarceration unless you understand the story of bail," Shima Baradaran Baughman told me. Shima is a law professor and one of the country's leading experts on bail and pretrial detention.

Shima's interest in bail grew out of a Fulbright fellowship to Malawi. Knowing that she would have the opportunity to conduct research while in Malawi, Shima spent some time before her Fulbright trying to identify what major criminal justice problems were facing the landlocked African nation. She discovered that Malawi had a serious problem with pretrial detention. One man had been detained for seventeen years before trial without charges, and there were many other people who had been detained for a year or more. During her two years in Malawi, she not only did research on the country's pretrial detention system, but she also did legal aid work. At one point her work made the newspapers because she was able to get fifty people at once released on bail pending trial.

When Shima returned to the United States, she was curious about how the bail system she studied in Malawi compared to the bail systems in the United States. She began by looking at the journals where academic articles about law are published, and she found that the last article written about bail was published in 1990. When she started updating the research in 2011, Shima discovered the staggering increase in pretrial detention that began in the 1990s. In the ten years since she has been writing about bail, many other law professors have begun writing on the topic, and legal advocacy groups like Civil Rights Corps have been filing lawsuits to challenge pretrial detention practices across the country.

Shima's research shows the problems with the harsh punishment in America aren't just about mandatory minimums and lengthy sentences; those problems begin the moment that someone is arrested.

"After arrest, bail is the most important decision that is made. Those two decisions—arrest and bail—are the most important when it comes to mass incarceration and to fixing the racial inequities that we see," she explained. She cited a series of studies from the past fifty years that showed that Black defendants are more likely to be arrested and detained before trial than White defendants. Studies also show that both Black and Hispanic defendants, as a group, have to pay higher bail amounts to be released than White defendants charged with the same crimes.

Shima knows a lot about the data behind pretrial detention because she worked with an economist to analyze data about recidivism—the rates at which people who have committed crimes in the past go on to commit new crimes in the future. They found that judges were detaining large numbers of people in jail who were unlikely to commit new crimes, especially not violent crimes. Shima and the economist concluded that judges could safely release many more people without increasing crime in those communities. Keeping those people in jail was not only harmful to the people detained but also expensive. Taxpayers were paying millions of dollars to keep people locked up—money that could be spent in much better ways because it wasn't necessary to keep people safe.

In recent years, a number of cities and states have adopted "risk assessment instruments," which are supposed to help judges make more consistent and more accurate decisions about who should be detained pretrial. A risk assessment instrument is basically a questionnaire. Its questions are designed to estimate how likely a person is to commit a crime if released before trial using data about past arrests. While Shima thinks that using data-driven approaches can lead to better decisions, she has concerns about the risk assessment tools that are currently available

She analyzed the various instruments that cities and counties are using and concluded that "they are mostly getting it wrong"—that is to say, the instruments weren't well designed to actually identify those few people who pose a real risk of violence if released. As a result, the risk instruments currently in use are going to continue to keep people in jail who aren't dangerous. In addition, those risk instruments also unfairly treat Black defendants worse than White defendants. "Because a lot of these instruments include questions like 'Do you own a home?' or 'Do you have a cell phone?' they end up having racially disproportionate impacts. I mean, most Black people *don't* own a home. Whites are ten times more likely to own a home than Blacks. We know that Whites are more likely to own a home than Blacks, so why would you put that in a bail release calculation? Do you have to own a home in order to show up at a court hearing?

Of course not. So we need to stop asking questions about socioeconomic status in bail questionnaires, especially since we know that those questions will harm people of color."

Elizabeth Rossi said that these sorts of questions were being used in Houston when Civil Rights Corps brought their bail lawsuit. "The background questions included things like 'Do you have a car?' and 'Do you have a landline.' And there were also questions about who lived in your household. These questions were all just really questions about poverty. And so the more indicators of poverty you have, the higher your risk score is, and the more likely you have to pay a high bail or be detained."

Elizabeth noted that this old risk assessment instrument was abandoned and replaced with a new instrument from the Arnold Foundation during their litigation. But Elizabeth wasn't convinced that the new instrument was something to celebrate, saying that even facially neutral risk assessment instruments rely on data from a system that is deeply racist. If the data being used to create a risk assessment instrument comes from a system that disproportionately targets, arrests, and convicts poor people and people of color, then we should expect that data—and any instrument that comes from that data—to be skewed.

Whatever the problems associated with risk assessments, those instruments didn't create the pretrial detention problem in this country. The dramatic increase in people held pretrial and the financial guarantees began many years before cities, counties, and states started using risk assessment instruments. The dramatic increase also can't be explained by the law-and-order crackdown that took place in the 1980s. Any changes attributable to the new focus on danger would have made its way through the system years before the increase that occurred in the 1990s and 2000s.

So I asked Shima: What changed?

"It took me a few years to figure this out," she replied. "It wasn't until I did a deeper dive into money bail practices that I discovered the role that the bail industry played."

The bail bond industry is made up of small companies that help provide the financial guarantee for defendants who are in jail before trial. Because most people who are arrested can't afford to pay the bail amount set by the judge, bail companies will cover the bail for defendants in return for a fee—usually 10 to 15 percent of the bail amount. If the defendant doesn't show up for a court appearance, then the bail bondsman might be required to forfeit the bail amount. But the defendant doesn't get the fee back from the bail bondsman if she shows up for all of her court appearances. Even if the defendant is acquitted at trial or the prosecutor ultimately dismisses the charges, the defendant still owes the bail bondsman the fee.

The bail industry is incredibly profitable. It makes an estimated $2 billion per year. And although the businesses that actually post bail for defendants tend to be small, the insurance companies that underwrite those small companies are quite big. They have a significant economic interest in having more cases where money bail is required and in having those bail amounts be higher. Sometimes they have even been successful in convincing courts and other public officials not to actually collect the money that is forfeited when a defendant doesn't show up for a court date.

"The bail industry is a multibillion-dollar industry. And the bail insurance industry is their lobbying arm," Shima explained. "In the 1990s the bail insurance industry designed a multijurisdictional campaign to convince people in state and local governments to make decisions that would be helpful for the bail industry. They gave money to people running for state legislature, for sheriff, for judge, and for local prosecutor. They did this because they wanted to change the default from having defendants released on their own recognizance to paying money bail instead.

"And they were so successful," she continued. "If you look from 1990 on, we've dramatically increased reliance on money bail. Now, in the United States, money bail is the most common way for a defendant to be released, while it used to be release on recognizance."

I pushed back a bit on the story that Shima was telling. I haven't found a lot of bail bond–related money in my own research on campaign contributions in local prosecutor elections. I'm generally somewhat skeptical of claims that the problems with the criminal justice system can be traced to the profit motive. For example, a number of people insist that the problems of mass incarceration are attributable to private prisons. But in reality, private prisons house less than 10 percent of the country's prisoners. And the incarceration rates in states that have private prisons don't appear to be growing any faster than states without them.

But Shima pushed back as well. "It actually *is* the profit motive," she insisted. She pointed to all of the major legal groups, including the American Bar Association, that have come out strongly against the concept of money bail. The groups have come out against money bail because it literally treats people differently depending on how much money they have—something that everyone knows is unfair. But the bail bond industry has repeatedly blocked attempts at bail reform, spending millions of dollars in campaign contributions and to lobby state lawmakers.

To give me a sense of how powerful the bail bond industry is, Shima spoke about her own experience with state bail reform. A few years ago, she was invited to a meeting of local officials and stakeholders who were looking to reform the bail system. Sitting around the table with public officials and experts like Shima was a representative of the bail lobby. Shima was very surprised to see the lobbyist, who had been invited as a "stakeholder."

"I'm thinking to myself, '*What?* In what world does *this* guy get to sit in here?'" But he did. And the reforms that came out of that group, Shima pointed out, didn't include any reforms that were going to meaningfully decrease the number of people being detained in jail.

* * * * *

Pretrial detention has become so common in this country that attempts to change it have met with serious resistance. The lawsuits that the Civil Rights Corps and other organizations file are hotly contested by local officials. And when those officials actually try to make changes themselves, they sometimes find that other local officials block their attempts at reform.

That's what happened in Boston.

Efrain Rivera was arrested for shoplifting at the Gap in a Boston mall. Mr. Rivera, who struggles with drug addiction, was no stranger to the criminal justice system at the time of his arrest. He had been arrested many times before. Some of those arrests had resulted in convictions, and others were still pending when officers arrested him for shoplifting.

Often, someone who has pending criminal charges will not be released if they get arrested on new charges. But Boston had a new prosecutor, Rachael Rollins, who was elected as Boston's district attorney in 2018. Rollins ran on a platform of criminal justice reform. One area she thought needed reform was bail.

"Bail is one of the biggest things that exposes the penalty of poverty—the penalization of poverty," Rollins said when we spoke on a Wednesday afternoon. "Imagine you are poor and I am not poor and we are charged with the exact same crime—say it is operating with a suspended license, and maybe bail is $250. If you don't have that money, you are going to stay in jail. But if I do have that money, then I'm getting out."

It's a powerful example of injustice, and Rollins knows it: "For non-lawyers it is so crystal clear that that has nothing to do with whether you're a good person, or I'm a good person, or you committed the crime, or I didn't commit the crime. It has everything to do with the fact I have money and you don't."

Rollins doesn't just talk about the problems with bail; she has also made changes within her office to help minimize the number of people held in jail pretrial. One change that she made involved the training for her prosecutors. As part of their training, she now requires all prosecutors to visit the Nashua Street jail, where Boston sends most people it detains pretrial. Rollins made the jail visit mandatory because, as she put it, the prosecutors "have the ability to set bail and send people away, and so they should have to set foot in the place where those people are going to go."

The changes that Rollins made meant that the prosecutors in her office treat Mr. Rivera differently. The prosecutor in that case told the judge that she didn't think Mr. Rivera needed to be kept in jail until his trial. His crime was minor, there was no reason to think that he wouldn't appear at his court dates, and he was getting treatment for his substance abuse problem. Sending Mr. Rivera to jail would interfere with that treatment, and so the prosecutor argued that releasing him pretrial was the best course of action.

But the judge disagreed. He ordered Mr. Rivera held in the local jail. "While commendable that the defendant has sought treatment, plainly his attendance at the program has not stopped the defendant from committing thefts to ostensibly fuel his drug habit," the judge explained. "Simply put, the court finds the defendant is incapable of confining his behavior to the law no matter what conditions of release this court could impose."

* * * * *

Judges have done a lot to ensure that people—especially poor people—stay in jail even though they haven't yet been convicted. To be sure, some judges have said that it is unconstitutional to keep someone in jail because they are too poor to post bail. But many trial court judges continue to set high bail amounts or refuse to let defendants out at all, even when the charges are minor. And some appellate judges have refused to reverse those decisions.

Sometimes judges are just doing what the prosecutors ask for. But as Mr. Rivera's case shows, sometimes it's the judges who are refusing to release defendants, even when the prosecutors ask for the opposite.

Why would a judge keep a person in jail before trial when the prosecutor is willing to let him out? Why are judges willing to treat rich people better than poor people? And why are judges content to keep people in jail even though they would return for trial, especially since the people who wrote the Constitution seemed to want the opposite?

The answer may be politics: judges may be afraid that they will be blamed if people they release commit other crimes while they are awaiting trial.

As Shima Baradaran Baughman noted, "Judges are really in the public eye. Every judge's worst fear is that someone they've let out on bail—even if the prosecutor said that the person should be released—will commit a crime. The buck stops with the judge. And the judge is the one that ends up in the newspaper with a headline that he or she let someone out who then committed a rape or committed a murder."

The prospect of a headline like that, Shima explained, makes judges very nervous—nervous because people wouldn't be able to put the story in context. "The media doesn't understand the bail right, and the public doesn't understand the right. They just think, 'This guy got charged. Why did you let him out?'"

Topher Sanders, the reporter who covered the Jerome Hayes story, agreed that politics played a role in that case. I asked him why the judge kept denying Jerome's requests for bail despite all the evidence that he wasn't guilty of the crime. Sanders said that judges in Florida knew that they would face "political blowback" if they went against local prosecutors or admonished their line prosecutors in court. Like many judges across the country, trial judges in Florida are elected, and so political blowback could knock them off the bench in the next election.

In a remarkable 2014 opinion, the New Mexico supreme court acknowledged the political pressure that judges feel about bail decisions. The trial judge in that case had refused to set bail for a defendant charged with a very serious crime even though the defendant had no prior criminal history and experts had testified that it was safe to release him.

> We are not oblivious to the pressures on our judges who face election difficulties, media attacks, and other adverse consequences if they faithfully honor the rule of law when it dictates an action that is not politically popular, particularly when there is no way to absolutely guarantee that any defendant released on any pretrial conditions will not commit another offense. The inescapable reality is that no judge can predict the future with certainty

or guarantee that a person will appear in court or refrain from committing future crimes.

The justices overruled the trial court and released the defendant, who had already spent more than two years awaiting trial.

Judges' fears about losing electronics are not unfounded. There are many examples of criminal justice decisions in favor of defendants being used as a wedge issue in judicial elections. But I think there is another reason, too: judges no longer think trials are necessary in order to impose punishment.

Because most defendants plead guilty, trials are no longer the defining moment when a defendant's guilt is established. Instead, guilt is basically presumed in most cases, and the defendant entering a guilty plea is just a formality that has to be observed. The idea that a guilty plea is just a formality may also explain why judges are so comfortable "counting" the time served before a conviction as part of a defendant's punishment. And because judges are told that they can make a quick and informal decision themselves about guilt at the bail hearing, they may be refusing to release defendants because they've already made up their minds that those defendants are guilty.

If judges already presume that defendants are guilty, then it shouldn't surprise us to see them using bail and pretrial detention as a way to punish those defendants before trial. One of the judges in Houston, Texas, admitted that he and the other judges in his courthouse had been using bail as a way to punish people if they showed up late to court. "You come in late? I was doubling, tripling bonds," he said. "Bond was a way to punish people. It's like a whooping. 'Go get the belt. You get three licks.'"

This doesn't just happen in Texas. A study of a Connecticut court found that police would use their power over bail to ensure that some defendants spent at least some time incarcerated. If a defendant was belligerent when the police interviewed him, the police would sometimes incarcerate the defendant to "teach him a lesson" or until he calmed down. Police would do this by initially setting a high bail, requiring the defendant to come up with a large amount of money in order to be released, and then reducing the amount of bail eight or twelve hours later.

In other words, judges and law enforcement *know* that pretrial detention is no different from actual punishment. And so they intentionally use it to punish people for behavior that they find annoying or disrespectful, even if it isn't a crime.

Those of us who care about plea bargaining can't overlook the central role that pretrial detention plays in the modern criminal justice system. People who are detained before trial—people like José and like Elizabeth's clients in Houston—often plead guilty because that is the only way that they can leave jail and go home. If they insist on their innocence, then they have to stay in jail for weeks or months waiting for a trial. There are a lot of people in this situation. A recent study by researchers at the University of Pennsylvania's law school found that people charged with misdemeanors were 25 percent more likely to plead guilty if they were detained pretrial than if they were released.

More important, when defendants accused of minor crimes are offered plea bargains for "time served," it shows that the legal arguments judges tell us about detention being different from punishment are really just lies. Detention is no different from punishment. So we shouldn't be surprised when police and judges use detention to punish people—people who are supposedly innocent until and unless proven guilty. And we shouldn't be surprised to see defendants pleading guilty just in order to escape jail. They are already being punished, so they may as well just get the formality of the guilty plea over with.

CHAPTER FIVE

LEGAL THEFT

As I mentioned in the last chapter, I am generally skeptical of claims that the criminal justice system operates on a profit motive.

At least, I *was* skeptical.

Once I started learning about forfeiture and fees, it became blindingly obvious that a desire to take money from people is motivating a number of deeply troubling practices in this country. Most of those practices target people who have already been convicted of a crime. But some of these practices are specifically designed to get money from people who have not been convicted. And sometimes the threat of conviction is used as leverage to get that money.

That's what happened to Eh Wah.

* * * * *

I can't imagine how anyone could think that Eh Wah was a drug dealer. He doesn't smoke. He doesn't drink. And he literally spends his free time trying to help people he has never even met. But for reasons that I cannot imagine, police in Muskogee, Oklahoma, assumed that this soft-spoken religious man was a secret drug dealer. And despite significant evidence to the contrary, they seized the money he was collecting for charity based on that assumption.

To understand how Eh Wah came to be in Muskogee, you need to know his life story. Eh Wah was born in Burma. He and his family were part of an ethnic minority group called the Karen (pronounced kuh-REN). Because the Burmese government was persecuting the Karen, Eh Wah and his family fled to Thailand when he was very young. Many other Karen also fled to Thailand, and Eh Wah grew up in a refugee camp.

When Eh Wah was in his early twenties, he and his family came to the United States as part of a federal program that allowed the immigration of Christians who had experienced religious persecution. (Many Karen are Christian, which means they are a religious minority in both Burma and Thailand.) Eh Wah settled in Dallas, worked hard, and never got in any trouble. He also became very active in the Karen church and community—a community that had settled in cities and small towns across the country.

Because of his involvement in his church, Eh Wah was asked to help a Karen band from Burma, the Klo & Kweh Music Team, organize a tour of the United States. The band wanted to tour the United States in order to raise money for a Karen college in Burma and an orphanage in Thailand.

The Klo & Kweh Music Team performs their own songs as well as covers of popular American songs. When they cover American songs, they sing the lyrics in the Karen language. The group is, according to Eh Wah, very popular. "They are the only Karen group that people know and want to see. That's the reason I agreed to help organize a tour—because I knew a lot of people would like to see them," he said.

The tour took nearly a year to organize. Eh Wah helped Klo & Kweh put together an itinerary that began in Utica, New York, and ended in Bakersfield, California, traveling across the country mostly by car. The cities they visited were dictated by where the Karen had settled. That's why, when the group came to North Carolina, for example, they didn't play in the big cities like Charlotte or Raleigh. Instead they played in New Bern, a small town on the coast with only 30,000 people. When they played their performances, the band also collected contributions for the Christian college and the orphanage.

It was grueling schedule, and so, when the band found out that their venue in Utah had fallen through, the performers and the other people on the tour decided to take the weekend off to relax, see friends, or do some sightseeing. The group scattered. A couple of people went to New York. Others went to Minnesota. The band leader—who goes by the name Marvellous—traveled with some friends to Florida. Eh Wah agreed to drop some band members off in Des Moines, and then he decided to drive down to Dallas to see his family for the weekend.

The drive from Des Moines to Dallas took him through Muskogee, Oklahoma, on February 27, 2016. When Eh Wah stopped at a traffic light in Muskogee, he noticed there was a police car behind him. At the time, Eh Wah wasn't concerned about the police car. After the light turned green, Eh Wah began to drive, and the lights on the police car started flashing. Eh Wah pulled over to the side of the road, and his ordeal began.

When he told me about his experience in Muskogee more than four years later, it was clearly still fresh in his mind. I asked Eh Wah approximately what time the police officer pulled him over, and he answered right away: "Six thirty or maybe 6:40." (His lawyer later confirmed for me that Eh Wah was pulled over at 6:35.)

When the police officer approached his window, he told Eh Wah that one of his brake lights wasn't working and asked to see Eh Wah's driver's license and insurance card. Eh Wah handed the officer his license, and he explained that he would need to get his insurance card out of his trunk. But rather than letting Eh Wah get his proof of insurance, the officer asked Eh Wah to step out of his car and get into the patrol car. Once he was in the car, the police officer started asking him questions.

The officer kept Eh Wah in the police car for more than twenty minutes, asking him a lot of questions about where he had been and where he was going. Eventually the officer told Eh Wah that he could leave. When he said, "You can go," the officer stuck out his hand for Eh Wah to shake. He noticed that Eh Wah's hand was shaking, and the officer became suspicious. "Why are you shaking?" he demanded of Eh Wah.

Eh Wah explained to me later that he was shaking because speaking to the police officer made him think about when he lived in Thailand as a refugee. "We always had to be afraid of the police back in Thailand. Because you are a refugee, you don't have any documents. So when you go out, you have to watch out for the police. Because if they stop you, you end up in jail." Although his immigration status in Thailand might have been precarious, Eh Wah immigrated legally to the United States, and he had become a U.S. citizen before being stopped in Muskogee. Nonetheless, as he explained, his background and his time in Thailand still made him feel nervous around police. And that was why he was shaking.

But the police officer assumed that Eh Wah was nervous or afraid because he had committed a crime. "He said, 'If you are shaking like this, you must have done something wrong.' And then things went on to another level. He asked me, 'Do you have any illegal drugs? Weapons?' He also asked me if I had any money."

Eh Wah did have money, but he didn't want to tell the officer about it. He was acting as the unofficial manager for the Klo & Kweh Music Team. As part of those duties, he was handling the band's finances. He had the money from their ticket sales, the money for their tour operating expenses, and the additional charitable donations that the band had collected. All told, Eh Wah had $53,000, which was stored in envelopes and bags in different places in the car. Even though he had this money, Eh Wah told the officer he didn't have any money in the car.

But when the officer asked to search Eh Wah's car, Eh Wah said yes. The officer found the envelopes and bags, and then things got worse.

The officer radioed for backup, and a whole bunch of other police cars descended on the scene. "I didn't see all of them, but I believe I saw at least six or seven patrol cars, and their lights were flashing all around me. I never imagined I'd be in that kind of situation—like what you see in a movie or on the news. It's not good when you are surrounded by police like that."

The officers kept Eh Wah on the side of the road for almost two hours. He stayed in the patrol car while different officers took turns asking him questions. He kept telling them the same story—the truth about where he had been, where he was going, and why he had the money—but they didn't believe him.

"They were pretty rude," Eh Wah said. "And it's changed my view about the police." He explained that he was raised in a very religious family and that he was always taught to respect the police, just as he was taught to respect his elders and all people in positions of leadership. When Eh Wah talked to the police that night, he did exactly as he had been raised to do. "I showed respect to them. But I didn't get any respect from them. Everyone's just, like, I'm a criminal."

After about two hours on the side of the road, police brought Eh Wah to the police station. At the station, several officers continued to interrogate him. Finally the officers said that they wanted to call Marvellous, the lead singer of Klo & Kweh Music Team, to confirm Eh Wah's story. Eh Wah gave them the number, and the police called Marvellous. But the police said that they couldn't understand Marvellous, whose English isn't as good as Eh Wah's. The officers told Eh Wah that, because it was too difficult for them to understand Marvellous, they couldn't confirm Eh Wah's story about where the money had come from.

"I know that during the whole conversation with Marvellous that they understand him and they know what is going on. They just don't *want* to believe him," Eh Wah said. He described the police rolling their eyes to one another while they were on the phone with Marvellous, as if they were signaling to each other that they thought Marvellous was lying. Then the officers just cut off the call, Eh Wah recounted, saying that they didn't want to talk to Marvellous any more.

"And I say, 'Okay, if you don't want to talk to him, I have other people that you can talk to.'" Eh Wah gave the officers the names of two pastors in the Karen Christian Revival Church. He explained to the police that these pastors were sponsoring the Klo & Kweh tour, and so they would be able to corroborate his explanation about why he had the money. But the officers wouldn't make the call. "They were just, like, 'Nope. We have enough. We don't want to talk to anyone.'"

The police suspected that Eh Wah's money had come from selling drugs. But rather than trying to confirm Eh Wah's story, the police sent him on his way home to Dallas and kept the money from his car. They kept the money because the law allows police to keep the proceeds of illegal activity, like drug dealing.

It's ridiculous that the police thought that Eh Wah was a drug dealer. And it is even more ridiculous that the law let them keep the money from Eh Wah's car based only on their unsubstantiated suspicion.

When Eh Wah got back to Dallas, he didn't know what to do. He wasn't a lawyer, and he didn't know any lawyers. But he did know that the band needed the money the police took. So Eh Wah asked lots of people what he should do. One friend he spoke to ended up calling a lawyer that he knew. And that lawyer said he knew exactly who Eh Wah needed to call: Dan Alban at the Institute for Justice.

* * * * * *

I first met Dan Alban in the summer of 2018 when I visited the Washington, D.C., office of the Institute for Justice. When I had mentioned to a friend that I was writing a book about how America's criminal justice system is designed to punish people without a trial, he said, "So you'll have a chapter about civil forfeiture, right?!" As someone who studies and teaches criminal law, I didn't know much about civil forfeiture, so I started researching the topic.

While doing that research, I kept coming across the policy and litigation work from the Institute for Justice, a libertarian public interest law firm that is commonly referred to as IJ. When I reached out to an acquaintance who worked at IJ, he put together the meeting for me with Dan and several of his IJ colleagues to talk about their work.

A committed libertarian, Dan went to law school because he wanted to work at IJ. When he started working there, he pushed to get assigned to the team that litigated civil forfeiture cases. Dan had learned about forfeiture in college, where he participated in speech and debate competitions. In fact, Dan made it all the way to the national speech and debate semifinals with a persuasive speech that he wrote about civil forfeiture. At the time, civil forfeiture didn't get too much public attention. The work of Dan and other people on the forfeiture team eventually led IJ to make civil forfeiture one of its major property rights issues. In 2014, IJ launched the End Forfeiture initiative. They not only bring forfeiture lawsuits; they also publish high-quality research on the topic and push legislative reforms in the area.

Because of their successes—and because they represent all of their clients free of charge—Dan gets calls from people like Eh Wah all the time. In fact, the Institute for Justice gets so many calls that they hired a full-time person just to field those calls and help jump-start the investigations that Dan and the other attorneys do before they take on a forfeiture case.

Dan began conducting one of those investigations after he spoke with Eh Wah. But he realized that time was short: the Klo & Kweh tour was drawing to a close, and the band members' visas were going to expire. Dan knew he wouldn't be able to conduct his investigation if the key witnesses were in Burma. So he got on a plane, flew across the country, and attended the band's last performance in Bakersfield, California. He met Eh Wah, he met Marvellous and the rest of the band, and he quickly concluded that Eh Wah was telling the truth: He wasn't a drug dealer. He hadn't committed any crime at all. He was simply helping people in his community to help other people.

That's when Dan decided to take up Eh Wah's fight.

Muskogee law enforcement had filed legal paperwork that would allow them to keep the money that they seized from Eh Wah. In order to get the money back, Eh Wah had to file a formal response, called an answer, which included legal statements from people swearing that the money wasn't from selling drugs. If he didn't file an answer—and a lot of people whose property is seized don't—then the state wouldn't ever have to give the money back.

Dan was hard at work, trying to get these sworn statement from the band members, who at that point were back in Burma. When there was less than a week left before the deadline for Eh Wah's answer, a paralegal in Dan's office got in touch with him. The paralegal had been helping Dan with Eh Wah's case and she had noticed something ominous: the Muskogee prosecutor had issued a felony arrest warrant for Eh Wah.

"It seemed really obvious that was an intimidation tactic. Like, if you file an answer, then you are going to have to face these criminal charges," Dan said. Dan sat in on my interview with Eh Wah. That interview took place while the coronavirus was still ravaging the country, and so the interview was conducted over videoconference, with the three of us all sitting in different states.

I asked Dan why he thought the arrest warrant was an intimidation tactic. He pointed to the fact that the prosecutor didn't bother to file charges until just before the answer was due, as well as the fact that the prosecutor only put the warrant into their electronic system rather than trying to have Eh Wah arrested. If the prosecutor actually thought Eh Wah was guilty of a crime, Dan told me, then she would have filed the charges earlier and she would have actually tried to arrest Eh Wah. Nothing had happened in the case in the many weeks between the time the police officers took the money and the time the arrest warrant was filed; the only thing that seemed to have prompted the arrest warrant was that the deadline for Eh Wah's answer on the forfeiture case was drawing close. The deadline meant he would have to decide whether to contest the forfeiture. Dan saw all of those circumstances and the timing as a clear signal that, if Eh Wah didn't file an answer and let Muskogee keep the money, then they wouldn't follow through with criminal charges. "They just put the charges out there. If you've got an attorney who is paying attention, the signal is 'Maybe you should tell your client to let this one go because now there are criminal charges pending,'" Dan explained.

Although the signal in this case was implicit—that the criminal charges would only be pursued if Eh Wah insisted on trying to get the money back—Dan said that in some cases law enforcement will actually say those things to a person. "There have been a few incidents at the Portland airport in Oregon where FBI agents or task force members with them have explicitly told someone, 'If you contest this forfeiture, we will show up at your house and arrest you.'"

In some places, the threat of criminal charges in order to scare people from challenging a forfeiture is routine. In 2013 the *New Yorker* magazine published an exposé on Tenaha, a small Texas town in which the local prosecutor routinely threatened to bring criminal charges against motorists stopped on the highway unless they agreed not to contest the forfeiture of their money and property. Police officers pulled one couple over for "driving in the left lane for more than half a mile without passing" and then seized all of the money in their car. The district attorney threatened to put the couple's children in foster care if they didn't agree to sign a document waiving their rights to the cash. The couple quickly agreed, and the DA let them go after making them sign a waiver that said: "No criminal charges shall be filed, and our children shall not be turned over to CPS [Child Protective Services]."

Because he knew about law enforcement using criminal charges as leverage in forfeiture cases, Dan was worried about the felony warrant. The warrant changed the stakes. This was no longer about just getting back the money that the police had seized from Eh Wah; now it was about protecting his freedom. If Muskogee officials asked police in Dallas to act on the warrant, Dan said, then a SWAT team could show up at Eh Wah's house to arrest him at any time.

So Dan decided to be proactive. As he finished the answer, Dan arranged for a criminal defense attorney in Oklahoma to represent Eh Wah in the criminal case. Eh Wah and his father drove to Muskogee, where they met the defense attorney, and then they all went to the police station so that Eh Wah could turn himself in. Once he'd turned himself in, there was no longer a threat of police showing up at his house to arrest him.

Eh Wah sat in jail for a few hours as they did the paperwork that allowed him to post a bond and be released. "That's not a nice experience," Eh Wah recalled. "I had to be inside of the jail and I got harassed by other people who had been brought in, people who had been arrested. And when you have to deal with those people—it's a nightmare."

Eh Wah was released, and his criminal defense attorney filed a motion with the judge for a hearing to see whether there was enough evidence to support the charges. There was a lot of evidence showing that Eh Wah was not a drug dealer, and so the attorney wanted the judge to hear all of the evidence and dismiss the charges. But the judge denied the motion. He was going to make Eh Wah go to trial.

"That scared the hell out of us," Dan said. "The last thing we wanted was Eh Wah facing felony charges, and we knew that we could get rid of the charges if we surrendered the money." It was a terrible dilemma: Dan and the folks at IJ only took this case as part of their broader litigation strategy to challenge civil forfeiture. If they gave up the claim for the money, there was no forfeiture case for them to litigate. But if they didn't give up the money, Eh Wah could end up in prison. Until then, Dan hadn't worried about Eh Wah getting convicted of a crime because there was so much evidence proving his innocence, and basically nothing in support of his guilt. But when the judge wouldn't even hold a hearing, Dan worried that maybe the weakness of the government's case wouldn't save Eh Wah after all.

But Dan had one more move left to play.

A reporter with the *Washington Post* had decided to write story about Eh Wah's case. The *Post* had previously published an extensive exposé on roadside seizures and forfeitures that analyzed years of data. The story about Eh Wah followed up on that reporting, and it was highly critical of law enforcement in Muskogee. Dan had called the reporter before Eh Wah's hearing to see when the story would be published. The reporter had assured him it would be published that morning.

So as Eh Wah was leaving the courtroom after the judge denied his motion, his criminal defense attorney stopped to talk to the prosecutor. The attorney told the prosecutor to look for a story in the *Washington Post*. The story had been published just before the hearing took place—and it did not make Muskogee look good.

In addition, a reporter for a local Oklahoma radio station interviewed Eh Wah after the hearing. Throughout the day, the reporter tried to interview the sheriff and the district attorney. But they were both holed up in the Public Safety Building. Between the *Washington Post* story and the local reporter, the officials must have felt a lot of pressure. Their subordinates had taken thousands of dollars that were supposed to support refugees and orphans, and it looked like they had basically no evidence to support that decision.

Just a few hours later, Dan received a call from the district attorney. He was calling to tell him that they were dropping the criminal charges. He also asked Dan for Eh Wah's address. They were cutting him a check for the $53,000 they took, and he wanted to put it in the mail right away.

Eh Wah's story had a happy ending. He, Dan, and Dan's wife, Emily, all traveled to Burma to deliver the money that the police had seized to the

Karen college and the Thai orphanage. The Klo & Kweh band members, who had raised the money, went with them as escorts and travel guides to ceremonies at the college and the orphanage when they delivered the money. ("I have some amazing photos," Dan told me when he described the trip.)

A while later, Dan and Emily traveled to Dallas to attend Eh Wah's wedding. And as I spoke with Dan and Eh Wah, it was clear that the two men had become friends. Before we finished the interview, Dan asked me wait so that Emily could join us and speak with Eh Wah; she had made Dan promise not to let the interview end before she could say hello.

As I watched Emily and Eh Wah catch up with one another, I couldn't help but think how lucky it was that someone referred Eh Wah to Dan. Most people whose property is seized don't have the help of someone like Dan Alban or the Institute for Justice. The laws surrounding civil forfeiture are complex and arcane. Even most lawyers find those laws hard to navigate, and so people who can't afford lawyers often don't understand how to file the necessary paperwork to get their money back. As a result, the vast majority of forfeitures go unchallenged, and those people end up losing their money forever.

* * * * *

Civil forfeiture can be very lucrative for law enforcement. A 2014 *Washington Post* investigation of federal forfeiture records found that law enforcement seized more than $2.5 billion in the years after 9/11 without either a search warrant or an indictment. State and local officials got to keep more than $1.7 billion, and the rest went to various federal agencies.

This money is incredibly important for local officials. Like many other government agencies, police and sheriff departments often receive less public funding than they need. And in times of financial crisis, law enforcement budgets sometimes get cut. Forfeiture gives law enforcement another significant income stream. Across the country, there are hundreds of police departments that receive as much as 20 percent of their total budgets from forfeitures. And there are counties in Texas where nearly 40 percent of the police budget comes from forfeiture money.

Forfeiture money doesn't just increase law enforcement budgets; it also gives some control to law enforcement over the size of their budgets. For example, in 1990 the attorney general of the United States distributed a memo to federal prosecutors encouraging them to "significantly increase" their forfeiture efforts "in order to meet the Department of Justice's annual budget target."

The way in which law enforcement exercises their forfeiture power is further evidence that they are driven by profit. For example, when police officers in Tennessee decided to use their forfeiture power to target drug trafficking on Interstate 40, they didn't focus their efforts on the eastbound lanes of the highway—the side where drugs were being transported. Instead, they stopped cars on the westbound lanes—the side where money was being transported. One would think that if law enforcement were using their powers to stop drug trafficking, then they would be worried about actually stopping the flow of drugs. But instead they made ten times as many stops on the westbound lanes, making clear that their priority was to seize money rather than drugs.

Nationally, criminal charges are never filed in 80 percent of civil forfeiture cases. That number should concern us. If police think that the people they are stopping are actually involved in criminal activity, then shouldn't they be bringing criminal charges and putting them in jail? It's only if forfeiture is about making money, rather than catching people who break the law, that these numbers make sense.

To be clear, law enforcement have used forfeiture to seize property that belongs to drug gangs and sophisticated criminal organizations. But their power isn't limited to criminal organizations. The police in Tenaha, Texas, for example, regularly seized items that were obviously personal property, like jewelry and DVD players, not instrumentalities of illegal activity. The town even confiscated a simple gold cross from around a woman's neck when she was stopped for a minor traffic violation. In Philadelphia, half of the forfeitures between 2011 and 2013 involved less than $193. That looks a lot more like taking property from ordinary people than seizing assets from criminal organizations.

* * * * *

How is the government allowed to take your property without first proving that you did anything wrong? After all, the Constitution requires that people can't be deprived of their property without due process of law.

The answer is complicated.

One reason is that these forfeitures are considered civil penalties rather than criminal punishment. That means the ordinary protections that are given to criminal defendants don't apply. The government can take your money or property based on nothing more than suspicion. If you want it back, you have to file a lawsuit. If you are poor, the state won't appoint a lawyer for you because it is not a criminal case. And even if you do file a lawsuit and get a lawyer, the government doesn't have to prove beyond a reasonable doubt that your money was obtained from the commission of a crime or that your property was used to commit a crime. Instead, it only has to satisfy the lesser standard of proof that applies in civil cases.

Another reason we have civil forfeiture is that it is a relatively recent phenomenon. If officials had tried this sort of thing in the early years of our country, there almost certainly would have been legal cases declaring it unconstitutional. The people who wrote the Constitution were deeply concerned about governments taking people's property. That's why they put various protections in the Constitution to limit those practices. To be clear, when the Constitution was written, you could find isolated incidents of civil forfeiture. But it was used for very limited purposes—such as dealing with pirates and customs violations. In those cases, officials often couldn't prosecute the owners of the property because they were not located in the United States. And while the history of those forfeiture cases is not entirely clear, it appears that some criminal procedure protections applied and that the sort of property that could be seized was much more limited.

It wasn't until after plea bargaining became normal and prison populations began to explode in the late twentieth century that law enforcement started using civil forfeiture with any regularity. As Michelle Alexander explained in *The New Jim Crow: Mass Incarceration in the Age of Colorblindness*, the War on Drugs played a prominent role in the rise of civil forfeiture. In 1970, Congress passed a law that allowed federal law enforcement to seize airplanes, boats, and cars used to transport drugs. When Congress passed new, harsher drug laws in the 1980s, it also established a program to share profits from drug busts with state and local governments. That profit-sharing program prompted law enforcement across the country to begin seizing cash, cars, and other property if they thought it might be connected to drug crimes.

Now civil forfeiture is huge. In 1986 the Department of Justice's Assets Forfeiture Fund collected only $93.7 million. By 2014 that number had ballooned to $4.5 billion per year. The Department of Justice does not track whether this money is connected to any existing or subsequent criminal investigation. And a 2017 inspector general's report that examined a subset of federal forfeitures found that federal officials could verify only that less than half of those forfeitures were even related to a criminal investigation.

Through all of this, the Supreme Court has permitted civil forfeiture to continue. They have even admitted that one reason for civil forfeiture is to punish people for committing crimes. And yet they allow state and federal officials to seize property without ever proving that someone committed a crime. Only Justice Clarence Thomas appears to have doubts about the constitutionality of this practice. The other members of the Supreme Court seem to have no problems with a system that allows law enforcement to punish people by taking their property and then placing the administrative burden on the people whose property was taken to get it back.

"The way that people who defend forfeiture view it is that it is too expensive and too difficult to actually bring all of these cases to trial and prove that the person actually did something wrong," Rob Johnson said. Rob is one of the other Institute for Justice attorneys that I spoke with when I first met Dan Alban to learn more about civil forfeiture. "I understand that some of the people they stop seem suspicious—like someone who is pulled over on the side of the road, whose car smells like drugs, and who has $200,000 in small-denomination bills wrapped up in a suitcase in the back of their car. I mean, I get it: that person seems like they might be a drug dealer or a drug mule. But the police should follow them, see where they go, maybe put out some sort of bulletin with their license plate number—you know, do some actual police work." If police did that, he explained, then they could turn their suspicion into an actual criminal case and prosecute all of the people involved.

But that isn't the approach that officers take, Rob explained. "Their response is 'We are 60 or 70 percent confident that this is drug money, so let's just seize it and see if they try to put up a fight to try and get it back.' If your goal is to be more efficient and to spend fewer resources, then I see how you arrive at that. But the problem is that they also take money from people who aren't drug dealers; they just happen to look suspicious. Is that the majority of cases? We don't know because no one is even keeping track." Rob added that the people who are running the system just don't seem to be concerned about innocent people having their property confiscated: "Protecting innocent people doesn't meet their cost-benefit analysis."

The lawyers at IJ don't just litigate individual cases; they also work to change state and federal laws. You would think that their work would be relatively easy, since 84 percent of Americans don't think that people should lose their property without first being convicted of a crime. That number is so high because, as Lisa Knepper, IJ's director of strategic research, put it, "civil forfeiture is completely outrageous. I think it challenges people's fundamental belief in American justice—that people are innocent until proven guilty."

Because of this public support, several states have begun to reform their forfeiture laws over the past decade. Lisa is part of an IJ team that collects data and laws. That team has analyzed forfeiture laws in all fifty states. She explained that, despite public opinion, most states continue to allow civil forfeiture to continue. She attributes the discrepancy between public opinion and state laws to the fact that law enforcement has been very effective at lobbying against change. "We can be winning in the court of public opinion but losing in the halls of the legislature," Lisa said.

* * * * *

Civil forfeiture is related to plea bargaining. For one thing, law enforcement tactics when seizing money or property can look a lot like the tactics that we see in plea bargaining. Law enforcement uses leverage in order to scare people away from exercising their rights. People have the right to challenge the government's seizure of their property. But law enforcement uses the threat of criminal charges to discourage them from exercising that right. Sometimes that threat is implied—as it was in Eh Wah's case, when a warrant was filed but not served until just before the deadline to challenge the seizure. But other times that threat is explicit, like the waivers that prosecutors used in Tenaha, Texas.

Forfeiture can also be a source of leverage in plea negotiations. Prosecutors can threaten to seize a defendant's house or savings account in order to pressure him into pleading guilty. These sorts of threats can be especially effective in white-collar cases where large amounts of money or property are at stake.

Another way in which civil forfeiture is related to plea bargaining is that it rests on the same basic principle as modern plea bargaining: that it isn't necessary to find out for sure whether the defendant committed a crime. Plea bargaining is predicated on the idea that, rather than asking a jury to decide whether she is guilty, a defendant will estimate her odds of winning at trial and then bargain with the prosecutor for a sentence that is below her expected punishment. When it comes to forfeiture, the disregard for the "search for truth" is even more blatant. We allow law enforcement to make seizures based on hunches, and we test those hunches only if defendants are willing to go through the time and expense of challenging them.

Most fundamentally, civil forfeiture is like plea bargaining in that it allows punishment without trial. The concept behind forfeiture is that people shouldn't be allowed to keep their money or property if they are using it to commit crimes or if they are the proceeds of crime. And, in theory, you can get your money back if you prove you didn't commit a crime. But the word "forfeit" literally means to lose your rights or your property because you have done something wrong. In fact, the FBI says on its own website says that it uses forfeiture to "punish criminals." So the mere fact that our government calls it a *civil* penalty rather than a *criminal* punishment doesn't change its nature.

Finally, I think we need to recognize how the timeline of civil forfeiture matches up with the timeline of plea bargaining. Congress started passing major forfeiture laws around the same time that the Supreme Court said plea bargaining was constitutional. In other words, civil forfeiture didn't become popular or widespread until after judges stopped treating a criminal trial as an absolute necessity before imposing any sort of punishment. There is also an interesting comparison to be made between the timeline of civil forfeiture and the timeline of bail. Civil forfeiture started to increase dramatically at the same time that states changed their bail laws and practices to keep more people in jail before trial.

When we look at it in context, the rise of civil forfeiture looks like one symptom of a broader disease: namely, the routine and accepted imposition of punishment without trial. That sickness has been around for quite some time. But only in recent decades has it become an epidemic.

* * * * *

Civil forfeiture isn't the only way that local officials profit off people in the name of the criminal justice system. Sometimes they charge people fees just for getting swept up in the system. And as with forfeiture, the profit motive seems to drive these fees.

Most criminal justice fees are triggered by criminal convictions. States tend to have a number of these fees, most of which are relatively modest. For example, in California traffic court, each convicted defendant has to pay a $4 emergency medical air transportation fee, a $1 night court assessment, a $35 conviction assessment, and a series of other small fees. But the overall effect of these fees quickly adds up. A person who is found guilty of a traffic violation in California and has to pay a $100 fine as punishment also has to pay an additional $490 in costs and fees. A study by the Brennan Center for Justice found that, in many states, defendants routinely have to pay hundreds if not thousands of dollars in fees. Many defendants are not able to pay these fees, and their failure to pay sometimes lands them in jail. Criminal justice debt can quickly spiral out of control, interfering with the ability of a person to get her life back on track.

Some of the fees are specifically targeted at those defendants who refuse to plead guilty. Many states impose "jury fees" or "jury taxes" on defendants who insist on their right to trial. There were no such fees when our constitution was first written, but within a half century of its ratification, states began to pass on to defendants the costs associated with trials.

When the Montana legislature passed a law in 2009 designed to offset the costs of providing appointed attorneys to poor defendants, they adopted different payment amounts for defendants who insisted on a jury trial and those who pleaded guilty or allowed themselves to be tried by a judge without a jury. For those who pleaded guilty or waived their right to a jury, charges were capped at $500. But those who insisted on a jury trial were required to pay for the entire cost of their attorney as well as any costs or fees for witnesses or interpreters. For some defendants, those costs were incredibly high; one defendant was ordered to pay more than $57,000.

The state senator who sponsored the bill, Jim Shockley, was quite clear that he wanted to pass the law because it would lead more defendants to plead guilty. He said if people "have to pay" for these costs, then "they're not going to be pleading not guilty. If you say not guilty doesn't cost you anything, hey, I'd like to meet the jury, but if you're paying for it, it makes a big difference." He also said that he was exempting bench trials—trials before judges without juries—from the higher fees because "a bench trial to me is like pleading guilty slowly." In other words, Senator Shockley assumed defendants who didn't have a jury trial would be found guilty anyway. He just wanted to make sure that defendants had to pay a heavy price for the chance to be acquitted by a jury of their peers.

Jury fees are only assessed at conviction. But others are due before then. Several states authorize local governments to collect "booking fees" that are assessed when people are arrested and booked into jail. Some local governments have decided to impose their own booking fees even without state law authorization. Sometimes these fees are refunded if charges are dismissed or if the defendant is acquitted at trial. But some governments put the burden on people who aren't convicted to seek a refund. And not all governments refund the fees. The courts have allowed governments to keep money from defendants who are never convicted on the theory that these fees are a legitimate way for governments to defray their costs.

For example, Illinois passed a law that allowed court clerks to keep 1 percent of a defendant's bail money even after a defendant made all of her court appearances. Illinois said that this money was for "bail bond costs" and it had to be paid by everyone, regardless of whether they were convicted or acquitted. When the law was challenged as unconstitutional, the Supreme Court refused to strike it down. It characterized the fee as "an administrative cost imposed upon all those, guilty and innocent alike," and said there was no problem with states imposing such fees. Rather than treating the fee as a question about the fundamental right of innocents to be free from punishment, the Court said "this smacks of administrative detail and of procedure." In other words, if state and local governments want to impose fees on those who get swept up in the criminal justice system, the courts will treat that decision no differently than a fee to collect your garbage or a fee to park in a municipal parking lot.

Ironically, the fact that these fees are collected from both innocent and guilty defendants actually shields them from certain legal attacks. If the government can prove that it is collecting these fees in order to recoup the costs of running its criminal justice system rather than as a punishment for convicted defendants, then the courts will say that these charges are fees rather than fines. If something is a fee, then the Constitution's prohibition on excessive fines doesn't apply. More fundamentally, if something is a fee rather than a fine, then a defendant can be ordered to pay it even if she isn't convicted because technically it isn't considered a punishment.

* * * * *

The payment of money has long played a role in criminal law. For centuries, criminal prosecutions in England were usually brought by a victim or a victim's family to recover "bot" or "wergild"—money from the defendant to compensate for the harm done. After criminal law became a public function, people who made arrests or prosecuted cases were often private contractors who were paid by the arrest or by the conviction. Even judges were sometimes paid for each affirmative action that they took, such as each time they signed a search warrant, and they didn't get paid if they didn't authorize the search.

Only in the early twentieth century did the courts start to recognize that these practices created incentives for overly aggressive criminal law enforcement. For example, in the late 1920s, the Supreme Court overturned the conviction of Ed Tumey, who had been fined $100 for unlawfully possessing intoxicating liquor during Prohibition. Tumey had been convicted in a local Ohio court. The mayor of the village served as the judge in that court, and the judge was paid for serving as a judge only if a defendant was convicted. The payments for the mayor came from the fees that convicted defendants had to pay.

The Court said this arrangement was unconstitutional. The justices explained that the Constitution's Due Process Clause guarantees defendants that the decision whether to punish them is made by a neutral decision-maker. Because the mayor, who was serving as the judge, would be paid only if Tumey was convicted, then the mayor had a personal stake in the outcome of the case. A person with a stake in the outcome of a case is not a neutral decision-maker.

Unfortunately, the Supreme Court has not consistently forbidden profit-driven criminal prosecutions. Soon after the Tumey case, the Supreme Court refused to reverse a conviction by a local court where the judge served as mayor and the mayor's town profited from convictions. But several years later it did reverse such a conviction. (These two cases appear to have come out differently because of obscure differences between the precise powers that the mayors had over the town's finances.) In addition to its inconsistent decisions, the Supreme Court has not required the same neutrality from police and prosecutors as it has from judges. As a result, lower courts have permitted practices that seem designed to encourage law enforcement to sweep more people into the criminal justice system.

For example, a federal appeals court rejected a constitutional challenge to a Mississippi law that paid constables $10 per charging decision that results in a conviction. The court said that, because the constable was performing an executive action, rather than a judicial action, the same neutrality wasn't required.

* * * * * *

Some may wonder whether we should think of payments to police, prosecutors, or the courts as punishment. After all, people have to pay for all sorts of government services, such as driving on toll roads, getting a driver's license, and applying for a construction permit. So perhaps we should simply think of the fees that people are required to pay in the criminal justice system in the same way—as an income stream to support government services. Rather than making everyone pay for those services with taxes, we fund those services by making those people who use the services pay for them. Indeed, the Supreme Court has adopted this logic, saying that these payments are fees for administrative costs rather than fines that are imposed to punish.

But there is an important difference between other user fees and fees associated with being booked into jail or posting bail: people have a choice whether to drive on a toll road, apply for a driver's license, or do the home improvements that might require a construction permit. People who are arrested have no choice in the matter. And when paying a fee is offered as an alternative to sitting in jail or being convicted, then it is hardly reasonable to say that the person "chose" to pay that fee.

Also, it is important to remember that money is a common punishment. People often think of imprisonment when they think about how people are punished for committing crimes. But we also impose fines as punishment. As with jail or prison time, fines are supposed to be imposed after a defendant has been convicted. But just as pretrial detention means that people—even innocent people—spend time in jail before they are convicted, these criminal justice user fees mean that people are forced to pay money before they are convicted and even if they are innocent.

Indeed, some jurisdictions have dropped any pretense about what these fees are meant to accomplish by allowing defendants to buy their way out of criminal charges by paying a fee. In Minnesota, for example, state law allows local governments to collect a "prosecution cost" from traffic violation and misdemeanor defendants who want to avoid a conviction. People pay that cost in addition to whatever fine they already needed to pay, and in return the case is considered "resolved" without a conviction. Washington, D.C., has a similar program in which people can have their charges dismissed if they agree to "forfeit" a small amount of money.

There is so much money to be made from fees that private companies have gotten in on the game. In Phoenix, Arizona, prosecutors set up their own pretrial diversion program in which people were sent to a private company that conducted drug and alcohol tests and held classes for people who had been charged with crimes. The prosecutors decided who was eligible for the program, and anyone who successfully completed it would have their charges dismissed. The program was very expensive. There was an initial fee of $900 or $1,000, and then additional $10 to $15 fees for each drug screening test.

Collecting money from participants was a major feature of the program. The company running the program made millions of dollars, and so did the local prosecutor's office, which received a kickback of $600 for every defendant enrolled in the program. Despite policies that were supposed to reduce fees for those who could not pay, in practice defendants who could not pay their fees were simply forced to remain in the program longer.

The Civil Rights Corps—the same organization that challenged the bail practices in Houston—brought a lawsuit against Phoenix officials, arguing that the program violated the constitutional rights of defendants who couldn't pay the fees. Since then, Phoenix prosecutors have changed their program to provide better screening for those who can't pay and to make the overall costs lower. But the new program still requires people to pay significant amounts of money in order to have their charges dismissed.

"It's like plea bargaining but without a formal guilty plea," Armando Nava, a criminal defense attorney in Phoenix, observed. Several of Armando's clients have gone through the Phoenix program. He explained that, in order for defendants to be admitted to the program, they have to give prosecutors a written statement admitting that they committed the crime in question. Prosecutors get to hold on to that statement and use it against any defendant who later tries to say he is innocent.

A formal plea bargain would require defendants to plead guilty, at which point the defendant would be placed on probation. Violating probation—say, by testing positive for drugs—could result in the defendant being sent to jail, but only after he gets a hearing in front of a neutral judge. But Phoenix's informal program allows the prosecutor to be the sole arbiter of whether the defendant has failed the program—a decision that could lead to a longer stay in the program (and a lot more fees). The prosecutor could even decide to kick the defendant out of the program and send him back to court, where he is certain to be convicted because the prosecutor has the statement in which he admitted his guilt.

Why would prosecutors set up this program? Armando explained that it gives them much more control than in regular cases and "prosecutors like to control their cases." But I'm sure that the money helps.

It isn't just prosecutors or private industry that have benefited from these fees. For many years the judges in New Orleans used the fines and fees that they collected from defendants in order to fund their courtroom operations. Only a civil rights lawsuit stopped the practice. Even public defenders have benefited from these fees. As law professors Ronald Wright and Wayne Logan have documented, public defenders in several states actively sought to have a new fee added in order to help fund their offices.

On some level I can understand why these officials turned to fees in order to finance their operations. The criminal justice system is woefully underfunded. But at the same time it is deeply troubling that those people who are supposed to protect criminal defendants—judges and defense attorneys—put the financial health of their institutions above their responsibility to those they are supposed to protect.

It is especially troubling because there is no getting around the fact that these fees look like punishment. And when some of those fees apply only when a defendant goes to trial—like the public defender fee in Montana or the jury "taxes" in other states—then there can be no doubt that the fees are also used to pressure defendants into pleading guilty.

* * * * **

Forfeiture and fees look a lot like punishment. They also give law enforcement more leverage in plea bargaining.

But there is another very important way in which forfeiture and fees actually increase the number of defendants who are punished without a trial: they create a financial incentive for law enforcement to investigate and arrest more people. When cities and states stand to profit from criminal law enforcement, then it should come as no surprise that they increase their enforcement. That's the "invisible hand" of market forces that economists tell us about.

There are clear examples of this profit motive causing law enforcement to arrest and charge more people. For example, the Department of Justice's investigation of the Ferguson, Missouri, police department found that the city relied on municipal fines and fees for a large percentage of its budget. City officials routinely urged the police chief to generate more revenue by arresting more people, and the municipal court served as essentially a collection agency for the city. And the incredibly high number of roadside forfeitures in Tenaha, Texas, began after a former state trooper told city officials that they could pay the town's expenses if they began stopping cars on the local highway.

If a system relies on fees for operational expenses, then it has an interest in bringing more people through the system. And the more people who come through the system, the more pressure there is to resolve those cases as quickly as possible rather than through trials. And so the cycle continues.

We should all be deeply concerned about a criminal justice system that is continuously expanding. An expanding system—especially a system that is driven by profit—can sweep in people who have done little or even nothing wrong. As Dan Alban observed, what happened to Eh Wah "can happen to anyone . . . It's really just a matter of luck."

CHAPTER SIX

THE PROCESS IS THE PUNISHMENT

"In this courtroom, the rule is no talking, no eating, no drinking, no using your cell phone, and no reading." This message was delivered to me while I was sitting on a bench in a courtroom in Brooklyn one April morning. The message was delivered in a low voice by Scott Hechinger, an attorney with the Brooklyn Defender Services, who was sitting on the bench next to me.

"Why no reading?" I asked.

Scott's eyes got a little bit wider, as if he was excited that I'd understood a point he was trying to make. "Exactly!" was all that he said in response.

Scott and I had been invited to speak at a conference at New York University about plea bargaining the day before. He was kind enough to agree to show me around the Brooklyn courts and talk to me about his experiences as a lawyer in the criminal justice system, and so I tacked an extra day on my trip to the city from North Carolina. I had practiced law briefly in New York City before becoming a law professor. My old apartment was only about eight blocks from the courthouse where we were sitting. But I had never been inside the building that Scott was showing to me.

When I was sworn in as a member of the New York bar, the ceremony took place in a courtroom just a few blocks away. It was a solemn but also celebratory affair, as all the young lawyers and their families crowded into the courtroom of the Appellate Division's Second Judicial Department.

That appellate courtroom had soaring ceilings and a beautiful dark wood bench where the judges sat to hear oral argument. Even though it was years ago, I still remember that day. My mom took the train down from Albany to attend the ceremony. She got choked up and even shed a few tears as she recalled how proud she was of me—the first person in our family to ever go to law school.

The Kings County (Brooklyn) Criminal Court building, where I sat with Scott, was geographically very close to the beautiful courtroom where I had taken the oath to become a lawyer. But it felt worlds away. The criminal court courtroom was dimly lit. The furniture was scuffed and a bit dirty looking. The judges sat behind several desks of court staff. The staff would occasionally call out a date or hand a piece of paper to a lawyer. But much of what they did—typing on computers, speaking quietly into telephones, and rarely looking at the people coming through the courtrooms—seemed inscrutable.

The only decoration in the room were large, block letters hung behind the judge, far above the people in the room. IN GOD WE TRUST, the letters said. But I've rarely been in a place where God felt more distant.

The benches in the courtroom were filled with people who had been arrested and whose families were there to show support for them. Some of the people had been unable to get child care, and so their young children sat on their laps as they waited on the hard wooden benches. No one smiled. Everyone sat staring at the front of the courtroom, waiting for their case (or a case for their family member) to be called.

At some point I mentioned to Scott how the courtroom looked and felt to me. He responded by saying that the courtroom had the ambience of a public restroom.

"The process is the punishment," he added.

* * * * *

That saying—"The process is the punishment"—was made famous by Malcolm Feeley, a law professor at the University of California, Berkeley. Feeley conducted an in-depth study of criminal courts that handled low-level crimes. Before Feeley published his findings, there were basically two theories of criminal courts: the due process model and the plea bargain model.

The due process model presents the criminal justice system as a fully adversarial model in which two sides battle each other and only one side wins: the prosecution wins if the defendant is convicted, and the defense wins if the defendant is acquitted. This adversarial battle has important, formal rules such as proof beyond a reasonable doubt and rules against considering certain types of evidence. Although the due process model sounds like what we teach high school students about the criminal justice system, it has been heavily criticized by those who are actually familiar with the system because it describes an ideal rather than reality.

The plea bargain model is considered to be a more realistic model because it recognizes that most cases are settled through plea bargains rather than trials. Unlike the due process model, there is no clear winner and loser in the plea bargain model; instead, the two sides negotiate in order to avoid some of the bad consequences that would occur if they lost but without getting all the benefits that would come with a win. The negotiation takes place in the "shadow of a trial"—that is to say, the two sides negotiate based on the facts of the case and settle on an outcome based on the likelihood that the defendant would have been convicted at trial and what the likely sentence would have been. The plea bargain model offers not only a more accurate description of the criminal justice system but also something that is valuable on its own terms: it helps deal with large caseloads more quickly and for less money than the due process model. In other words, unlike the due process model, the plea bargain model seeks to make the criminal justice system more efficient.

Feeley blew up both of these models. He showed that the plea bargain model does not, as its champions claim, accurately describe the criminal justice system. It is true that most cases are resolved by guilty pleas; in fact, Feeley did not find a single trial in his yearlong study of more than 1,600 cases in a Connecticut courtroom. But he cautioned that a guilty plea does not necessarily mean that the defense and the prosecution actually negotiated with one another or that any negotiation was based on the facts of the case and the likely outcome at trial. Instead, prosecutors and defense attorneys routinely bargained without carefully reading the case files and thus not knowing or understanding the facts. They also bargained over issues that were irrelevant to whether the defendant would have prevailed at trial, like the relationship between the defendant and the victim before or after the crime was committed.

Sometimes, Feeley reported, the bargaining occurred across cases: a prosecutor would tell a defense attorney that he could not dismiss charges in a case because that defense attorney had already had his "quota" of dismissals that day. Or a defense attorney would argue in favor of a dismissal by noting that he hadn't asked the prosecutor for anything yet that day.

As for the due process model, Feeley didn't just say what everyone already knows—that it doesn't accurately describe the criminal justice system. Instead, he turned the due process model on its head, presenting it as a problematic approach to criminal justice. Most people praise the due process model as an ideal (if impossible to achieve) system. But Feeley tells us that defendants may actually try to avoid some of the process that they are due. As he explained, any contact with the criminal justice system was unpleasant and costly for defendants. Invoking the process that they were entitled to would often prolong the defendants' interactions with the criminal justice system, and so defendants readily give up their ability to test the prosecution's evidence or even secure a lawyer because those rights meant more time and effort for the defendant.

This was nothing short of a bombshell when Feeley's book was published. The process that he tells us defendants were trying to avoid exists, in large part, to protect those defendants. It is part of the "due process of law" guaranteed by the U.S. Constitution. But more important, Feeley demonstrated that the system could "punish" people merely by bringing them into the system. Even those defendants who were acquitted or whose cases were dismissed had to endure an arrest and court appearances. Such experiences impose costs on and demean everyone who is subjected to them.

For defendants, one of the major costs of the criminal process is having to show up at court. Feeley found that cases dragged on for unbelievably long amounts of time: "Cases in which there was no trial, no witnesses, no formal motions, no pretrial involvement from the bench, and no presentence investigation still required as many as eight or ten different appearances spread over six months." These appearances not only discouraged people from insisting on their right to a trial; they also discouraged defendants from having protracted negotiations to get a better plea bargain from prosecutors. As a result, defendants with complex cases would plead guilty at arraignment rather than trying to wait and convince the prosecutor to give them a better deal.

As Scott Hechinger said when we spoke in Brooklyn, the costs of coming to court are literal and figurative. It literally costs defendants $5.50 round trip on public transportation to travel to the courthouse for every appearance. That might not seem like a large amount of money to a middle-class defendant. But for those who are not financially secure, that is an added expense they can ill afford. For some of his clients, Scott said that this $5.50 is "the difference between eating and putting food on the table" or going without.

The figurative costs—which academics call "opportunity costs"—are all of the other things that a defendant can't do when they have to appear in court. They can't go to work, take care of their children, go to a doctor's appointment, or do any of the other dozens of things that we all need to do every day just to keep our lives on track. "Just having to come to court in and of itself—let alone the six or seven times that they would have to come if they ever wanted to possibly get to the point where they'd get a trial—is a horrible, punishing process," Scott stated.

Appearing in court is not the only source of "costs" for defendants. The right to have a lawyer represent them also imposes either literal or figurative costs. Any defendant who wants to hire her own lawyer will have to pay the costs of that lawyer's fee out of her own pocket. And lawyers are not cheap. Of course, defendants who can't afford lawyers can ask judges to appoint lawyers for them. But, as I explained in chapter 5, some places still manage to charge defendants money for their "free" lawyers.

Even in those places that don't charge defendants money for their appointed lawyers, defendants still have to expend significant time and effort to prove that they are entitled to free lawyers. The defendants have to fill out forms that ask invasive financial questions, and they have to be prepared to answer further questions by judges or other court personnel who might be skeptical of their claim that they can't afford to pay for a lawyer.

The process of getting a court-appointed lawyer can also be humiliating. When I clerked for a judge after I graduated from law school, one defendant asked for a court-appointed lawyer, but the prosecution objected. My judge held a hearing at which the prosecutor argued that the defendant should sell his car to pay for an attorney. When the defendant pointed out that the proceeds from selling his car would not be enough to pay a lawyer for his whole case, the government attorney responded that the defendant should sell his car, use that money to pay for a lawyer, and then come back to the court and ask for a court-appointed lawyer after the money ran out.

There was little doubt in my mind that making the defendant switch lawyers partway through his case would be inefficient: the first lawyer wouldn't be able to accomplish much, and then the new, court-appointed lawyer would have to get up to speed. So making the defendant sell his car wouldn't really save the taxpayers much money, but it would leave the defendant without his car even after the case was over.

Feeley also documented that the people who worked in the system saw contact with the system itself as a form of punishment. He saw prosecutors tell defendants to plead guilty at arraignment—including a defendant a with complex case that could have benefited from further investigation and negotiations—on the theory that they should "be smart and get it over with today."

The inconvenience associated with being arrested was also perceived as punishment. Feeley observed: "Officials are often willing to drop minor charges, feeling that the arrestees have learned their lesson by spending a night in jail." That sort of attitude makes sense if pretrial incarceration is a punishment; after all, many misdemeanors are very minor offenses that don't deserve more than a night in jail. But as chapter 4 explains, our criminal justice system constantly maintains the fiction that pretrial incarceration is not punishment.

By tearing down that fiction—that nothing we do to defendants before they are convicted is punishment—Feeley exposes perhaps the greatest injustice of our modern system: it indiscriminately punishes the guilty and the innocent. The costs of the pretrial system are borne by everyone who is swept up in it: guilty defendants, innocent defendants, and even their family members.

* * * * *

Looking at the people seated around us in the Brooklyn courtroom, I could see what Feeley (and Scott) meant. The people waiting in the courtroom were being subjected to a form of punishment; they resembled children in detention at school as they sat on the benches, not permitted to talk or even to read. The way in which the judge spoke to them—not rudely but somewhat condescendingly—also reminded me of a principal or a teacher telling a student what he had done wrong.

Most of the people whom Scott and I saw in that courtroom had been released, sometimes on bail. They were home with their friends and families while their cases wound their way through the system. Because they had been charged with misdemeanors, even if they lost at trial, they were not facing particularly severe punishments. As Scott explained, even though misdemeanors could result in a sentence of up to a year in jail, the prosecutors in Brooklyn rarely sought jail sentences, and judges rarely imposed them. Nonetheless, the vast majority of these people will plead guilty rather than insist on a trial.

Scott said that approximately 40 percent of misdemeanor defendants plead guilty as soon as they are able to see a judge. And for those cases that don't plead guilty at their first judicial appearance, they steadily trickle out of the system before a trial takes place. Some of the defendants have their charges dismissed. Others eventually decide to plead guilty; some decide to plead because the prosecutors are willing to reduce the charges against them, others because they get sick of having to come back to court so many times. Some of the defendants will enter an alternative treatment program. At the end of the day, Scott estimated that, at most, 1 percent of misdemeanor cases in Brooklyn go to trial.

That cases were leaking out of the system became clear as Scott took me from courtroom to courtroom in the Brooklyn courthouse. The first courtroom—the one that resembled the public restroom—was where misdemeanor defendants made their initial appearance before a judge. It was the largest and most crowded courtroom that I'd ever seen. The subsequent courtrooms we visited—the ones where people would make additional appearances before judges, where suppression hearings were held, and where defendants facing felony charges appeared—had fewer defendants in them. The courtrooms were also smaller, more formal, and less dingy, but still far from welcoming.

One of the last courtrooms we visited was part of a specialized court—specifically a court that dealt with defendants whose crimes were related to substance abuse. When we entered the courtroom, a man who had been arrested for drunk driving was being admitted into the program. The man was tall and broad-chested. He seemed like the sort of person who would take up two or three seats on the subway, not only because of his size but also because he'd feel entitled to the extra space. But in the courtroom, the man did not exude an air of self-confidence or entitlement. His broad shoulders drooped as he listened to the judge tell him, very sternly, the consequences of failing out of the program.

The Brooklyn substance abuse treatment program is structured as an alternative to incarceration. It requires defendants to plead guilty in order to enter the program and avoid jail. For defendants facing felony charges, that means they plead guilty to two crimes, a felony and a misdemeanor. After they plead guilty, their sentences are withheld—that is to say, the sentences aren't imposed until after they complete the treatment program. If a defendant successfully completes the program, then the judge will vacate the felony plea, removing the guilty plea on that charge from the defendant's criminal record. Since felonies often carry mandatory minimum sentences, getting the felony pleas vacated and those charges dismissed is really beneficial for defendants. Once a felony plea has been vacated, the only charge left is the misdemeanor, and then the judge will impose a sentence on the misdemeanor—not incarceration but some other small punishment.

The man whom we saw pleading guilty in the drunk-driving case was facing felony charges because this wasn't his first DUI. If he successfully completes the program, then he will be sentenced just for a misdemeanor—a sentence of only a $500 fine. But if he doesn't complete the treatment program successfully, he won't get the felony vacated. He'll be sentenced for that felony, and he will end up in jail.

As the judge explained all of this to the defendant, it sounded really daunting. The judge emphasized that the treatment would be demanding and that if the defendant did not do everything required of him, then the prosecutor would be free to seek the maximum sentence on the felony. In other words, the judge told the defendant that if he failed to complete the treatment program, he would almost certainly end up spending no small amount of time in jail.

The judge also explained the requirements of the treatment program. One of the requirements was that the defendant had to pay for the costs of treatment. But as the man told his defense lawyer, the treatment itself was going to interfere with his work hours. And if he couldn't get enough hours at work, then he wouldn't have the money that he needed to pay for the costs of the program.

The lawyer explained the problem to the judge. The judge understood that the defendant was in a catch-22. But it was quickly made clear to the defendant that the problem was his, not the court's. It was up to the defendant to figure out how to attend treatment and still work enough hours so that he could pay for that treatment and all of the other expenses in his life.

After we left the courtroom, I asked Scott what would happen if the defendant couldn't attend all of the treatment sessions or if he couldn't pay for them.

It's complicated.

Scott stressed that the judge in the treatment court wouldn't kick the defendant out of the program right away; they generally give people a number of chances if they miss an appointment, don't make their payments, or have a urine sample test positive for marijuana. But there would be smaller punishments along the way for these lapses: an outpatient treatment regime might get converted into an in-patient regime, forcing the defendant to live in an institution while undergoing substance abuse treatment. Or the time in the treatment program could be extended from twelve months to eighteen months. Judges in the treatment programs could also give a lapsed defendant a short jail punishment of a week or two at Rikers Island.

Obviously, ending up in an institution or in jail would prevent the defendant from working and being able to pay for his treatment. And if the defendant's treatment got extended because he was missing payments, he would probably just end up missing even more payments. The drunk-driving defendant was warning his lawyer and the judge about these problems, but it didn't matter. He was pleading guilty anyway, even though he could see that there was a significant chance that he might fail the program and end up in jail.

Substance abuse treatment courts have been touted as a good alternative to incarcerating people who break the law. The basic idea behind these courts is that some people commit crimes because they are abusing drugs or alcohol, and their criminal activity is more likely to continue so long as they continue to abuse these substances. If the system can get them to stop abusing alcohol or drugs, so the argument goes, then they will also stop committing crimes. So the objective in substance abuse courts is to treat the substance abuse problem and use the threat of criminal punishment to get defendants to comply with the terms of the treatment program.

But drug courts are only a good alternative to jail if they actually work. "I've had clients who have succeeded. But I've had more clients who have not succeeded and ended up in jail," Scott told me. And sometimes, he added, the clients who enter these treatment programs and who fail end up worse off than if they had just pleaded guilty in the first place. Scott recounted the story of one client who could serve as a poster child for ending up worse off.

Scott's client was charged with burglary in the third degree for stealing some things from a bodega. The client wasn't eligible for bail, so he was sitting in jail. After he'd been in jail for nine months, Scott convinced the judge to let the client enter an alternative-to-incarceration plea. The plea required the client to do eighteen to twenty-four months of treatment, the first year of which would be in an inpatient program. The year of inpatient treatment was very successful and, against the odds, the client appeared to have actually kicked his substance addiction. But when he was released from the inpatient program, no one helped him set up his outpatient appointments, and he didn't have any insurance to cover those treatments. So the client relapsed, and he ended up getting rearrested for assaulting another man and taking his phone.

Because the client was already in the treatment program, he wasn't eligible to be released from jail pending trial when he was arrested for the new charges. So he ended up pleading guilty in the new case, just so that he could be released from jail, even though he disputed taking the phone and assaulting the other man. The new charges resulted in the drug court judge sending him back to the inpatient treatment program, but at that point the client wasn't interested in receiving treatment. "He was just kind of gone at that point," Scott said. The client ended up failing out of the treatment program, and he was facing sentencing on the bodega burglary charges when I interviewed Scott.

"He faces a mandatory minimum of one and a half to three years, which means he'll be eligible for parole after one and a half years. But I don't think he'll be released on parole," Scott said. His client actually ended up worse off by entering the treatment program than if he'd just pleaded guilty to the charges in the first instance. In addition to spending more than a year living in an institution for his inpatient substance abuse treatment, he's going to have to serve the same sentence that he would have gotten if he'd never entered the program in the first place.

"This started out as an eighteen- to twenty-four-month program, but this whole ordeal has been going on for four years," Scott said. At this point the client wants to put the ordeal behind him and he is frustrated with the prosecutor, with the judge, and with Scott because these petty charges have kept him in the system for years. "He keeps saying 'y'all' like I'm a part of this, and that hurts: 'Y'all have had me for four years for stealing a few things from a bodega to support my drug habit. When is enough, enough?'" Scott paused for a second and then added, "Apparently, the answer is 'Not yet.'"

* * * * *

Like many public defenders, Scott Hechinger developed a passion for criminal justice in law school. He went to NYU, where he met Bryan Stevenson, a modern hero in the fight for criminal justice reform. In addition to teaching law at NYU, Stevenson runs the Equal Justice Initiative, a human rights organization that has been very successful in exonerating wrongfully convicted defendants and winning Supreme Court victories. Stevenson's memoir, *Just Mercy: A Story of Justice and Redemption*, was a *New York Times* #1 bestseller and has been made into a major motion picture starring Jamie Foxx and Michael B. Jordan.

As a student, Scott did some legal research for Stevenson on juveniles serving sentences of life in prison without the possibility of parole. That research was part of a broader litigation strategy that culminated in Stevenson arguing before the Supreme Court. Scott camped out the night before the oral argument, sleeping on the sidewalk in front of the Supreme Court, so that he could get one of the small number of public seats in the audience. Stevenson ended up winning the case, resulting in a landmark ruling that the Eighth Amendment forbids mandatory life-without-parole sentences for juveniles.

Stevenson was a mentor for Scott. When Scott told Stevenson that we wanted to pursue a public interest career and that he wanted to use his law degree to help tell compelling stories, Stevenson told him that the path was obvious: he should become a public defender. Scott took Stevenson's advice and spent one of his law school summers in New Orleans interning with the public defender's office. It was a new office, established in the wake Hurricane Katrina. New Orleans had never had public defenders before, and Scott was in their second class of summer interns.

Public defenders are in a difficult situation. They are supposed to zealously protect the rights of their clients, but they also have to get their funding from public sources. Many chief public defenders are appointed by judges or by other elected officials in their jurisdictions, so they can get dragged into political fights as well. Sometimes zealous advocacy can ruffle feathers and get the defenders in trouble. For example, the top public defenders in Montgomery County, Pennsylvania, were fired recently after they filed a brief with the state supreme court criticizing how judges in their county set cash bail. The judges appear to have complained to the county commissioners, who fired the defenders.

The new public defenders in New Orleans also upset the judges, who were not used to defense attorneys sticking up for their clients and questioning how the courts dispensed justice. "I remember seeing supervising attorneys getting dragged out of courtrooms in handcuffs for making simple legal arguments," Scott said as we sat down for lunch after my tour of the courthouse.

As an intern, it was Scott's job to help the public defense lawyers who would appear in court on behalf of indigent defendants. "My main job was helping in arraignments, which would be held en masse," he said. "A hundred people or so would be marched into the loading dock of the Orleans Parish Prison, in front of an oversized TV. As an intern, I would run and try to interview as many people as I could to find out as much about them as I could. Then I would run the three blocks from the prison to the courthouse, where there was one public defender sitting next to the judge, looking at a television screen full of Black faces in orange jumpsuits. Then bail was set, basically just depending on the charge."

According to Scott, the New Orleans public defenders would lose all the time. Nonetheless, he was inspired by his experience. It impressed on him that even if the defendant was going to lose, it made a big difference have someone speak to them face-to-face and treat them like human beings. The defendants felt listened to instead of just feeling forgotten by the system.

And so Scott decided to become a public defender. After a short fellowship and a clerkship with a judge, Scott joined Brooklyn Defender Services in 2012. Since joining the organization, Scott has developed a national reputation as a critic of the criminal justice system. He is the founder and director of Zealous, an organization devoted to training and helping public defenders across the country to advocate outside the courtroom for an end to mass incarceration. We met at an academic conference organized by NYU, but his reputation extends beyond legal academics. *Teen Vogue* did a profile of him. And he has a large following on Twitter.

When I ask Scott about his rise to prominence, he tells me a story about sitting in the Brooklyn courthouse one day, covering arraignments. He watched a middle-aged woman being arraigned for failing to pay a surcharge. The woman had pleaded guilty to stealing beef jerky from a bodega two months before. Because she'd been convicted, she had to pay a $250 surcharge. But she hadn't paid the surcharge, and so she got arrested again. The penalty for failure to pay a surcharge, Scott explained, was fifteen days in jail, which could be reduced to ten days for good behavior.

"The whole thing took about two minutes," Scott said. And while the facts of the case and the implication were buried in technical language, Scott understood those technicalities and knew what was happening. "What I saw was a person who had pleaded guilty for stealing food because she was hungry—something that shouldn't be criminalized in the first place—and then she added to her criminal record. She tried to pay her fine but failed. She spent the night in jail, got brought to court, and then got sent back to jail for ten days for simply not having any money—which is what got her in trouble in the first place. And when she gets out, she's going to be even more damaged."

During his time as a public defender, Scott has tried hard not to lose the inspiration from his early experiences or to allow himself to become desensitized to what he sees: "I try not to become blasé about everyday injustice. It's so easy to because you see the same patterns and the same things happen every day." But he knows that many people who work in the system do become desensitized. And as he looked around the courtroom at the woman's arraignment, he saw the other lawyers not even paying attention to the case because it was so routine.

So he wrote about the case on Twitter. He wanted to remind his fellow public defenders about how awful these cases are and hoped that it could serve as a kind of call to action for the small group of colleagues who followed his Twitter account. "I wanted to tell them not to lose sight of this stuff—that we have an obligation to bear witness, both because we see it happening, but also because we understand it in a way that other people don't."

Scott's tweet about the woman's case was retweeted ten or fifteen times, which he said with a self-deprecating laugh "was about ten or fifteen more than I'd ever gotten before . . . except maybe from my wife, who would sometimes retweet my stuff to make me feel better."

The positive feedback, though modest, encouraged Scott to tweet more. He started bringing his laptop with him to arraignments. And while he's waiting between cases, he'll sometimes tweet about the cases that he observes. "I want people to see what I saw and understand it the way that I understood it," he said.

Scott's tweets have gone viral, giving him a platform not only to speak about the everyday injustices that he witnesses but also to lift up the voices of others in the system. One inmate in Texas reached out to Scott during the coronavirus pandemic. The seventy-one-year-old man, who was charged with a drug crime, suffered from non-Hodgkin's lymphoma. He had been in solitary confinement for six months, and jail officials weren't supplying him with any medical care. Scott's tweet about the man was retweeted more than 6,000 times. One day later, the local prosecutor issued a statement saying that the man was being released.

In helping people learn about and understand what happens in these courtrooms, Scott hopes not only to bring about change in specific cases but also to help other public defenders tell the stories of people who are caught up in the criminal justice system. And as those stories are told more widely, and as more people see the everyday injustice that Scott and his colleagues do, he hopes that more people will see the criminal justice system as the wrong way to deal with problems like poverty and addiction.

* * * * *

David Jaros, a public defender turned law professor, tells a frightening story about how the pretrial process can lead defendants to give up their right to a trial. The story is about his former client, James.* James had left his apartment one day when he the police were in his building. When officers confronted him in the hallway of his building, they ordered James to show them his identification to prove that he lived in the building. Because his wallet was still in his apartment rather than with him, he couldn't show them his ID. So police arrested James for trespassing even though he was in his own building.

David was appointed to represent James on the trespassing charge. Because he had been arrested, James first met with David while he was still locked up in the back of the courthouse. At that point James had spent almost twenty-four hours in jail. His meeting with David took place right before James was scheduled to appear in front of a judge for the first time. During the meeting, David had to learn about James's case, tell him what his options were, and counsel him about what decisions to make.

David explained to James that there were only two possibilities about what could happen at his first hearing: he could either plead guilty or have the judge decide whether bail was required for his release. David assured James that, in cases like this, the judge would almost certainly release him without bail, but the judge was not going to be willing to dismiss the charges at that first hearing. If James wanted to fight the trespassing charge, he would be released, but he would have to return to court for another appearance and bring proof with him that he lived in the building.

If James didn't want to fight the charges and return to court again, David explained that James would have to plead guilty. Pleading guilty to trespassing would be considered only a "violation" rather than a misdemeanor, which meant that James wouldn't have to serve any more time in

---

* James is not his real name.

jail. He wouldn't even have a criminal record. He would have to pay $100 in court costs, and there was a chance he would have to do some community service too. But if he pleaded guilty, not only would he be released immediately, but he would not have to return to court.

James told David that he wasn't willing to take off another day of work for a second court appearance: he had already missed work because of his arrest, and he was worried that more absences might result in him getting fired. David told James that in order to avoid returning to court, he would have to plead guilty then and there. James said he wanted to plead guilty right away. David said, "As his lawyer, I could explain the ramifications, but it's ultimately his decision about whether or not he's better off taking that plea or missing work."

David is right that defendants need to make their own decisions about their cases, but I was horrified by James's story. James pleaded guilty to trespassing in his own building. He was completely innocent of that charge, and it would take only one more trip to court to clear his name. I couldn't understand how James could make that decision.

But David helped put the situation in perspective. "Can you imagine spending almost twenty-four hours in jail and then having to take another day to return to court just to prove that you in fact had a right to be in your building?" he asked me. David did, of course, have clients who would go home, get proof that they lived in the building or that they were legitimately visiting someone in the building, and then bring that proof with them to the next court date to get the charges dismissed. "But someone who doesn't want to lose his job, or someone who makes more in a day than the court costs, might rationally say, 'I don't want to spend a day sitting in court and waiting around for my lawyer to show up and the prosecutor to get there and then have my case called. I'd rather just have this case resolved and never have to come back here.'"

I would like to think that I would have made a different decision—that I would stand on principle and insist on proving that the police who arrested me were wrong. But, as David explained, getting the charges dismissed wouldn't feel like a victory. "At the end of the day, all you get is that the case is no longer there—it's been dismissed—but you don't get back that time or that experience."

James's story is not unique. He had been arrested during a regular sweep of buildings in the Bronx. Officers would swarm the hallways, and, to avoid being arrested, people had to demonstrate that they were there to see someone or that they otherwise had a right to be in the building.

David has many stories about clients being arrested during these sweeps. A lot of those clients had perfectly legitimate reasons to be in those buildings. One client was arrested when he was at a building to visit his aunt. Another was at a building to see some friends from school—friends who lived only two doors away from his own building. David explained that officers would take the people over to the door of the person they said they were visiting. They would knock on the door, and if no one answered, they'd arrest the person. David's clients would try to tell the officers that their family members or friends actually lived in those apartments; they just must not be home at the moment. But officers would just say, "Fine, that's your defense," and arrest them anyway. Then the police would take David's clients to booking and make them sit in a jail for a day before David would meet them for the first time and they would get to see a judge.

As a lawyer, I couldn't understand how these people were being arrested for trespassing. "Trespassing" means entering or remaining on someone else's property without permission. Visiting family and friends certainly isn't trespassing. And it is legally impossible to trespass in your own home. More important, police can't arrest you unless they have probable cause to believe that you've committed a crime. Not having your wallet in your pocket isn't evidence that you've committed a crime, nor is the fact that the friend you went to visit ends up not being at home.

James and David's other clients were arrested under a program called Operation Clean Halls in New York City. The idea behind Operation Clean Halls was simple: to make New York apartment buildings safer and more pleasant for their residents. The operation targeted people who were hanging around those buildings, hassling residents, and selling drugs. Of course, proving that someone is selling drugs isn't always easy, and people aren't likely to harass someone else where the police can see them. So, in order to keep people out of these apartment buildings, the NYPD used the trespassing laws rather than having to prove that these people were engaging in any other illegal activities.

Operation Clean Halls began in 1991. At one point, more than 8,000 buildings were participating in the Clean Halls program; that meant that the owners had invited the NYPD in to make these arrests. More than 3,000 of the Clean Halls buildings were in the Bronx, which resulted in thousands of arrests. During David's time as a public defender in the Bronx, Clean Halls cases were, as he put it, "extraordinarily common." "It would be a rare day if you had an arraignment shift and didn't have people who had been arrested for trespass in a Clean Halls building."

The problem, of course, was that police weren't particularly careful when it came to deciding who had a legitimate reason to be in a building and who didn't. They would clear the hallways, sometimes arresting anyone that they found without an ID. And even if you did have an ID, you had to prove to officers that you had a legitimate reason to be in the building, even though the Constitution requires the opposite: It requires police to have evidence of illegal activity before arresting someone rather than requiring people to provide proof of their innocence in order to avoid arrest.

A 2013 study by New York City's Civilian Complaint Review Board found that 40 percent of fully investigated complaints by people who had been caught up in of Operation Clean Halls were "substantiated." That's a bureaucratic way of saying that the officers acted improperly if not illegally. As the report noted, this rate was twice as high as the rate for complaints against officers outside of Clean Halls buildings. The report strongly suggests that police were routinely violating people's rights in the Clean Halls sweeps. Unsurprisingly, people of color were disproportionately swept up in Operation Clean Halls. Of people who complained to the Civilian Complaint Review Board, nearly 90 percent were either Black or Hispanic.

In 2012, three organizations—the ACLU, the Bronx Defenders, and a group called LatinoJustice—filed a lawsuit against the New York City Police Department, saying that Operation Clean Halls was illegal. The groups won a preliminary injunction against the program and ultimately entered into a settlement with the NYPD. Under the terms of the settlement, the police could not conduct sweeps of Clean Halls buildings in which they forced everyone present to provide identification. Instead, police could only approach people when they already had some evidence that the person was trespassing in the building or committing some other crime. In other words, these groups had to sue the NYPD in order to force officers to follow ordinary constitutional rules. The settlement also required police to keep records about every person they stop or frisk near a Clean Halls buildings—something that will allow more scrutiny of police behavior in the future.

But before the lawsuit forced the program to change, tens of thousands of people were swept up into the criminal justice system. Between 2007 and 2012, the NYPD made at least 16,000 trespassing arrests every year under Operation Clean Halls. Many of the cases were dismissed by judges or weren't prosecuted by district attorneys. But more than 60 percent of Clean Halls arrests ended either in a guilty plea or another unfavorable disposition for the person arrested. We don't know how many of the thousands of people arrested in Operation Clean Halls were innocent or how many of those innocent people pleaded guilty. But David's stories make clear that the burden of the court process itself caused at least some innocent defendants to plead guilty.

At the end of our conversation about James and his other clients, I asked David: Why couldn't he have gotten James's charges dismissed without making James come back to court and miss another day of work? Why couldn't James just send David a copy of his ID and then have David show up at the next court date without James to provide that evidence to the judge and the prosecutor in order to get the case dismissed?

David explained that James was legally required to appear at the next court date. The default rule in criminal cases is that defendants have to show up for all court dates—even the ones when nothing is going to happen and the lawyers are just going to set another date for the next status update. In an incredibly small number of cases, David had been able to convince the judge to allow the defendant to "waive" his appearance at the next court date when the case was clearly just going to be dismissed. But it was "stunningly rare" how often judges were actually willing to do that. David sighed as he noted, "There was absolutely no recognition by the actors in the system about the level of inconvenience for all of the people caught up in the system."

* * * * *

It is very important to understand the plea bargaining dynamic in misdemeanor cases because most criminal cases are misdemeanor cases. But studying misdemeanor cases can be difficult because state and local governments do not keep particularly good records of misdemeanors. Until recently, we didn't even have a good estimate of how many misdemeanor cases are filed in the country. Law professor Alexandra Natapoff undertook the difficult task of combining data from across the country and found that there are approximately 13 million misdemeanor cases filed every year. Those cases can range from serious criminal behavior like domestic violence to trivial misconduct like littering.

Because misdemeanors make up 80 percent of all criminal cases in the country, most of the people who are arrested and charged with a crime will be accused of committing a misdemeanor. And because misdemeanor offenses can be so trivial, any of us might find ourselves charged with one. So it should deeply concern all of us that those people who are swept up in the misdemeanor criminal justice system see *the system itself* as a form of punishment.

To be clear, the process can also look like punishment in felony cases. People accused of felonies who are lucky enough to be released pending trial also have to return to court time after time. But that inconvenience doesn't drive plea bargaining in felony cases—at least not serious felony cases—the same way that it does in misdemeanor cases. In serious felony cases, defendants can't risk going to trial because the stakes are too high. In misdemeanor cases, defendants don't push for trials because the stakes are so low. Unlike felony defendants, who face much more severe sentences if they are convicted at trial than if they plead guilty, the difference between a guilty plea and a conviction after trial for a misdemeanor defendant is likely to be much, much smaller. But while the difference in sentencing gives prosecutors a lot of leverage in felony cases, the similarity in sentences make the punishment of the process more obvious and more important for misdemeanor defendants.

Imagine a misdemeanor defendant who is facing a $250 fine if she is convicted at trial. She could avoid the fine if she is acquitted at trial, but it will take anywhere between three and seven court visits before she will actually get that trial. It will probably set her back more than $250 in transportation costs and lost wages for her to attend all of the court appearances—and she might even lose her job for missing so much work—so she is probably better off just pleading guilty right away. If she can make the fine just a little bit lower by pleading guilty at arraignment, then it would be even more irrational for her to insist on a trial.

David Jaros emphasized that the risk of losing their job isn't the only gamble that misdemeanor defendants take when their cases drag on for extended periods of time awaiting trial. There is also the risk that a defendant could miss a court date or get arrested again for something else. If a defendant misses a court date, then the judge will issue a warrant for her arrest. And if you are arrested when you already have charges pending on another case, you usually won't be released on the new case. As we know, defendants who are incarcerated before trial feel enormous pressure to plead guilty in order to be released. "So," David concluded, "all of these things snowball into creating a system that functions more around resolving pleas rather than going to trial."

That the stakes in misdemeanor cases are lower does not mean that a misdemeanor conviction has no effect on a person. Even if a defendant isn't going to go to jail when she is convicted of a misdemeanor, there are still collateral consequences associated with that conviction. For example, a misdemeanor conviction can affect a person's eligibility to get a student loan or live in public housing. A misdemeanor conviction can keep people from getting a job at the many businesses that require a criminal background check. It can even result in a person who is not a U.S. citizen being deported.

But those consequences seem smaller when compared to the costs of the prolonged contact with the system while waiting for trial. The very act of being brought into the criminal justice system—even if you are never convicted—can also have severe consequences. Defendants have to miss school or work to attend court dates, and so the defendants may perform poorly in class or lose their jobs if they keep returning to court while waiting for a trial. And an arrest record—even if the arrest never turns into a conviction—is often used by landlords, employers, and immigration officials when they make important decisions about people's lives. It doesn't matter to these people outside of the criminal justice system that the defendant wasn't convicted. As law professor Eisha Jain has explained, these people use arrest records because those records are relatively easy and inexpensive to find, and because they think arrests are good proxies for the potential for violence, unreliability, or instability.

Because the difference is so small between the consequences of a trial and the consequences of a plea bargain, misdemeanor plea bargains might seem unimportant, especially when you compare their outcomes to the outcomes in felony cases. But it would be a mistake to ignore the problems that misdemeanor plea bargaining causes. And it would be an even bigger mistake to ignore misdemeanors when thinking about how to reform our system.

Scott Hechinger sometimes makes a stink about the silly misdemeanor cases that he sees at arraignment. He'll say, "Why is this case even in the system?" The assistant district attorneys get annoyed that he is objecting when they are giving his client a favorable deal. "The ADAs turn to me and say, 'They are going home, Scott. Why are you making such a big deal?'

Then I'll say, 'If it's not a big deal, then why are you prosecuting?' They don't have an answer."

Scott's question is an important one. The 13 million misdemeanor cases filed each year clog up our criminal justice system. Especially in large urban areas, the people inside the system have made the decision that these cases aren't really worth it: they think that a few hours in jail or a small fine are enough to "teach a lesson" to these defendants. The system doesn't even care whether it has swept up an innocent or a guilty defendant; only the defendant who is willing to endure the costs of additional appearances has the opportunity to prove that he is innocent.

So why do we have this bloated misdemeanor system? Sure, some misdemeanors are serious: domestic violence, for example, should be taken seriously by law enforcement. But many other crimes should not. In fact, it might be less efficient for us to treat certain behavior—especially behavior that is caused by poverty—as a crime rather than as a social problem to be solved.

How much does it cost us to prosecute a person who jumps the turnstile in the subway rather than pay the $2.75 fare? How much does it cost us to jail the woman who can't pay the surcharge from her previous misdemeanor case? If we put the resources that we currently use to arrest, prosecute, and jail these people into social service programs aimed at alleviating poverty, we would almost certainly save money. And those social services would help a lot of people who are hungry and who can't afford public transportation but who *haven't* stolen food, jumped a turnstile, or committed another crime.

Unfortunately, the judges, prosecutors, and defense attorneys who work in the criminal justice system don't get to make those decisions. Decisions about poverty prevention programs and the costs of public transportation are made by other public officials who set local budgets and decide on public priorities. And those officials are making those decisions—at least to some extent—based on what the public wants. Yet I can't help but wonder whether the public would feel the same way if they sat in those courtrooms, saw the people shuffled through, and began to understand that we can't arrest our way out of poverty and addiction.

* * * * *

Months after I'd been to visit Scott Hechinger in Brooklyn, I was still bothered by the courtroom rules that he had told me about—especially the rule about no reading. I could understand why talking on the phone could disturb others in the courtroom, and I could understand why eating and drinking in the courtroom could cause a mess. But reading doesn't bother anyone, so why should it be prohibited?

I began to wonder whether the no reading rule was just a random inconvenience imposed by someone who worked in the Brooklyn courthouse. But when I spoke with David Jaros, he mentioned that they had the same rule in the courthouse where he practiced in the Bronx. That made me think the no reading rule might actually be a formal policy.

I did some poking around and found the rule against reading on the Brooklyn criminal court website:

Courtroom Rules

No eating, drinking, talking, reading or sleeping. No use of laptop computers or personal stereos. All beepers and mobile phones must be turned off.

The bookworm in me recoiled against such a rule. I have always loved books, and I'd read for hours at a time when I was a kid. In fact, when I would get in trouble, my parents would sometimes punish me by saying that I couldn't read that day. (It was a more effective punishment than saying I couldn't watch television because we didn't have cable in our house.) So, to me, a rule prohibiting reading seems like a punishment. And it doesn't seem right to me that we should punish the people in that courtroom: they had only been accused of a crime, not convicted. Some people in the courtroom hadn't even been accused of a crime; they were there only to support their friends and family.

In addition, a no reading policy seems counterproductive. Reading is an activity that our government should be encouraging. People who read are informing and educating themselves. And informed and educated people are less likely to get in trouble and end up in court. In fact, there are several studies showing that those people who end up in prison have very high rates of illiteracy. So shouldn't courtrooms get rid of their no reading policies?

That's what Noor Ahmad thought. Ahmad is a Legal Aid Society lawyer who represents juvenile defendants for free in the Brooklyn courts. And when I looked into the no reading rule some more, her name came up. She, too, had questioned why the Brooklyn courts prohibited reading, and she had done something about it.

Like the adult courtroom that I visited, the Brooklyn juvenile courtroom had a no reading policy—a policy that Ahmad sought to change when she saw some her clients get kicked out of the courtroom for talking. Ahmad could tell that her clients were bored just sitting there, so she asked to speak to the judge overseeing the courtroom. She explained to the judge that banning reading was counterproductive. She reminded him that a lot of the juvenile defendants were missing school to appear in the courtroom, and so it would be a good idea to give them something educational to do while they waited—sometimes for hours—for their cases to be called.

The judge agreed. He was willing to change the policy. Ahmad then fought for permission to actually install a bookcase in the courtroom so that even those defendants who hadn't brought a book with them would have something to read. It took more than a year to get permission for the bookcase. Some courthouse officers said they were worried that the young people might use the books as weapons. Ahmad sensed that those officers seemed to think the kids were not entitled to pass their time in the courtroom in a productive manner. But the rule was changed, the bookcase was installed, and the kids who appear in juvenile court can now read as they wait for their cases to be called. Ahmad's employer, Legal Aid, even has plans to expand the program to juvenile courtrooms across New York City in a partnership with publisher Penguin Random House.

But while the rule changed in Brooklyn's juvenile court, reading is still prohibited in adult court. Because I was sworn in as a member of the New York State Bar in Brooklyn, I felt an obligation to find out why the court of which I am a member has such a rule. I sent a letter from the courthouse to the judge who handles administrative matters, and I sent copies of the letter to the court clerks. The letter asked the judge to consider changing the rule or at least to explain why such a rule had been adopted.

No one responded to my letter. I followed up by phone and email, but I never got a response. The rule is still on the website. The people who arrive in that courtroom still are not allowed to read. They must sit in silence—as if being punished.

CHAPTER SEVEN

THE POLITICS OF REFORM

Shon Hopwood is the best spokesperson for criminal justice reform I've ever met. He's not only incredibly smart; he's also very personable. A former high school and college basketball player from Nebraska, Shon is a friendly, down-to-earth person you can immediately feel comfortable talking to. The first time I met Shon was at a conference for law professors—the sort of place where small talk usually consists of abstract discussions about academic research or recent Supreme Court cases. But Shon had me talking about my family and my childhood growing up on military bases, and I felt completely at ease within minutes of our first conversation.

But it isn't just Shon's quick smile and Midwestern twang that makes him such an effective advocate for changing the criminal justice system. He has a personal story that is so compelling that it could be the plot for a movie.

Today, Shon is a law professor. But he used to be a bank robber. He robbed five banks in the late 1990s, and he spent more than ten years in federal prison. While in prison, he used books from the prison library to teach himself law, and he wrote legal briefs for his fellow inmates. Sometimes Shon wrote petitions to the U.S. Supreme Court, asking them review the cases of his fellow inmates. It's nearly impossible to get the U.S. Supreme Court to review a case; the Court grants review in less than 5 percent of the petitions it receives. As a federal prisoner, Shon got the Supreme Court to grant review in two separate cases—a track record that is better than many high-priced lawyers. Shon did all of this without any formal legal training or even a college degree.

When he was finally released from prison, Shon worked for several years, finished his college degree, and applied to law school. He attended the University of Washington's law school on scholarship from the Bill & Melinda Gates Foundation.

Since graduating from law school, Shon has used his law degree to help others. He continues to bring cases for people who are serving prison sentences. In addition, he has started lobbying Congress for criminal justice reform.

Shon worked tirelessly to get the First Step Act passed in 2018. The act increases rehabilitative programming in federal prisons and includes some modest sentencing reforms. Shon's work was so instrumental to the passage of the First Step Act that President Trump publicly thanked him for his efforts and asked Shon to speak at a White House event celebrating the legislation.

I asked Shon how he started lobbying for criminal justice reform, and the answer was interesting: he was invited to work with the White House by President Trump's son-in-law, Jared Kushner. Shon explained that Kushner "is a lot like most Americans. He never thought about the criminal justice system—never thought about the injustices—right up until the point where a family member was charged and sentenced." (Jared Kushner's father, Charles, was a real estate developer. In 2005 he pleaded guilty to various crimes associated with illegal campaign contributions, tax evasion, and witness tampering. Charles Kushner served more than a year in federal prison for those crimes.)

Shon came to Kushner's attention when the television show *60 Minutes* aired a segment on Shon in 2017. Shon had written a book about his redemption story that was published in 2012. At the time the book was published, Shon was a law student. By 2017 he had been hired by Georgetown—one of the top law schools in the entire country—as a full-time professor on the tenure track. The idea that a person who had served more than a decade in federal prison could one day attend law school makes for a good story. The idea that such a person could get one of the most competitive legal jobs in the entire country is like a fairy tale.

So it is no wonder that Kushner—whom Shon credits with being a very smart and savvy person—decided to have Shon help sell reluctant members of Congress on criminal justice reform. There are other formerly incarcerated people who served prison sentences who now lobby for criminal justice reform, including the leadership of Families Against Mandatory Minimums (FAMM), the American Conservative Union, and #cut50. But Shon was the only person with conservative connections (he's a member of the Federalist Society) who had served a lengthy sentence for a non–white-collar crime.

"I introduce myself the same way whenever I'm asked to speak—paid speaking events, Rotary clubs, churches, before the president and senators. I say, 'My name is Shon Hopwood. I'm an associate professor of law at Georgetown University Law Center. I committed a violent crime, but I am not a violent criminal,'" Shon recounted.

It's an effective introduction, Shon explained, because it introduces people to the idea that someone could commit a violent crime because he is at a certain stage in his life. But as he grows older, he finds himself at a different stage where he wouldn't dream of doing anything violent or breaking the law. The idea resonates with people—people who otherwise think that a person who commits a crime is a criminal and can't be changed.

Shon reminds those people that, of course, "everyone changes from their late teens and early twenties until their forties. Everyone goes through pretty profound changes. And nobody wants to be the same person they were when they were twenty." Once he reminds people of this idea of change—a change that they've witnessed in their own lives and with their own children—he asks them why they would think that someone in prison can't change. And then he tells them stories—stories about people he knew in prison, and stories about his current clients.

Shon isn't the only person whose personal story can cause government officials to change their minds. He explained to me that Matthew Charles is an especially effective advocate for criminal justice reform. Matthew served twenty-one years of a thirty-five-year prison sentence, and he applied for and was granted early release in 2016. After his release, he built a life in his community. But unfortunately his sentence reduction was reversed on appeal, and so he was sent back to prison in May of 2018 to serve out the rest of his sentence. But Matthew qualified for sentencing relief under the First Step Act. Matthew was actually Shon's first client who was released from prison under the First Step Act.

"Matthew had an ugly criminal history," Shon said. "Domestic violence. Kidnapping. He'd shot someone in the head. So when the judge gave him thirty-five years for a federal drug offense, it's hard to fault the judge for thinking, 'Man, this guy's dangerous. He's done this for ten years. We can't let this guy back out.'

"But what judges can't measure at the front end of sentencing is the capacity of people to change. And there were lots of people I saw in the federal prison system who I wondered how they ever ended up there. Because by the time I saw them they had been rehabilitated. They had been clean and off drugs for several years. And they were delightful people."

As Shon described the people he knew in prison and his clients, it reminded me of his book. Even though he spent more than a decade in prison, Shon wrote about his experience as an opportunity for growth—a chance to turn his life around and to help others. In the book, Shon sometimes talked about injustices that other inmates endured. But when he talked about his own case, Shon did so with an unflinching and unflattering tone. Throughout the book he never took less than full responsibility for what he had done and the pain he had caused his family.

I asked Shon about this—about why he never made excuses for what he did or otherwise let himself off the hook.

"It's an interesting question," he said. After a pause, he continued: "I don't have the baggage of many people that I saw in prison. I grew up really poor. My dad made, like, $35,000 for a family of seven throughout the 1990s. So we were really poor. But I was at a decent school. I had good parents. Other people I saw in prison never really got a first chance, let alone a second chance. And so, to me, their sentences always seemed more unjustified because of that."

Shon also explained that his sentence, given what he'd done, didn't seem very harsh at the time he wrote the book. "A twelve-year-and-three-month sentence for running into five banks with guns—even for a first-time offender—didn't seem that bad, especially when I compared it to everyone that was around me, including a bunch of African American men who got twenty-year mandatory minimums for a handful of crack cocaine. And so, in comparison to all of the other injustices I saw in federal prison, in my mind my case didn't seem unjust."

But was that sentence actually unjust? Shon noted that his judge gave him the lowest sentence that was permitted at the time and said that he is not angry with the judge. "But, yes," he added, "twelve years and three months for a crime—which was violent but in which no one actually faced physical violence and no one was physically hurt—that's just too long. Especially when you consider all of the punishments that a person faces in prison."

When he mentioned "all of the punishments," I thought Shon was talking about the time he didn't get to spend with his family. He speaks movingly in his book about his father's cancer diagnosis and death while he was in prison. But that's not what he meant. He meant the threat of violence from other prisoners—the need to be constantly vigilant, to understand who you can talk to, and to have to sometimes preemptively engage in violence yourself in order to avoid being victimized.

A few months after Shon went to prison, he started lifting weights, trying to bulk up his skinny frame. He did this because he narrowly escaped being raped by another prisoner—a prisoner who was HIV positive and who had a history of preying on young inmates. The prisoner told Shon that he was going to "come see him" in his cell the next morning. Shon told the other prisoner to leave him alone, and he spent the night in his cell clutching a sharpened toothbrush.

"I spent the entire night thinking I'm either going to get raped or I'm going to stab this guy and then probably get more time and never get out of federal prison. And fortunately for me, at 5:30 in the morning the guards came in and said, 'Hopwood, pack your stuff. You're on the transport out today.'

"I tell that story because if I hadn't got transferred that day, then my story turns out much differently. That nice little story about the guy that did time and then gets out and has this wonderful life no longer exists."

Shon paused: "It isn't fun for me to have to tell that story. It's a story I had only ever told to my wife. But I want people to know that when you send someone to jail—even for three or four years—this is what you are sentencing them to."

Shon first told that story publicly because he was asked to write something that he knew was going to be sent to federal judges. He knew that his optimistic tale of redemption might be appealing; it got him a heartwarming interview on *60 Minutes*. But it might also let people ignore the brutality and cruelty of prison.

Because the truth of the criminal justice system is that it is a brutal and terrifying place. It treats people unfairly both before and after they are convicted. And it is in desperate need of reform. But it is unclear whether that reform will take place—and if so, when—because although people generally think that the government should treat people fairly, they also are afraid of crime.

* * * * *

Newspapers are full of stories about how the politics of crime have changed.

For years the conventional wisdom was that voters were afraid of crime and that anyone who was "soft on crime" would lose an election. But more recently newspapers run stories that say something else.

Some of those stories focus on district attorney elections in which the winning candidates ran on criminal justice reform platforms and won. These reform candidates have won elections not only in large cities like Chicago and Boston but also in smaller cities like Jacksonville and Durham. These successes, we are told, are a sign that the era of tough-on-crime politics is coming to an end.

Other stories focus on how political conservatives are joining the cause of criminal justice reform. They highlight new reform efforts in red states like Texas and Mississippi. Or they point to the proliferation of conservative organizations like Right on Crime, which are devoted to reforming the criminal justice system. Even Donald Trump—whose January 2017 inaugural address appealed to law and order while decrying "American carnage"— granted a number of pardons to people serving long drug-related sentences and helped pass the First Step Act, one of only a couple of federal criminal justice bills to pass Congress in the past ten years.

In light of these stories, some people think that America is ready to reform the criminal justice system and make it much less harsh and much more fair.

I'm not so sure.

Don't get me wrong: there have certainly been reforms. The election of reform-oriented prosecutors and the conservative movement to overhaul the criminal justice system are both proof that there are a sizable number of people in this country who think that the criminal justice system is too harsh. But, on closer inspection, many of these success stories have been modest and do not suggest that people are looking to make it more difficult for the state to punish people. Reform prosecutors have focused their efforts almost exclusively on low-hanging fruit. And at the same time that conservative-led groups have managed to get some criminal justice legislation enacted, those same state legislatures have continued to enact harsh criminal justice legislation at a steady pace.

Most people remember election night in 2016 because of the surprising win of Donald Trump over Hillary Clinton. Clinton had been the heavy favorite in polls, and Trump's campaign was marked by a series of missteps, including outrageous comments and behavior from the candidate as well as the release of a recording of Trump bragging about grabbing women's genitals. For criminal justice reformers, the election of Trump was a horrible setback. American was enjoying one of the lowest crime rates in decades, yet Trump's speech at the Republican National Convention railed against violence in the streets and insisted on the need to restore law and order.

Despite the election of a fear-mongering president, criminal justice reformers found reason to celebrate the morning after the 2016 election. Although Trump defeated Clinton, there were a handful of important elections of local prosecutors across the country in which reformers challenged entrenched incumbents and won.

In Houston, Kim Ogg defeated incumbent prosecutor Devon Anderson. Ogg campaigned on a platform of reform, saying that nonviolent offenders should be diverted from the criminal justice system rather than incarcerated. She also promised to change the bail bond system so that fewer defendants who could not afford the money required to be released were no longer incarcerated pretrial. Ogg's victory marked the first time in nearly forty years that a Democrat would serve as the district attorney in that county.

Progressives won another key victory in Chicago. There, Kim Foxx, who had defeated two-term incumbent Anita Alvarez in the Democratic primary, soundly defeated her Republican opponent. Foxx had campaigned on diverting low-level offenders to treatment programs rather than prisons, addressing wrongful convictions, and dealing more aggressively with police misconduct. In contrast, Alvarez's campaign had been mired in a police shooting scandal. Seventeen-year-old Laquan McDonald had been shot by police in October 2014. The police report of the shooting said that McDonald had been behaving erratically and refused a police order to put down a knife he was carrying. But police video released more than a year after the shooting contradicted the report, showing that McDonald was not threatening officers but instead walking away when he was shot. Alvarez didn't file criminal charges until after the video of the shooting was released by court order. But by then it was too late. There were calls for Alvarez to step down, and she lost to Foxx in a landslide.

Ogg and Foxx were not the only progressive prosecutors elected in 2016. Reform candidates also won in Denver, Jacksonville, St. Louis, Santa Fe, Tampa, and a few other races in counties without large cities. Many of these victories were supported by significant campaign spending by billionaire activist George Soros. And criminal justice advocates interpreted these wins as a sea change in public opinion. As Ronald Sullivan, Harvard Law professor and cofounder of the Fair Punishment Project, said: "These results signify that overzealous prosecutors that resort to draconian sentences and pursue convictions with a win-at-all-costs mentality will soon see themselves being replaced with leaders who have rejected these failed policies of the 1980s and 90s, and are truly committed to reforming the justice system with proven, evidence-based, equitable solutions that increase public safety."

Since 2016, several more progressive prosecutors have been elected. Larry Krasner won the 2017 Philadelphia district attorney race, running on his record as a criminal defense attorney and civil rights lawyer who had filed dozens of lawsuits against the Philadelphia police for violating citizens' constitutional rights. In Boston, Rachael Rollins was elected local prosecutor in 2018 after publicly releasing a list of low-level crimes that she vowed not to prosecute. And in San Francisco, Chesa Boudin was elected district attorney in 2019 after openly campaigning not only on a platform of reform but also on his personal story of visiting his own parents in prison while growing up. (Boudin's parents, who were members of the radical group the Weather Underground, were arrested and convicted of participating in an armored car robbery when Boudin was a toddler.)

To be sure, progressive prosecutor candidates have not been uniformly successful. There were two-high profile losses in California's 2018 district attorney elections. The Sacramento DA, Anne Marie Schubert, fought off a progressive primary challenger who had received financial support from George Soros and other progressive groups. Schubert prevailed, thanks in part to hundreds of thousands of dollars spent by law enforcement groups who did not want a reformer elected. And Summer Stephan, the incumbent prosecutor in San Diego, soundly defeated a progressive challenger who also received millions of dollars in support from Soros. Stephan painted her challenger as "anti-prosecutor" and claimed that her "reform agenda endangered public safety." More recently, Julie

Gunnigle failed in her attempt to unseat Phoenix prosecutor Allister Adel in the 2020 election. Adel had faced criticism for her failure to charge police who had shot and killed civilians, and Gunnigle ran on a platform of criminal justice reform.

When they are elected, reform prosecutors have indeed changed the criminal justice system from inside. In Chicago, the jail population decreased almost 45 percent during Kim Foxx's first term. Satana Deberry, the new district attorney in Durham, North Carolina, reduced the jail population by more than 10 percent within the first six months of taking office in 2019. In Brooklyn, District Attorney Eric Gonzalez changed his office's bail policy, reducing the number of people held on bail before trial more than 50 percent. And in Tampa, State Attorney Andrew Warren significantly increased the number of juveniles diverted from the justice system.

These reforms matter. But district attorneys do not work in a vacuum; they are part of a larger political system, and other actors in that system can frustrate or even block their reforms. Prosecutors who move too fast or aim too high may not be able to accomplish their agendas, while those who move slowly or who make technical or incremental changes are more likely to succeed.

"In order to avoid being vilified by law enforcement, reform prosecutors can be most successful when they look for the most effective and least controversial reforms possible," Sarah Staudt said. As a senior policy analyst at Chicago Appleseed Center for Fair Courts, Staudt works on issues related to the criminal courts, and in that capacity she has performed research about and made recommendations to Kim Foxx.

"Ideally," Staudt explained, "policy makers and politicians can adopt a reform that affects a lot of cases, but that is so esoteric that it won't even be noticed—that it won't end up in the newspaper." One example she pointed to from Chicago was Foxx's decision to allow pleas for probation for juvenile gun possession cases. That sort of change "isn't going to make headlines, but it helps immensely on the ground if it gets consistently implemented."

The relative success of incremental or esoteric change versus radical and high-profile change has been on full display in Florida. Jacksonville prosecutor Melissa Nelson and Tampa prosecutor Andrew Warren have taken a "measured" approach to reform. Nelson and Warren have proceeded cautiously, seeking input from career prosecutors in their offices and from people in the broader community. They have adopted targeted reforms that are relatively narrow and do not touch on controversial topics. This approach appears to have largely insulated Nelson and Warren from criticism.

In contrast, Orlando prosecutor Aramis Ayala tried to move quickly in tackling a controversial subject: the death penalty. Ayala was elected in 2016 in a surprise victory against the incumbent prosecutor, her former boss. She ran on a platform that promised transparency and building bridges with the local community, especially the African American community. George Soros spent more than a million dollars to help elect Ayala, and she was the first African American to be elected prosecutor in the state of Florida.

Soon after taking office in 2017, Ayala declared that she would not use her power to seek the death penalty. The response was swift and negative. Florida governor Rick Scott used his power under state law to remove more than twenty murder cases from Ayala and reassign them to other prosecutors in the state. Ayala fought the governor's move, but the Florida Supreme Court sided with Governor Scott against her. Ayala was forced to reverse her anti–death penalty policy. She established a panel that reviewed each capital case to see whether to seek the death penalty. By the middle of 2019—a year and a half before she was slated to stand for reelection—Ayala announced that she would not seek a second term. Rather than continue to serve as a prosecutor, Ayala said that she wanted to "continue the pursuit of justice in a different capacity."

Before Ayala's announcement that she would not seek reelection, she had already drawn multiple challengers. One challenger announced his candidacy only days after Ayala's death penalty announcement. Another challenger—a prosecutor from within Ayala's own office—was endorsed by the police union. That endorsement conveyed the powerful message that Ayala had lost the support of law enforcement.

Ayala's decision not to seek a second term may indicate that she was worried about losing to one of these challengers. Or it might also reflect the fact that anything other than moderate, incremental reform isn't politically feasible: other officials can countermand liberal reforms, and voters may not be ready to embrace candidates whose views on crime are more liberal than their own. A person who wants to abolish the death penalty, for example, can't accomplish that goal by being elected prosecutor—at least not in Florida.

* * * * *

As a group, progressive prosecutors have embraced reforms that decrease the number of people who are swept up in the criminal justice system and the number of people who are held in jails. Those reforms include changing money bail practices to ensure that more poor defendants can be released, diverting more cases from the criminal justice system, and refusing to prosecute certain low-level crimes, such as marijuana possession.

But some progressive candidates have promised to be harsher and pursue more cases—for certain types of crimes at least. Police shootings are probably the most obvious example of this. Progressive candidates have sometimes won elections because incumbent prosecutors were unwilling to bring criminal charges against police officers who shot unarmed civilians. That was a major theme in Kim Foxx's victory in Chicago. Something similar happened in Cleveland: the incumbent prosecutor lost his primary election when he failed to secure an indictment in the police shooting of twelve-year-old Tamir Rice.

Progressive candidates have also promised to increase prosecutions in non-police cases as well. For example, in the 2019 Democratic primary for district attorney in Queens, New York, Tiffany Cabán, a thirty-two-year-old public defender, ran an outspoken progressive campaign that promised to increase prosecutions of corporate crime, crimes by landlords, and employers who failed to pay workers what they had earned. Although Cabán lost narrowly to Melinda Katz, her campaign succeeded in getting Katz to promise to investigate and prosecute constructions companies and real estate developers who failed to appropriately pay their employees or who didn't maintain safe work sites.

Cabán received endorsements from many prominent progressives, including Senator Elizabeth Warren. During her time in the Senate, Elizabeth Warren has also sought to increase corporate crime prosecutions, including by introducing legislation that would allow criminal prosecutions of corporate executives who were negligent about wrongdoing at their companies, rather than requiring prosecutors to prove that the executives *knew* about the wrongdoing. Warren said that the new legislation was necessary because it was too difficult for prosecutors to prove their cases under the existing standard. To be clear, Warren didn't seem to think that negligent executives actually deserved punishment; instead, she wanted to make it easier for prosecutors to win their cases.

As these examples show, even those who call themselves "progressive" want to use the criminal justice system to punish more people; they just want to punish different people. For example, animal rights activists have been successful in making animal cruelty a crime in states across the country and in getting people who abuse animals sent to jail. Similarly, feminists have fought to increase prosecutions and lengthen sentences for domestic violence and rape. There are so many examples of people on the left seeking to use the criminal justice system to achieve their political goals that academics have coined a term for the phenomenon: "carceral progressivism."

I can understand why progressive prosecutors and other public officials want to use the criminal justice system to achieve their political goals. After all, the criminal justice system is incredibly powerful. People will often change their behavior to avoid the possibility of criminal prosecution. So if you want to make someone stop doing something—say, if you want employers to stop cheating their workers out of overtime pay—then criminalizing that behavior might seem attractive.

Another reason that carceral progressivism is so popular is that it allows people to bring about change by affirmatively using their powers rather than by refraining from using their powers. For those officials who are elected, it is natural to campaign on the accomplishments that you've had. It is more difficult to paint yourself as successful by talking about all of the things that you *didn't* do. This holds true for prosecutors as well: it is easier for them to campaign on the convictions that they obtained in high-profile cases than on the criminal charges that they never brought.

Even if progressive prosecutors don't want to use their power to increase cases against corporate officials, domestic abusers, or other groups, it is unclear whether they would be willing to give up some of their power and make it more difficult to punish people that they *do* decide to prosecute. As chapter 3 explained, one of the major justifications for our current system of plea bargaining is that it gives prosecutors leverage and flexibility. It seems unlikely that any prosecutor—including a progressive prosecutor—will tell lawmakers that she wants less leverage and less flexibility.

Indeed, when the New York University School of Law hosted a conference on plea bargaining in 2019, someone in the audience posed this very question to some of the progressive prosecutors who appeared to speak. The audience member asked whether progressive prosecutors should use their power not just to prosecute fewer crimes in their office but to convince the legislature to change the laws to legalize more conduct and reduce the leverage that prosecutors have.

The question didn't go over well.

The elected prosecutors all said that their top priority was using their power and discretion to achieve better outcomes for their communities. And while they all recognized that other prosecutors were free to use their power and their discretion differently, they were more concerned that introducing any limits on prosecutorial power would keep them from being able to charge fewer cases and keep more people out of the system. There was, they explained, simply too much resistance from other law enforcement and legislatures to the progressive goals that they were trying to achieve, and so they were not interested in trying to help limit prosecutorial power.

* * * * *

Texas had a reputation for being tough on crime. In 1990 the Republican candidate for governor ran a campaign ad in which he promised to double the number of prisons and teach drug offenders "the joy of bustin' rocks." The candidate lost, in part because of a public campaign statement joking about rape, but his views on punishment appear to have been widely shared. The state increased the number of people in its prisons by 300 percent between 1985 and 2005.

But in 2007 the legislature's budget committee delivered startling news: if the state continued its rate of increased incarceration, then it would have to add more than 17,000 prison beds within the next five years. The costs of adding those additional beds was estimated at more than $2 billion—a number that was so large that it sent a shock wave through the state. Officials who had previously opposed criminal justice reform efforts as "soft on crime" scrambled to figure out how they could send fewer people to prison. The legislature decided to fund more treatment programs and take steps to help released prisoners reintegrate into society so that they were less likely to commit new crimes and end up back in prison.

The results were striking. Not only did Texas not have to build new prisons, but the incarceration rate actually declined for the first time in decades, while crime rates fell as well. Suddenly other states were sending their officials to Texas in order to try and mimic the state's criminal justice reforms.

Texas is not the only red state to pass criminal justice reform legislation. In 2014 the Mississippi legislature passed a law allowing defendants convicted of nonviolent crimes to be released on parole after serving

25 percent of their sentences. The state tried to go even further in 2020. The legislature passed the Mississippi Correctional Safety and Rehabilitation Act, which would have made the new parole rule retroactive. But Republican governor Tate Reeves vetoed the bill.

In the federal system, Congress passed the First Step Act, a federal sentencing and prison reform bill, in 2018. After decades of making the federal system more punitive, the First Step Act was one of only two pieces of modern legislation to reverse that trend. The Fair Sentencing Act of 2010 decreased the punishments associated with crack cocaine crimes. The First Step Act made those sentencing changes retroactive; that is, they made them apply to people who were already convicted and serving their sentences. It also reduced other statutory maximum and minimum drug sentences as well as reducing the number of federal gun enhancement charges that could be brought in some cases.

Remarkably, the First Step Act passed with the help of the Trump White House. News outlets reported that President Trump's son-in-law, Jared Kushner, convinced Trump to support the bill. And that political support appears to have made a real difference: it allowed the legislation to pass both Republican-controlled chambers of Congress. The Trump campaign even ran an advertisement during the 2020 Super Bowl touting his grant of clemency to a woman who had been jailed for years on drug charges.

Importantly, the reforms achieved through legislation are fragile: they can be rolled back if the political winds change. That's what happened in Missouri. In 2019 the state legislature passed several criminal justice reform bills. Among other reforms, those bills eliminated mandatory minimum sentences for some nonviolent offenses, and they prevented the state from keeping people in jail just because they couldn't pay various court-related costs. Together, the reform bills were passed with a specific purpose in mind: to reduce the prison population because the state had one of the nation's highest rates of incarceration. These reform efforts were spurred by estimates that, if the incarceration rate continued to grow, the state would have to spend hundreds of millions of dollars to build new prisons.

But then, within a year, an uptick in the Kansas City homicide rate and several shootings involving children in St. Louis created pressure on Missouri lawmakers to act on the issue of crime. The mayors in those cities wanted a new law to create a witness relocation and protection fund for the people who cooperated with homicide investigations. The mayors thought this fund could help police solve shooting cases. Police had been struggling to solve those cases, and so the fund was considered uncontroversial. But for some reason the legislature never passed a law to create it.

Instead, the legislature passed a bill to make sentences longer and to create new crimes. The bill required certain prison sentences to run consecutively—that is, one after the other—instead of concurrently. Under existing law, judges and juries were given the choice whether sentences could be served at the same time. The push to create new crimes and lengthen sentences probably undid any reduction in prison populations that had been achieved though the 2019 reforms.

As the Missouri experience demonstrates, criminal justice reform depends heavily on context. Arguments about the costs of mass incarceration can prompt lawmakers to take some action. But if the crime rate goes up or sensationalized crimes occur, then increasing punishments once again becomes the legislative priority. Remarkably, in Missouri, local officials were asking for help in solving crimes, but the legislature opted to increase sentences and expand the criminal code instead. Even when they could have made the criminal justice system more *effective*, they chose to make it more *punitive*.

Not only are the legislative gains in these red states fragile, but there appears to have been a lot of fanfare for some relatively modest reforms. "I think there is some soft bigotry of low expectations," Kevin Ring, president of Families Against Mandatory Minimums (FAMM), told me.

I asked Ring—who served as a Republican staffer in Congress and who lobbied for Jack Abramoff when he was younger—for his insight into the conservative movement to reform the criminal justice system. Ring was enthusiastic about the conservative reform movement. He pointed out that attitudes toward crime have changed in the Republican Party. The party has become more libertarian and less punitive. In addition, more Republicans now view drug crime as a public health issue rather than as an individual moral failing.

Nazgol Ghandnoosh, a senior researcher at the Sentencing Project, also said that she believes a lot of Republican lawmakers are willing to make real policy changes when it comes to drug crimes. She described the issue as one of "bipartisan agreement." Even if those reforms are, in themselves, quite modest, she added: "If everyone were doing these kinds of things, then we'd be in a better place right now in the criminal justice system."

Despite the modest nature of some red state reforms, Kevin Ring emphasized that a criminal justice "win" in a Republican state or in a Republican Congress could send an important message. He compared it to a "Nixon in China" moment and said that those moments could give cover to Democrats to enact more sweeping reforms than they otherwise might have. But he also seemed quite convinced that Democrats were still willing to do more than Republicans to accomplish criminal justice reform: "I mean, if you think that we wouldn't be getting more out of Andrew Gillum than we are out of Ron DeSantis, then I don't know what to tell you." (Republican Ron DeSantis defeated Democrat Andrew Gillum in the 2018 election for governor of Florida.)

While there is no doubt that conservative states have begun to enact criminal justice reforms, those states still have very harsh criminal justice systems. Ring made this point when we spoke: "For all of this talk about Texas 'leading the way,' I wouldn't want to go before a Texas judge. I wouldn't want to be in a Texas prison where it's 110 degrees and there's no air-conditioning."

Also, at the same time that Republican-led states have enacted criminal justice reform, they have continued to enact laws that do the opposite. In my own research on state criminal justice legislation, for example, I found that Texas enacted many more laws that increased the scope of the criminal justice system than laws that reformed the system. In the years 2015 to 2018 the Texas legislature passed four laws that either shortened sentences or narrowed the category of conduct that qualifies as a crime. During that same time period, the legislature passed *forty-eight* laws that lengthened sentences or expanded crimes. That hardly seems like a state that is "leading the way" on criminal justice reform.

As these numbers from Texas show, it's important not to overestimate how criminal justice politics have changed, especially in red states. Republican-controlled legislatures are still quite committed to expanding the criminal justice system even if they sometimes pass reforms as well.

In addition, not all criminal justice reform legislation is created equal. When a state reduces the number of people who can be held in jail pretrial, for example, that reform can be very powerful. As chapter 4 explained, the desire to be free leads innocent defendants to plead guilty in order to be released. And studies of bail and pretrial detention show that defendants who are released are less likely to plead guilty than those who are jailed pretrial.

But other reforms—including some of reforms that are being aggressively touted by conservative reform groups—are unlikely to change plea bargaining dynamics. Occupational licensing is one example of such a reform. Many states require people who want certain jobs—like hairstylists, florists, and building contractors—to obtain a license. People with criminal records are often prohibited from obtaining these licenses.

Occupational licensing reform—allowing people with convictions to get these licenses—has been successful in several states. Occupational licensing reform actually sounds like a good idea because licensing restrictions can make it more difficult for people who have been released from prison to get their lives back on track. But it is hardly the most important issue facing people who have been charged with a crime. Allowing a person a license to give manicures at a nail salon after she has been released from prison doesn't make it any harder for the government to pressure her to plead guilty and then punish her in the first place.

Also, it's hard not to see the push for occupational licensing reform as a bit opportunistic. Conservatives who believe in free markets and small governments have long tried to get rid of occupational licenses altogether. As Kevin Ring observed, "It's funny: I see everybody on board with occupational license reform and I think, 'That's been a libertarian goal forever.' I mean, I'm sure Cato [the Cato Institute, a libertarian think tank] had papers on that thirty years ago, and now they've got everybody signed on to it as a criminal justice reform."

That some criminal justice reforms—like reducing the number of occupational licenses—may further other ideological goals of conservative groups isn't necessarily a problem. But it does make me wonder whether those conservative groups would be willing to support the big-picture reforms necessary to address the problems I identify in this book. Especially if reforms require more government spending—for example, spending to hire more judges and public defense lawyers—then some conservatives' political preferences for small government and low taxes might win out over their commitment to criminal justice reform.

Nazgol Ghandnoosh also expressed concern about criminal justice reform collaboration across the ideological spectrum. "There is sort of a bipartisan agreement to some extent about scaling back incarceration levels," she acknowledged, "but that agreement doesn't extend over to what the alternative should be to incarceration."

* * * * *

Once I started looking closely at people's ideological or political motivations for criminal justice reform, I became concerned that the current bipartisan coalition for criminal justice reform might be built on shaky ground. The coalition has been able to achieve some reductions in sentence lengths and some changes to the cash bail system. But are more sweeping reforms possible?

I don't know. But I worry that sweeping reform might not be possible because the liberal and conservative reform movements aren't necessarily fighting for the same things—or for the same reasons.

Conservatives and liberals frame their calls for reform very differently. While conservatives tend to talk about limiting government powers, liberals tend to talk about how the criminal justice system disproportionately affects people of color. As a result, the groups sometimes seem to talk past each other. As one criminal justice advocate put it, "Reformers on the left try to make all criminal justice reform issues about race, while reformers on the right don't want to talk about racial justice at all."

That comment stuck with me. There is no denying the fact that many problems in the criminal justice system disproportionately affect Black and Brown people. That the government uses its power differently against different groups is disturbing and needs to be acknowledged and addressed. But it's wrong to think that the government uses its power *only* against people of color.

James Forman, a professor at Yale Law School, has written eloquently about this issue. As he notes, there is no disputing that Blacks are drastically overrepresented in America's prisons. But Forman has pushed back on the idea (popularized by Michelle Alexander's *The New Jim Crow*) that White people swept up in the machinery of criminal justice are just "collateral damage" in a system explicitly designed to disenfranchise Blacks. When it comes to absolute numbers, there are nearly as many Whites in prison in this country as Blacks. As Forman says, "That's a lot of 'collateral damage.'"

In a sense, then, both liberals and conservatives are correct: we have given the government too much power to punish people, and we have made it too easy for them to use that power. In addition, the government uses that power in an unequal way that hurts already marginalized groups, and it's undeniable that the unequal treatment has deep roots in racism, both past and present. But the amount of power we have given the government would still be objectionable even if the government were using that power equally against the rich and in White communities.

Disagreement between liberals and conservatives isn't just limited to this overall framing. In addition to the abstract question about whether criminal justice reform ought to be focused on issues of equality or issues of liberty, the groups also seek different types of reform. Especially in the wake of the death of George Floyd at the hands of police and the intense protests that rocked the nation in the summer of 2020, people on the left have started to call for dramatic funding cuts to police departments. And the abolition movement—a progressive movement to abolish prisons and/or police departments and instead address crime and public safety through other means—has begun to gain traction in mainstream discussions.

At the time that I am writing these words, abolition has not yet made the jump from activists and academics to policy makers. Congressional Democrats moved quickly to quash any talk about defunding the police. In the 2020 presidential election, Joe Biden said that he was "totally opposed" to defunding the police, and his campaign platform actually called for more funding for law enforcement. A majority of the Minneapolis city council pledged to defund the city's police department in the wake of George Floyd's death, but many later backed away from the pledge.

It is unclear whether the abolition movement will gain the sort of traction that is necessary to actually spur reform. Ironically, the abolition movement *is* proposing the sort of radical reforms that would make it more difficult for the government to punish people, but they are also insisting on abolishing the criminal justice system altogether rather than reforming it; indeed, many abolitionists speak about their movement as affirmatively hostile to the idea of mere reform. As a result, abolitionists may not be willing to work with other groups—especially with more conservative groups—to achieve sweeping reforms that stop short of getting rid of police and prisons.

Of course, even if these groups do not succeed in their goal of abolishing police and prisons, they may help change the conversation in the country in a way that makes sweeping reform seem more palatable. By earnestly proposing a policy that seems radically unthinkable—getting rid of prisons—abolitionists may make other radical policies that stop short of abolition—like decriminalizing most misdemeanors—seem more reasonable.

The emergence of radical groups can also encourage more moderate groups to cooperate. Kevin Ring, who's seen groups from the right and the left work together well in a number of states, said that more radical groups can help move reform forward by refusing to support it. If, for example, a more radical group refuses to support a bill because it doesn't go far enough, then that can reassure moderate or conservative lawmakers that the reform legislation is reasonable enough that they can vote for it.

* * * * **

When I first met Shon Hopwood, he was very optimistic about criminal justice reform. He had just helped pass the First Step Act, and I got the distinct impression that he thought even more aggressive criminal justice reform was possible. Shon had even written an academic article encouraging people to have patience with modest, incremental reforms because those reforms were a step in the right direction.

That optimistic message is very powerful coming from Shon. When he helped pass the First Step Act, he did so even though it excluded people serving sentences for violent crimes. That meant Shon himself wouldn't have qualified for any relief under the First Step Act if he had still been in prison. He also helped pass the act despite all of the compromises that were necessary in order to get law enforcement groups on board with the legislation. At one point they had to change the bill so that it wouldn't apply retroactively to federal gun charges. "I had all of those friends in prison who were pushing me," Shon said—friends who would be able to get shorter sentences or even be released from prison if changes to gun sentencing laws applied to people who had already been convicted. "To find out that it was no longer on the table—that was hard."

But when I spoke to Shon in the spring of 2020, he was much more pessimistic about the possibility of meaningful criminal justice reform. I asked him why. Shon replied that he felt less hopeful about reform because the Department of Justice had not done what it was supposed to do in implementing the First Step Act and Congress had failed to move on any additional reforms. He didn't think that more change was going to occur because the Department of Justice usually opposes criminal justice reform. And while the Trump administration was willing to ignore the wishes of Department of Justice when it was led by Jeff Sessions, it seemed unwilling to go against the wishes of the DOJ now that it was led by Bill Barr.

Neither Shon nor I stated the obvious difference between the Department of Justice under Barr as opposed to the DOJ under Sessions: while Sessions had recused himself from the investigation into Russia's interference in the 2016 election, Bill Barr had proven himself to be a staunch political supporter of President Trump. Barr took a series of actions that seemed designed to discredit and unravel the criminal matters related to the Russia investigation. President Trump stood to benefit personally from those actions, and so he was unlikely to countermand Barr on matters of criminal justice policy.

To appreciate the role that the Department of Justice plays in federal policy, imagine if the president of the United States decided to take advice on criminal justice reform only from criminal defense attorneys. The president would send only defense attorneys to Congress to testify about criminal justice bills. Defense attorneys would be solely responsible for the running of prisons, testing of forensic evidence, and deciding who should be eligible for a presidential pardon.

No president would ever give such an important and exclusive role to criminal defense attorneys. If he or she did, there would be a firestorm of disapproval. People would immediately object that we can't rely on criminal defense attorneys to play these roles because they will only bring one point of view to criminal justice issues: the view of the defendant.

And yet our country does precisely this. It enshrines one single view of the justice system over all others. But it isn't the view of criminal defense attorneys: It is the view of prosecutors.

The two law professors who came up with this thought experiment—Rachel Barkow and Mark Osler—have explained at great length how the views of prosecutors dominate federal criminal justice policy. The Department of Justice advises the president on criminal justice issues. The DOJ testifies in front of Congress, giving the views of "the executive branch" on new legislation. And the DOJ houses those portions of the federal government that are responsible for prisons, forensic testing, and clemency recommendations.

As Barkow and Osler show, the Department of Justice has used its role as adviser, spokesperson, and agency head to repeatedly and nearly uniformly block meaningful criminal justice reform. When Congress passed the First Step Act, for example, it did so over the vocal objection of the DOJ. And when President Obama instituted a system to process large numbers of clemency applications for drug offenders, the person who was hired to oversee those efforts ended up quitting in protest because the DOJ frustrated her efforts, denying her sufficient funding, reversing her favorable recommendations, and forbidding her from speaking to the White House to explain why she thought the prisoners actually deserved relief.

Even when Department of Justice leadership is willing to move forward with criminal justice reform, there is still resistance from the rank and file. Shon Hopwood has published research in which he documents that, in addition to resistance from the DOJ, the National Association of Assistant U.S. Attorneys (NAAUSA) will often lobby Congress for harsher laws and against reform. The organization, which represents career federal prosecutors, even went so far as send a letter to President Obama in which they told him that he shouldn't be granting clemency to nonviolent drug offenders who had already served decades in prison.

Prosecutors are sometimes a stumbling block to reform in the states as well. My own research has shown that, in many states, prosecutors are very successful at blocking or watering down criminal justice reform legislation before it can become law. For example, during the years 2015 to 2018, the legislatures in Arizona, Oklahoma, and Pennsylvania did not pass a single bill that prosecutors opposed.

Importantly, voters themselves often support making criminal laws harsher. When polled, many voters say that they think the criminal justice system isn't harsh enough—that sentences are too short and that judges are too lenient. Some of this public opinion can be traced to the fact that, as Professor Rachel Barkow puts it, "voters are relatively uninformed, both in general and specifically about criminal justice issues." One Illinois study, for example, demonstrated that voters incorrectly assumed that criminal defendants were receiving overly lenient sentences. Roughly two-thirds of people surveyed thought that judges sentenced burglars too leniently. But when those people were given a sample burglary scenario and asked to suggest an appropriate sentence, 89 percent suggested imposing sentences that were below the statutory minimum sentence. In other words, the survey respondents thought that defendants should receive a sentence that was actually *lower* than what judges were allowed to impose, and yet, because they don't know much about criminal sentences, they still assumed that judges were giving out sentences that were too light.

Why are voters so misinformed? Part of the answer is that people are misinformed about a lot of things. For example, most Americans can't name all three branches of government, and more than a third of Americans can't name a single right that is guaranteed by the First Amendment.

In addition to their general ignorance about important issues, Americans are particularly uninformed about the criminal justice system. This ignorance stems, in part, from misleading media coverage. That coverage also helps to explain why voters want more punitive policies.

When it comes to sentencing, for example, the media tends to report only unusual sentences. When a sentence is unusually lenient, it is easy to write a story about how the defendant should have received more punishment: the reporter can simply quote a victim who is angry at the light sentence. It's harder to write a story about sentences that are too harsh. To write such a story, the reporter would need to gather information about sentences in other, similar cases; only if she had that information would the reporter be able to write a story about how the sentence was longer than normal. The reporter might also need to find and summarize studies about recidivism so that she could explain that a sentence doesn't need to be so long in order to keep people safe. And, of course, a sentence that seems about right isn't newsworthy, so there is no reason for the media to cover it.

It isn't just media coverage about the lengths of sentences that misinform the public. As Rachel Barkow explains in her book *Prisoners of Politics: Breaking the Cycle of Mass Incarceration*, the media is "obsessed with crime stories. The lead story on local news outlets is either a crime story or an accident story 77% of the time, and 32% of all local television news stories are about crime."

Media coverage also tends to focus on violent crimes; as the old saying goes: "If it bleeds, it leads." But this focus on violent crimes gives people the wrong impression about what the criminal justice system is dealing with. As chapter 6 explained, the criminal justice system is dominated by misdemeanor prosecutions—many of them for nonserious nuisance behavior. And yet, as Barkow notes, "Murder stories dominate the news whether overall homicide rates are up or down."

To be sure, there are media outlets that provide high-quality reporting about criminal justice issues, rather than just sensationalized stories about particular crimes. In recent years, two new online outlets—*The Marshall Project* and *The Appeal*—have been founded to provide precisely this sort of coverage about criminal justice issues. ProPublica, another relative newcomer to the media landscape, also routinely publishes in-depth reports on the criminal justice system, though its coverage extends to other areas.

Existing national outlets have also begun to publish articles and air news stories that present a more critical view of mandatory minimum sentences, prosecutorial power, and even plea bargaining.

But despite those recent improvements in reporting, survey results continue to show that Americans still believe that crime rates are going up—even when they are actually dropping dramatically. Especially disturbing is a 2017 study that found that people who lived in conservative areas and watched a lot of local news had more punitive attitudes than people who lived in high-crime areas or had themselves been a victim of crime.

That isn't to say that voters will not support any criminal justice reforms. They will. There is significant support, for example, for getting rid of mandatory minimum sentences, especially for drug crimes. But discussions about making the criminal justice system less harsh still seem to gain less traction than discussions about how to make it more harsh. As Barkow says:

> Any discussion about overall strategies or long-term responses and results can be derailed with a single story. All it takes to kill a reform proposal's chances is one example of an individual convicted of a violent crime who would benefit from the proposed change. That one person ends up being the public's image of the reform, and if it looks like the law is going to coddle that individual, the public will resist, no matter what the overall benefits are.

Of course, public opinion may not always stay the same. News media coverage skews people's perceptions about the criminal justice system. But attitudes toward the criminal justice system still moderated as crime has gone down. A recent Gallup poll shows a smaller number of Americans who say that the criminal justice system is not tough enough and a larger number who say the system is too tough than in years past.

In addition, as the criminal justice system sweeps more people into its net, those people, their friends, and their families start to form their own views about the system—views that are not filtered by the news media. The people who come into contact with the system are usually unhappy to learn that the system is designed to punish people quickly and efficiently.

Kevin Ring—who joined FAMM after having been swept up in a public corruption prosecution and spending nearly two years in federal prison—identified this phenomenon as one reason that criminal justice reform has become more popular: "Every time I go speak, like at a college campus, I say 'Who here has an immediate family member or close friend who's been to prison?' and half the class always raises their hand."

"That's amazing," I told him.

"It is amazing," he responded. "And when my house was raided by the FBI, neighbors would come up to me, one by one, for the next week or so and say, 'Hey, I've never told anyone, but my brother is in prison.'"

So perhaps the system itself will be the best hope for reform: the injustices people see when their own families are pressured to plead guilty will cause them to demand change.

"It's like that quote from Abraham Lincoln," Kevin said. "'The best way to get a bad law repealed is to enforce it strictly.'"

In the days after the 2020 election, I reached out to Shon Hopwood to see what he thought about the chances of meaningful criminal justice reform. President Trump had lost his bid for reelection, and it was unclear whether the Republicans would keep control of the Senate. Shon sent me an email after teaching class, expressing optimism about election results from the states. He was particularly positive about state referenda that had further decriminalized drugs. "The 2020 election was a further referendum on American drug policy," he wrote, "with more states (and hence more Americans) joining the notion that substance abuse is better handled as a public health issue rather than a crime and punishment issue. And, more broadly, it is encouraging that nearly every criminal justice reform referendum passed."

I don't know whether Shon is right that criminal justice politics are moving in the right direction. But I certainly hope that he is.

CHAPTER EIGHT

THE COSTS: TRUTH AND JUSTICE

Multimillionaire Jeffrey Epstein was accused of sexually exploiting dozens of underage girls, but he served only thirteen months in jail. His case largely escaped public notice until the *Miami Herald* published an exposé in the fall of 2018. The paper reported the sordid facts of sexual coercion as well as a secret plea deal in which Epstein pleaded guilty to two prostitution charges in state court. In return for that guilty plea, the federal government agreed to close its investigation into sex trafficking and other crimes.

The public was outraged. The *Herald* identified approximately eighty women who claimed that they had been sexually abused by Epstein when they were teenagers. Epstein paid the girls not only to give him massages and engage in sex acts but also to bring more girls to him. With his victims acting as recruiters, Epstein was able to secure a steady stream of underage girls for his sexual gratification over the course of several years, sometimes molesting multiple girls in a single day.

Many of the accusations involved sexual abuse by Epstein at his home in Florida. But there were also allegations that Epstein had supplied underage girls to other men at sex parties that he hosted. These sex party allegations were especially explosive because Epstein's social circle at the time included former President Bill Clinton, England's Prince Andrew, and Donald Trump, who was president when the story broke. After the *Herald*'s story was published, a 2002 quote from Trump surfaced in which he said that Epstein was "terrific" and that he "likes beautiful women as much as I do, and many of them are on the younger side." Trump made that comment at the same time that accusers say Epstein was cycling dozens of underage girls through his Florida home.

The sordid facts and the mere implication that powerful people may have attended Epstein's sex parties would have been enough to ensure a media firestorm. But the *Herald*'s reporting also indicated that Epstein received unusually favorable treatment from law enforcement. Despite what seemed like significant evidence of sex trafficking, federal prosecutors decided not to pursue charges against Epstein. They entered into a deal with Epstein in which he could plead guilty to state prostitution charges and, in return, no federal charges would be brought against him or any of his accomplices.

The deal was shrouded in secrecy. The meeting to arrange this deal was held at a hotel rather than at the prosecutor's office. Federal prosecutors worked with Epstein's defense lawyers to limit press coverage of the case. Prosecutors also failed to notify Epstein's victims, who were entitled to know about the deal under federal law.

The federal prosecutor who agreed to the extremely lenient plea deal, Alexander Acosta, quickly became the focus of intense public outrage. Acosta was serving as President Trump's secretary of labor when the story broke. He gave an awkward press conference in which he tried to defend himself. But the press conference didn't work. Acosta resigned two days later.

As the furor over the story crested, federal law enforcement took action. Epstein was arrested on sex trafficking charges in New York. The FBI raided his Manhattan town house, where they found nude pictures of underage girls. Prosecutors claimed that Epstein and his employees brought underage girls to the town house so that Epstein could molest them. Epstein was denied bail and awaiting trial in federal custody when he committed suicide in August 2019.

Epstein's story captured the public's imagination at least in part because of his wealth and personal connections. The media reporting on the case emphasized that Epstein was able to use his significant personal wealth and his relationships with powerful people to obtain favorable treatment. If not for Epstein's money and connections, the stories suggested, his victims would have had their day in court and Epstein would have served the lengthy sentences that we impose on sex offenders.

I'm not so sure.

Don't get me wrong: the criminal justice system treats wealthy people better than those without money. And I have no doubt that knowing powerful people can get you even more favorable treatment.

But favorable plea deals that sidestep terrible facts—especially when it comes to crimes involving sexual abuse—are the rule, not the exception, in the criminal justice system. You don't have to have millions of dollars or be friends with a president and a prince. You just have to convince a prosecutor that it isn't worth the time or the effort to try and prove a particular set of facts. As long as you are willing to plead guilty to something, some prosecutors do not need a lot of convincing. Their goal is to ensure that the case is disposed of efficiently—that the defendant is convicted and receives at least some punishment. Getting at the truth would require a jury and a trial, neither of which is convenient or efficient, and so prosecutors want to avoid both.

* * * * *

The envelope was so large, my assistant took it out of my faculty mailbox and kept it at her desk for me to pick up. I was in the middle of a big research project collecting records from district attorney elections, and so she was used to taking giant envelopes out of my mailbox.

But this envelope didn't contain copies of the dusty, somewhat boring election records that I was collecting. It contained evidence that would rattle most Americans, shaking their faith in the criminal justice system—provided they had the ability to understand it.

When I first opened the envelope, I didn't appreciate what I saw. It contained a document that was more than 130 pages long. The document listed hundreds of cases from Cuyahoga County, the second-largest county in Ohio, which includes the city of Cleveland. The cases were sex crimes that had been pleaded down to far less serious charges, oftentimes having nothing to do with sex. And there were a lot of them.

As I read through the descriptions, I was astounded by what I saw. One defendant had been charged with raping a child, but he had pleaded guilty to "interference of custody" and served only six months in jail. Another defendant was charged with kidnapping and anal rape but pleaded guilty to aggravated assault and attempted abduction. His sentence was three years of probation.

A third defendant engaged in a sexual relationship with a girl who was only twelve years old. They had sex multiple times a week for years.

He pleaded guilty to one count of aggravated assault and was sentenced to five years of probation. The list of cases went on and on. A small handful of cases involved child pornography or soliciting a minor to engage in sexual activity. But the overwhelming majority were cases of child molestation, rape, or sexual assaults against adults and children—literally hundreds of very lenient plea deals for very serious crimes.

I was surprised by how little punishment these defendants received. Legislatures routinely pass laws that increase punishments for sex crimes. There are so many laws because sex offenders are some of the most reviled people in the criminal justice system. At the beginning of the twenty-first century, several states started to adopt laws that imposed the death penalty on defendants who raped children. But the U.S. Supreme Court struck those laws down, saying that it was unconstitutional to execute people who hadn't killed anyone. While they couldn't execute sex offenders, state legislatures did what they could to eliminate them from society. They passed laws that not only kept sex offenders in prison for long periods of time but also restricted where they could live, work, and even walk once they were released.

Ohio is no exception when it comes to these laws. It imposes long mandatory minimum sentences on people convicted of rape. Rape carries a mandatory sentence of three years in prison. And other sex offenses carry mandatory minimum penalties of five, ten, or fifteen years. Ohio also requires sex offenders to register with the state and imposes residency restrictions on them. Based on these laws, the people of Ohio probably think that anyone who commits a rape or molests a child will spend a long time in jail and will be monitored after release.

But that isn't what happens.

The list of cases that I read showed that these harsh laws are routinely circumvented. The list spanned a little over a decade, from 2005 to 2017. Of the hundreds of cases included, fewer than 60 resulted in prison sentences longer than a year. And nearly 250 cases resulted in no jail time whatsoever for defendants: they were sentenced to probation or a fine, or their jail sentences were suspended by the judge at the time of sentencing. In other words, because of plea bargaining, these defendants spent much less time in jail than the mandatory minimum sentences required—and many didn't have to go to jail at all. And for the many defendants who weren't pleading guilty to sex crimes, they were not subject to sex offender registration requirements or residency restrictions.

Of course, as I read through the case descriptions, I didn't know whether the defendants actually committed the crimes that they were charged with. The mandatory minimum sentences, the sex offender registry, and the other restrictions on convicted sex offenders no doubt placed a lot of pressure on all of those defendants to plead guilty. So it was possible that I was looking at a list of innocent people who had been forced to plead guilty. Or I might have been looking at a list of people who committed heinous crimes and suffered very few consequences. I couldn't tell. But either way the list was deeply troubling: if these people hadn't committed crimes, then they shouldn't be convicted; if they *had* committed these crimes, then their punishments seemed much too lenient.

Even more troubling was that people in Ohio almost certainly didn't know that this was happening. Unless they or someone they knew was involved in one of these cases, they don't know that prosecutors are willing to bargain serious sex crime charges down to less serious convictions. And because the public doesn't know, they can't make their public officials tell them why little or no jail time seemed like a good resolution in these cases. To put it simply, since the plea bargaining process wasn't transparent, voters couldn't hold their officials accountable.

One man in Ohio wanted to change that.

* * * * *

Judge Michael Donnelly has deep concerns about plea bargaining.

As a former prosecutor, Donnelly was both familiar and comfortable with plea bargaining in 2005, when he was elected to serve as a trial court judge in Cuyahoga County, Ohio. At first he thought of plea bargaining the same way that he did when he was a prosecutor: that is to say, he thought that plea bargaining was a good way for the two sides in a criminal case to negotiate a resolution. Just as two lawyers in a real estate transaction might haggle over the sale price or the closing date, plea bargaining allowed the prosecutor and the defense attorney to haggle over what the right punishment would be for a defendant. Or so Judge Donnelly had been taught as a prosecutor.

Once he was on the other side of the bench, Judge Donnelly started to look at plea bargaining differently. He was no longer one of the lawyers engaged in a negotiation. Instead he was the judge, and so he was supposed to be a neutral party in the process. Soon that process began to concern him.

Initially, Judge Donnelly was concerned only about the judge's role in the off-the-record hearings that occurred in Cuyahoga County before guilty pleas. In those hearings, the prosecutor and the defense attorney would tell the judge about the case and then would ask whether he would be willing to accept the plea that they had negotiated. Sometimes the judge would say no, but more often than not the judge would say yes. If the judge decided to accept the plea bargain, then he had to decide what sentence to impose on the defendant.

Unlike in the federal system and some other states, judges in Ohio have a lot of flexibility in deciding what sentence to impose. Judge Donnelly noticed that the lawyers were saying things in the off-the-record conference that they wouldn't say in open court—things that could make a serious difference in a judge's sentencing decision. This made him uncomfortable.

For example, a former trial court judge told Judge Donnelly about a prosecutor who would appear in her courtroom. The former judge had thought very highly of this prosecutor, but she knew that he was often in trouble with his supervisor for not being aggressive enough. The supervisor wanted the prosecutor to demand higher sentences, but the prosecutor didn't agree. The prosecutor told the judge about the problem with his supervisor. And sometimes, in off-the-record hearings, the prosecutor would give a sentencing recommendation and then warn the judge that he was going to argue for a harsh sentence later, in open court. As he told the judge, he would argue for the harsh sentence in open court in order to satisfy his supervisor, even though he personally didn't think that such a severe sentence was necessary. This was a clear signal to the judge that she should impose a lower sentence than what the prosecutor would argue for in open court.

The judge who told Judge Donnelly this story thought it showed the benefits of off-the-record hearings and why they should continue. Those hearings allowed her to get a candid sentencing recommendation from the prosecutor without getting him in trouble with his supervisor. But Judge Donnelly didn't see it that way. He saw the story as an illustration of why these hearings should be stopped.

"What good did that do to anybody?" he asked me. "Was there a victim in that case who didn't know that the prosecutor was being disingenuous?"

Judge Donnelly began to realize that prosecutors and defense attorneys were striking deals that left victims and the public in the dark about what actually happened. And he worried about the role that judges played in all of it. He noticed that the on-the-record proceedings in which the defendant pleads guilty sometimes made reference to facts that were completely different from those in the off-the-record conference. He realized that some defendants were pleading guilty to entirely different sets of facts or even crimes than what had been discussed beforehand.

Judge Donnelly was especially concerned about this practice in cases involving rape and sexual assault. Based on the difference between what was discussed in the off-the-record conferences and then what was said in the courtroom, he realized that prosecutors were repeatedly letting defendants accused of serious sex crimes plead guilty to charges that had nothing to do with sexual assault even though the prosecutors appeared to think that the defendants actually had committed sex crimes.

The more of these cases Judge Donnelly saw, the more concerned he became. How many sexual assaults were being treated like other, less serious types of crimes? He looked into it, and the result was a long list of cases—the large document that showed up in my mailbox.

Judge Donnelly was horrified when he found all of these cases. As a judge, he was especially worried that those plea bargains obscured whether the defendants were repeat offenders. If one of these same defendants committed another rape in the future, the next judge would not know that the defendant had committed sex offenses in the past. As a result, the defendant would probably get a lesser sentence than if he were a repeat offender. Or he might be permitted, once again, to plead guilty to a lesser, nonsexual offense.

Judge Donnelly also worried about the victims in these cases. Some cases had been pleaded down to a particular type of low-level assault that was available only for defendants whose victims were partially at fault for the crime. Those were the sorts of charges that prosecutors might bring against a defendant who was in a bar fight if the victim had started the fight.

"Could you imagine being the victim in that sort of case?" Judge Donnelly asked me when we spoke on the phone. "The defendant sexually assaulted you. And the public record in that case says you were partially to blame."

As his uneasiness grew, Judge Donnelly changed plea bargaining practices in his own courtroom. He ended all off-the-record conferences for plea bargaining, and he informed lawyers that he wasn't going to accept pleas for charges that weren't supported by the facts.

Not content to allow these plea bargaining practices to continue in other courtrooms, Judge Donnelly also tried to change the court rules that allowed them. He drafted a new state rule that would bring more transparency to plea bargaining by requiring that plea-bargained convictions be based on the facts of the defendants' crimes. He brought the rule to the Ohio Supreme Court—which is responsible for writing the court rules in the state—but the justices there rejected it.

Undeterred, Judge Donnelly took his fight to voters. Ohio, like many states, elects its judges. And so Judge Donnelly ran for a seat on the Supreme Court of Ohio. As part of his campaign, he talked about the need to change plea bargaining in the state. And he won. Judge Donnelly is now Justice Donnelly. As of January 2019, he sits on the Ohio Supreme Court. And he is now one of the people who will make decisions about court rules.

* * * * *

You might think that the problem of overly lenient plea bargains is limited to sexual assault cases because those cases often get treated differently. Sexual assaults are rarely reported. Police are less likely to believe victims of sexual assault than victims in other types of cases. And prosecutors will often refuse to bring charges even when police have arrested a suspect. As a result, even when they are reported, sexual assault cases rarely result in convictions. So it shouldn't be surprising that prosecutors are more likely to offer overly lenient plea deals in sexual assault cases; after all, they are less likely to pursue those cases in the first place.

But sexual assault is hardly the only area of the law where plea bargains routinely and systematically obscure the facts. Take, for example, cases involving guns. Many places have passed laws that impose harsh punishments on people who possess or use guns illegally. But prosecutors routinely use those laws only as a way to pressure defendants into taking a plea to a lesser crime rather than to actually make defendants serve long prison sentences. This practice is so common in federal court that it has a name: "swallowing the gun."

Importantly, government officials mislead the public about how often these harsh gun laws are enforced in practice. That's what happened when one of the New York Giants' wide receivers, Plaxico Burress, was arrested for accidentally shooting himself in a New York City nightclub in 2008. New York has a harsh law that requires a mandatory sentence of three and a half years in prison for people who possess a loaded gun without a license. When Burress's arrest made headlines, the mayor of New York, Michael

Bloomberg, gave a press conference in which he stated that Burress should be prosecuted to "the fullest extent of the law." He told the press that the law imposed mandatory three and a half years minimum sentence for anyone who carries a loaded handgun. And then he went on to say, "I don't think that anybody should be exempt from that . . ."

What Bloomberg didn't tell the press was that *lots* of people are exempt from the law. People who possess loaded guns in New York City are routinely allowed to plead guilty to a different crime—attempting to possess a weapon—which carries a lower sentence. So the question wasn't, as Bloomberg suggested, whether Burress would be the rare defendant who would be treated better because he was a football star. Instead it was whether he would be the rare first-time offender who had to serve the mandatory minimum sentence.

Initially it looked as though Plaxico Burress would receive worse treatment than the average defendant. Prosecutors presented the case to a grand jury, which returned an indictment that carried the mandatory minimum sentence. Only when the publicity surrounding Burress's case finally died down was he offered a more lenient plea deal. Burress took that deal and ended up serving two years in prison.

Like the sexual assault plea bargains in Ohio, these gun deals keep the public in the dark. People may think that they know what the mandatory punishment is for a certain crime. But many—or maybe even most—defendants don't serve the mandatory sentence. And when celebrities and other high-profile cases are treated differently, it reinforces that mistaken impression.

The public isn't just mistaken about how much time people who break the law spend in prison. The public is also misled about whether those long, harsh sentences are actually necessary. As we've seen, legislatures routinely pass laws with long sentences in order to give prosecutors more leverage at plea bargaining. But lawmakers don't tell voters that's why they have passed those laws. Instead they say that the long sentences are necessary to keep people safe.

Michael Bloomberg echoed this idea when he gave his press conference about Plaxico Burress. He said:

> Our children are getting killed with guns in the streets. Our police officers are getting killed with guns in the hands of criminals. Because of that we got the state legislature to pass a law that if

you carry a loaded handgun, you get an automatic three-and-a-half years in the slammer.

But the three-and-a-half-year sentence wasn't about keeping guns off the street. If it were, then prosecutors would insist on having defendants serve that sentence. Instead the three-and-a-half-year sentence was about keeping cases out of the courthouse. And Bloomberg's press conference—in which he said it would make "a mockery of the law" not to pursue the mandatory minimum sentence—misled the public about when, how, and why those sentences are imposed.

* * * * *

It may not seem like a big deal if a politician misleads the public. Politicians aren't known for being particularly honest, and so we may even expect that we can't take what a politician says at face value. But plea bargaining doesn't simply let politicians lie in the so-called court of public opinion. It also encourages lies in the courtroom—a place where people are supposed to tell the truth.

Plea bargaining encourages lies because it replaces fact-finding with compromise. In a system of trials, lawyers present evidence and arguments to a jury, then it's the jury's responsibility to decide who is telling the truth and what really happened. If the prosecutor doesn't convince the jury beyond a reasonable doubt, then the defendant goes free. But if the jury is convinced that the defendant committed the crime, then they convict the defendant. That conviction tells the judge what the defendant is guilty of doing, and the judge can impose a sentence based on those facts.

In plea bargaining there is no jury to decide what really happened. Instead, it is all a matter of negotiation. The attorneys negotiate about what the punishment will be, and then the defendant pleads guilty to a crime that carries that punishment. When mandatory minimums or other sentencing laws would interfere with the negotiated punishment, the lawyers negotiate over the crime.

Sometimes the negotiated crime is a lesser version of the crime the defendant is accused of committing. For example, a defendant who is accused of stealing jewelry worth $10,000 might plead guilty to petit larceny—that is, stealing property worth up to $1,000—rather than grand larceny—stealing property worth more than $1,000. But other times the defendant pleads guilty to an entirely different crime with entirely different facts.

Rutgers University law professor Thea Johnson calls these cases "fictional pleas." Under her definition, a case qualifies as a fictional plea if the defendant pleads guilty to a crime he has not actually committed with the full knowledge of the defense attorney, the prosecutor, and the judge. The rape cases Judge Donnelly found in Ohio certainly qualify as fictional pleas. Many of those defendants pleaded guilty to a crime called aggravated assault. In Ohio, aggravated assault is less serious than other assault crimes. That is because a defendant is guilty of aggravated assault if he hurts someone during a sudden fit of rage that was brought on by the victim provoking the defendant into using physical force against her. Neither the prosecutors nor the defense attorneys in the rape cases could have believed that the victim had provoked the defendant into committing a sexual assault. In one case, the victim was asleep and woke up to find the defendant sexually assaulting her. How is a sleeping person supposed to have provoked a sexual attack? Yet, the lawyers and the judge in that case allowed the defendant to plead guilty to a crime that the defendant didn't commit rather than resolve whether the defendant had actually sexually assaulted the victim.

Fictional pleas are not simply tolerated but actually encouraged. Johnson points out that the U.S. Supreme Court endorsed the practice in a case called *Padilla v. Kentucky*. That case established that criminal defendants are entitled to competent lawyers who not only can assist them if they go to trial but can also provide them with accurate advice about the immigration consequences of their choice whether to go to trial or to plead guilty. Because many—though not all—criminal convictions can result in a noncitizen being deported from the United States, charge bargaining can make the difference between being deported or being allowed to stay in the country.

A lawyer who knows the immigration consequences of different convictions, the Supreme Court tells us, can engage in "plea bargaining creatively with the prosecutor." Sometimes the facts of a particular case will allow convictions for multiple different charges—some with immigration consequences and some without. But when the facts don't allow for a creative solution, Professor Johnson wrote in an article about this topic, then defense attorneys must "turn to fiction."

Johnson gives an example from Washington State, where a noncitizen had been charged with a marijuana crime. Drug convictions are a common reason for deportation, so the defense attorney convinced the prosecutor to allow the person to plead guilty to a different crime: inhaling toxic fumes. Inhaling toxic fumes carried the same penalty under state law as the marijuana charge, but it didn't threaten the defendant's immigration status. Specifically, because it wasn't a drug crime, it didn't make him eligible for deportation under federal immigration law.

The defendant's lawyer did exactly what the Supreme Court suggested a competent lawyer would do: negotiated a plea bargain that had better immigration consequences for the client. But the crime of inhaling toxic fumes is limited to a list of certain chemicals—a list that does not include marijuana. So the defendant pleaded guilty to a crime he did not commit.

Plea bargaining doesn't simply encourage lying; sometimes it actually requires it. That is because, in some places, defendants have to tell the judge that they were not promised anything in return for their guilty pleas. But what is a guilty plea other than a response to a promise—or a threat? The threat is that a defendant will receive more punishment if she insists on going to trial; the promise is that she will get less punishment if she waives her right to a trial and pleads guilty.

The defendant is required to say this during what is called the plea colloquy, the exchange between the judge and the defendant before the judge will accept the defendant's guilty plea. Although the precise wording of the colloquy differs from place to place, its purpose is always the same: to make sure that a defendant's guilty plea is "knowing and voluntary." Judges conduct the colloquy to make sure that defendants are pleading guilty as a matter of their own free will and conscience rather than in response to threats or promises.

Judge Donnelly calls it "the biggest lie that is said in court every single day." In the Cuyahoga County courthouse, the defendant is asked during plea colloquy whether anyone in the case told him what sentence he will receive or the sentence he's likely to get when he enters a guilty plea. Defense attorneys tell their clients that they have to answer this question with "No" even though the entire plea process has been about trying to ensure that the defendant gets a particular sentence. The lie that defendants are instructed to tell is even more outrageous because, as Judge Donnelly explains, some judges will actually tell defendants what sentence they will impose on them during the off-the-record hearing and then turn around several minutes later and ask the defendants to swear in open court that no one has made any representations to them about what sentence they will receive.

* * * * *

How have our courthouses have become places of routine and systematic lies? A courthouse is where we are supposed to find out the truth. It's the place where people have to *swear* to tell the truth. In fact, defendants swear an oath to tell the truth before the plea colloquy. We make them swear to tell the truth right before we make them lie.

What's worse, when defendants try to expose the lies at the heart of plea bargaining, they can actually be punished for it. Look at the case of Michael Flynn, President Trump's former national security adviser, who pleaded guilty to lying to the FBI about his telephone calls with the Russian ambassador. After pleading guilty but before sentencing, Flynn hired a new lawyer who challenged the government's case against him. The new lawyer sought evidence from the FBI about its investigation, and she used that new evidence and an affidavit from Flynn to argue that Flynn should be permitted to withdraw his guilty plea because he wasn't actually guilty.

The Flynn case quickly turned into a circus because President Trump's attorney general, Bill Barr, abruptly filed a motion to dismiss all of the charges against Flynn. That motion was one of several actions that Barr took to undercut a special counsel's investigation into Russian interference in the 2016 presidential election—actions that President Trump publicly encouraged from his Twitter account and press statements.

Largely ignored in the political frenzy surrounding the Flynn case was the fact that the judge handling the case contemplated holding Flynn in contempt for his affidavit in support of withdrawing his guilty plea. In that affidavit, Flynn said that he did not know that the statements he gave to the FBI were false when he spoke to the FBI agents about his telephone calls with the Russian ambassador. He wasn't lying, Flynn said. He just couldn't remember what he'd talked about with the Russian ambassador.

Because the crime that Flynn pleaded guilty to required him to "knowingly" lie to federal officials, the affidavit (a sworn written statement) contradicted Flynn's sworn statement at his plea colloquy that he knew that he was lying when he spoke to the FBI. The statement Flynn made when pleading guilty and the statement he made to withdraw that plea couldn't both be true—one of them had to be false—and so the judge in his case made quite clear that he thought Flynn had committed perjury. Perjury—lying under oath—is a crime.

After reading through the media coverage and the documents filed in the Flynn case, I am unconvinced that Michael Flynn is actually innocent. The report by special counsel Robert Mueller on Russian interference in the election contains many references to interviews with Michael Flynn—references that contradict Flynn's later claims that he couldn't remember the content of his conversations with the Russian ambassador. Put bluntly, I don't think Flynn is innocent, and I think President Trump's decision to pardon him is one of several examples of the Trump administration playing politics rather than seeking justice.

But even though I don't think Flynn is innocent, I am deeply troubled by the idea that a judge would consider punishing a person for trying to withdraw a guilty plea on the theory that he committed perjury. There is no doubt that innocent people sometimes plead guilty. And if those people are lucky enough to uncover evidence that proves their innocence after they've pleaded guilty, they should not be punished for lying under oath. Many judges will not allow defendants to enter a guilty plea unless they first say that they are guilty. So when innocent defendants decide not to risk the additional punishment associated with going to trial, they should not have to worry about perjury charges if they later find evidence supporting their innocence. They shouldn't be punished for lying because our system not only encourages that lying; it sometimes requires it.

University of Virginia law professor Josh Bowers has a theory about why we accept these lies associated with plea bargaining but then react with horror when we hear that innocent people plead guilty to crimes they didn't commit. Bowers points out that the criminal justice system accepts many lies. So long as the defendant admits that she did "something wrong," then the system is willing to tolerate those other lies. But, as Bowers explains, the system "finds something sacrosanct and inviolable—even magical—in the bottom-line accuracy of the defendant's admission that she behaved (in some fashion) illegally." We are comfortable with all of those other lies as long as it is true that the defendant has done *something* illegal.

But the very system that we created to pressure guilty defendants to plead guilty creates a situation in which innocent defendants are actually sometimes better off pleading guilty than going to trial. It's this pressure on innocent people and the proof that some innocent people have pleaded guilty that are the most obvious examples of what is wrong with criminal justice in America.

Criminal justice reformers who criticize plea bargaining often tell stories about innocent people who plead guilty. I myself tell such a story—Damian Mills's—at the beginning of this book. And it is no wonder why many criticisms of our criminal justice system focus on innocent people who get convicted. Stories like Damian's shock us.

But we should be shocked by the system even when the defendant is not innocent. That's because ours is still a bad system, even when the people pleading guilty are, in fact, guilty. It is a system that not only abandons the search for truth but also encourages—or even requires—lies. All of those lies obscure what is happening in the criminal justice system. We can't evaluate the decisions that are being made by public officials and we can't judge whether defendants are receiving the appropriate punishment. This is why everyone should be outraged by Mayor Bloomberg's lies about the Plaxico Burress case. We should be outraged that we are being told that these heavy sentences are absolutely necessary and that they are imposed on everyone—when the truth is the precise opposite.

* * * * * *

That guilty defendants are forced to lie during the plea colloquy is not the only problem with a system that pressures guilty defendants to plead guilty. The system also deprives those defendants of important rights—rights that everyone has, regardless of whether they have committed a crime.

A trial does more than just sort the innocent from the guilty. It also forces the government to play by certain rules. For example, police aren't allowed to violate people's constitutional rights in order to collect evidence against them. If the police do violate their rights—say, if they search some-one's house without a warrant—then people can often keep this evidence from being used against them at trial, or they may be able to sue the police and collect money damages.

Our system of plea bargaining deprives people of those constitutional rights because it allows the prosecutor to make defendants bargain those rights away to get a better deal. As chapter 3 showed, the "free-market" approach to plea bargaining allows prosecutors to insist on the waiver of additional constitutional rights as part of the bargain, including the right to file a motion to suppress evidence that was discovered in an unconstitutional search. And while some courts allow defendants who plead guilty to file a civil suit for money damages if the police search was illegal, others will not allow those civil suits unless the defendant first gets the guilty plea withdrawn or the conviction overturned. These legal rules preventing civil lawsuits are not limited to cases involving illegal searches; they also prevent civil suits in cases of police brutality and other types of law enforcement misconduct.

"When you have a system in which cases basically never go to trial—and I looked in 2016, and only 0.3 percent of cases made it to suppression hearings—then it leads to the insulation of bad police practices," Scott Hechinger informed me when I visited him in Brooklyn.

"And it's not just misdemeanor cases," he added. "The majority of the felony gun cases that I see are the result of bad stops-and-frisks, or pretextual stops that turn into full-blown searches.

"Police officers know that they can do anything. They can make up a story, they can violate people's rights, and they so very rarely will ever have to take the stand in court. In misdemeanor cases, they know that they are going to wake up the next day and start their tour and already the cases of the five, six, or maybe ten people they arrested the day before—the ones that they stopped and searched unconstitutionally—have already turned into a successful prosecution."

Scott related a story about one of his clients who had been arrested because of unconstitutional conduct by the police. It was, he emphasized, one of the very few cases that resulted in a hearing that could expose police violating defendants' constitutional rights.

The client had been driving and was pulled over by plainclothes police officers on what was obviously a pretext. The officers were part of a unit that dealt only with violent crimes and gangs. The officers decided to pull over Scott's client—a young Latino man who was in a car with his three friends—for failing to signal before making a turn. As Scott explained, the officers obviously didn't care about traffic infractions; they were just using them as an excuse to stop the car and perform a search. In fact, the officers didn't even approach the client's car until after they called for backup to arrive—hardly the sort of thing a police officer would do if he just wanted to give someone a ticket for a traffic infraction.

A traffic infraction alone doesn't give police the right to search your car. Ordinarily, police need a good reason to believe that they will find evidence of a crime before they can search your car, especially the trunk.

But if you tell them that they are allowed to search it, then your consent makes an otherwise illegal search constitutional. And so, when the police approached Scott's client, they claimed that they smelled marijuana. In their police report, the police said that they asked Scott's client about the odor, and the client responded by saying he'd smoked marijuana earlier that day and then told officers that they were free to search his entire car. Of course, it is entirely unbelievable that Scott's client would confess to a crime and then invite the police to search his car.

"It was pretty obvious to me, for a lot of reasons, that the police were lying," Scott explained. "But they did find a gun, and my client's DNA was all over the gun."

The police found the gun in the trunk of the car, which was full of the client's dirty laundry. Scott had a theory for trial—namely, that his client hadn't touched the gun, and that the DNA from his client's laundry must have been transferred from the laundry to the gun, either because one of the passengers used the laundry to wipe off his fingerprints or because the police officers used the laundry to pick up the gun.

Because this was a New York gun case, Scott's client was facing the same mandatory three and a half years that Plaxico Burress faced. The prosecution made the standard two-year plea bargain offer. But the client wanted to go to trial. Between the DNA transfer theory and the unbelievable story from the police officers, there were good reasons to think that they could get a better plea bargain. So Scott filed a motion to suppress the gun.

When the day of the suppression hearing arrived, the prosecutors reached out to Scott with a new plea offer: instead of two years in prison, they were willing to offer Scott's client a sentence of probation.

"I knew that meant they had finally talked to their police officers and realized that they had an issue. So I go talk to my client and tell him the good news." But, much to Scott's surprise, his client told him he was not taking the deal.

Scott tried to reason with his client. He told him that as soon as the suppression hearing started, the prosecutors would rescind the probation offer. If they lost the suppression motion, then the gun would be admitted at trial, and the client would likely be convicted. Scott explained to the client that if he was convicted, he would get a sentence of at least three and a half years because of the mandatory minimum. So an offer of probation was a very attractive offer—especially when compared to a high probability of conviction and a sentence of three and a half years in prison.

Nonetheless, Scott was in an impossible position. "I *know* that these officers are lying. I believe, not only based on what my client tells me but based on their own paperwork, that they have violated the Constitution," he said. "I was *eager* to cross examine these police officers. But I was still arguing with my client not to exercise his constitutional rights to challenge them because of mandatory minimums and because of the prosecutor practice of refusing to hold open a plea offer if they are required to do more work."

Scott emphasized to his client that it was unreasonable for him to turn down the prosecution's offer. But the client stood firm. By a stroke of luck, the case got assigned to a judge who Scott knew had previously suppressed evidence when police officers had acted unconstitutionally. (Not all judges were willing to do that, Scott stressed in our conversation. There were some judges who were unwilling to suppress a gun no matter how unconstitutional the police behavior or how implausible their testimony.)

The hearing went well for Scott. He was able to show that the officers were lying about smelling marijuana, and they were lying about his client consenting to the search of the car. The judge ended up issuing a written opinion in the case in which she called the officers' testimony "not credible"—in other words, she decided that the officers had lied in court—and that the search had been unconstitutional. So the gun was suppressed and the charges against Scott's client were dismissed.

This was a good outcome for Scott's client; perhaps he was guilty, but the police still violated his rights by illegally searching his car. It is the sort of outcome that is very rare. As Scott noted: "It was one of those infinitesimal percentage of cases that gets beyond the pressure to plea. And in this case it happened because my client made an actually unreasonable decision not to accept a plea."

There is a postscript to Scott's story that is quite disturbing.

Scott later learned that, a month after the gun was suppressed in his client's case, the same police officers made an arrest under nearly identical circumstances and told an almost identical story. The latter case was handled by the same prosecutor, who put those officers on the witness stand in another suppression hearing even though the prosecutor knew that the officers had just lied in Scott's case.

Not only did the prosecutor continue to rely on these officers, but so did the judge. Scott said that two months after his suppression motion, he saw one of the officers who testified waiting in the judge's courtroom in order to ask the judge to sign a search warrant. Ordinarily, police officers can't search someone's home or business unless they get a judge to sign a warrant. A judge will sign the search warrant only after the officers tell her all of the information that they have gathered that makes them confident that they are likely to find evidence of a crime at the location. This judge knew that the officer had lied on the witness stand, under oath, during Scott's suppression hearing. But she signed a search warrant for someone's home based on his statements to her anyway.

We may never know how many people have had their cars illegally searched by these officers—officers who have made it clear that they are willing not only to violate people's constitutional rights but also to lie about their behavior under oath. Yet, rather than forcing them to testify and allowing judges to acknowledge those lies, our system protects them. In the vast majority of cases, the system keeps these officers off the witness stand, and it protects them from civil rights lawsuits. It does this by getting defendants to plead guilty. And even in those unusual cases where officers do testify and judges acknowledge that the officers are lying, there are no consequences for those officers. They keep their jobs, and both prosecutors and judges continue to rely on them to convict other people and send them to jail.

* * * * *

Even when defendants haven't been deprived of other rights, pressuring them to plead guilty still deprives them of an important right protected by the Constitution: the right to a trial. The right to a trial before a jury of peers isn't just about separating the innocent from the guilty. Most defendants who go to trial are ultimately convicted. But even if they would be convicted anyway, a system without trials deprives guilty defendants of their day in court and the sense that they were treated fairly. Trials allow defendants to hear the evidence that shows their guilt, and it allows them to tell their own stories. When we punish people without this process and this opportunity, then it doesn't feel fair.

A system without trials doesn't just seem less fair; it can also deprive defendants of the message that criminal trials send—the message that they have done something wrong. Law professor turned judge Stephanos Bibas refers to this feature of trials as "morality plays." Morality plays were popular during the Renaissance period; the plays taught moral lessons to audiences using allegories. As Bibas explains, trials also teach moral lessons;

in particular they teach defendants that their criminal behavior was unacceptable while reaffirming society's commitment to its criminal laws.

I agree with Bibas about the moral message of criminal trials. The quick, assembly-line–like process of guilty pleas seems more like the system is checking a box on a form than sending a message about a defendant's behavior. And in checking that box rather than sending a message, even the bare facts of what the defendant actually did can sometimes be completely lost in plea bargaining.

I saw this firsthand when I observed criminal court proceedings as a law student in Connecticut. Like many law students, I wanted to get some practical experience when I was enrolled in law school, and so I worked as an intern at the local prosecutor's office. As part of the internship, I would shadow prosecutors in court. One day I was sent to the court that handled arraignments. I sat on a bench toward the front of the courtroom, taking notes by hand as the prosecutor I was following around handled cases.

One of the cases that the prosecutor handled involved a young woman who could not have been more than twenty years old. The prosecutor and her defense attorney stood up and told the judge that they had agreed to postpone the case for a certain amount of time. They had also agreed that, if the young woman did not get in trouble again during that time, then the charges would be dismissed. This arrangement, which is called a deferred prosecution agreement, isn't unusual. These agreements are related to plea bargaining except that they allow defendants to avoid convictions if they stay out of trouble. Deferred prosecution agreements are very common in some courthouses, especially in cases involving first-time offenders or low-level crimes. The judge in this case readily agreed to the arrangement, and the court quickly moved on to the next case.

But the defendant looked confused. She and a family member walked over to where I was sitting and asked me what just happened. I wasn't entirely sure myself—I'd only just started the internship, and I was still more than a year away from graduating law school—so I recommended that the young woman ask her lawyer.

The defense lawyer must have been busy with something else, and so instead of talking to the lawyer the two women kept talking to me. "What about the gun?" asked the other woman—a woman who looked a lot like the defendant but older. I assumed she was the defendant's mother or aunt.

"I'm sorry," I told the women, "but I don't know anything about a gun." The charges—which I can't precisely remember these many years later—had nothing to do with weapons of any kind. The prosecutor and defense attorney must have either agreed to some nominal charges or a fictional plea.

"They arrested me for a gun," the young woman explained. "There was a gun in my car when the police stopped me. That's why I'm here."

"I'm not really sure," I said again, feeling uncomfortably out of my depth. "Maybe that's another case? You'll have to ask your lawyer."

"This is my only case," the young woman said before turning to her relative and saying that she thought they could leave.

The deferred prosecution agreement was probably a good outcome in the case. It certainly put the defendant in a better position than if she had been convicted of illegally possessing a gun. Perhaps if the agreement had been explained to her by the judge, then the defendant would have heard a valuable message: that she was getting a second chance so long as she stayed out of trouble.

But she never heard that message. She didn't even know whether the prosecutor understood why she had been arrested. Because the defendant thought that the resolution of her case might have been a big mistake, it is hard to believe that she heard any message at all.

* * * * *

Defendants aren't the only group of people who have lost rights and opportunities; victims also suffer in a system of plea bargains. Trials of guilty defendants allow victims an opportunity to participate in the criminal justice system and have their voices heard. A system of plea bargains not only eliminates that participation but also shrouds the resolution of cases in secrecy, sometimes leaving victims unable to understand what happened or why.

This lack of understanding can be incredibly difficult for victims to deal with. When I first started teaching, I had a student whose father had been killed several years before. The student had gone to law school, in part, because of her father's death. The prosecutor gave the defendant who had caused her father's death a plea bargain under which he pleaded guilty to something other than murder and served a few years in jail. Years later, the student and her family were still devastated: not only was her father dead, but they never understood why the man who killed him got that deal. They didn't think the sentence was long enough, and they didn't understand why the prosecutor didn't insist on the defendant pleading guilty to murder.

The student said that they had asked the prosecutor these questions but he didn't really answer them. Instead, he made some vague statements about the strength of the evidence in the case—at least, the statements were vague to my student and her family. During the years that she was in law school, the woman came to my office several times to give me more details about her father's case. She wanted me to help her understand the decision the prosecutor made. But I couldn't help her. I could explain how plea bargaining works generally, but I didn't have access to information about her father's case.

This is the other side of the morality play that Bibas describes. Trials don't just send messages to defendants; they also send messages to victims. Trials tell the story of what the defendants did and how that behavior affected the victims. Sometimes the victims themselves get to testify, allowing them to tell their own stories. Having the opportunity to tell his story in open court and hear a jury say that the defendant is guilty can give a victim a sense of closure. Guilty verdicts don't undo the harm that a victim suffered, but the verdict lets the victim know that his community agrees with him that what the defendant did was wrong.

Not everyone agrees that trials are better for victims. Sometimes crime victims don't want to testify at trial—maybe because they are afraid of the defendants or maybe because they don't want to relive the terrible experiences of the crimes themselves. And those who see the victims' rights movement as just another way to push for harsh law-and-order policies might worry that having victims testify at trial could lead to more convictions or harsher sentences.

Those victims who don't want to testify shouldn't be forced to do so. But some crime victims *do* want to testify at trial; they want to be a part of the process that decides guilt and punishment for the people who harmed them. This was one of the complaints that Jeffrey Epstein's victims raised. They were outraged not only by the lenient way he was treated but also by the denial of an opportunity to speak out about what happened to them and to have that pain and violence acknowledged. A system without trials deprives victims of the ability to participate and the ability to feel heard.

As for whether victim participation might result in more convictions or harsher punishment, that's far from clear: juries might be skeptical of victim testimony, and a clearer picture of the harm victims suffered might actually result in less punishment for those defendants who cause less harm. But even if it did result in more convictions and more punishments, those convictions would be the result of more and better information about what the defendants actually did. Trials allow us to draw more accurate conclusions about what defendants did and the effects of their actions. That accuracy is important, even if it makes us think some punishments are too lenient.

* * * *

A system without trials doesn't just affect victims and defendants; it also deprives the general public of the opportunity to participate in the criminal justice system by serving on a jury. It might seem strange to argue that people should have the opportunity to sit on a jury, since most people probably think of jury duty more as a chore than as an opportunity. Jury duty can involve long waits on uncomfortable chairs, and the whole exercise may seem somewhat pointless.

Personally, I've been called for jury duty three times. Two of those times I just sat in a big waiting room all day and never saw the inside of a courtroom. The third time I made it into the courtroom as a possible juror in a criminal case, but I was quickly excused once I said I was a criminal law professor. Although I would have been professionally intrigued by the opportunity to serve on a jury, even I breathed a sign of relief that I didn't have to endure the inconvenience of a trial.

Maybe if it were run more efficiently, and maybe if people were more likely to actually serve on a jury, then jury duty wouldn't seem like such a hassle. After all, jury duty gives us the chance to see what the justice system looks like in regular cases, not just the cases that happen to show up on the news. When my students tell me that they have served on criminal juries, they always speak about the experience as a positive one. And they are eager to learn more about the law that they had to apply in a particular case.

Jury duty might also seem like a positive opportunity if people better understood the power that it gives them. Jurors have the power not only to decide guilt or innocence but also to declare what is just in particular cases. This is an extremely important power that many people do not know they have.

When a person serves on a jury, she is asked to make decisions about the facts in a particular case, such as whether she believes a particular witness or whether she thinks the prosecutor proved the defendant's guilt beyond a reasonable doubt. But a juror also has the ability to nullify—to refuse to punish a defendant even if that defendant is guilty.

The power to nullify, like the power to vote, is an important feature of our democracy. It allows public opinion to constrain government actors in individual criminal cases. Voting gives citizens a voice in deciding what laws to pass. Sitting on a jury gives citizens a voice in deciding how those laws will be applied.

The people who wrote our constitution thought that this power of the jury was incredibly important. Thomas Jefferson once said that if he had to choose between democratic participation in the legislature and democratic participation in the judicial branch in the form of juries, he would choose juries. Similarly, John Adams said, "The common people, should have as complete a control . . . in every judgment of a court" as in the legislature. More recently, Justice Antonin Scalia—a modern proponent of interpreting the Constitution according to its original meaning—called the jury "a fundamental reservation of power in our constitutional structure."

The jury's power to push back against the government isn't just a historical relic of a bygone era. There are modern examples of jurors refusing to allow public officials to enforce the law in cases where the defendant violated the letter of the law but not the spirit.

Think of the people who help their terminally ill relatives end their lives. Assisting another person in committing suicide has long been a crime in this country—it is murder to intentionally end the life of another person—but helping sick people end their suffering doesn't fit with our ordinary understanding of what it means to murder someone. Nonetheless, prosecutors have sometimes charged and prosecuted those who helped terminally ill patients end their lives. When they do, jurors will sometimes nullify. For example, Dr. Jack Kevorkian, who assisted more than one hundred people in their suicides, was prosecuted multiple times. Three juries acquitted him—clear cases of nullification—although he was later convicted of second-degree murder by a jury that decided not to nullify.

Some communities are especially active when it comes to nullification. For example, jurors in the Bronx are so skeptical of police officer testimony—especially in drug cases—that they have acquired a nationwide reputation for nullification. The "Bronx jury" has the highest rate of acquittals in New York City. The New York Post reported that in the years 2017 to 2019, Bronx juries acquitted nearly half of all defendants, as compared to less than 20 percent in the rest of the city.

Some people say that jurors in the Bronx are more likely to acquit because they distrust police. Others say that the acquittals are evidence of a backlash against harsh drug laws that have been disproportionately enforced against people of color. Jurors who acquit for these reasons are sending a signal to public officials that they disapprove of how those officials are wielding their power.

In some instances, jurors nullify because they are trying to achieve just results in particular cases. For example, in the early 1990s, a Bronx jury made headlines when it acquitted a defendant who shot an unarmed man in the back. The shooting occurred on the courthouse steps, in broad daylight, and there were multiple witnesses to the shooting. But there was more to the case than just the shooting itself. The shooting victim, who survived, had previously shot and killed the defendant's son. After the killing, the victim was released on bail and then proceeded to harass the defendant for months. The defendant complained to the district attorney's office about the harassment, but they wouldn't revoke the victim's bail. So the defendant shot him.

The jury thought these facts excused the defendant's crime. They saw the defendant as the true victim who was acting in self-defense, even though the defendant didn't qualify for the defense as a technical legal matter.

Reasonable people could disagree with the jury's decision to acquit. But it matters that the decision was made by regular citizens. Without jury trials, the decision whether to apply a broader definition of "self-defense" is made by police and prosecutors; the general public doesn't get a say in those decisions. But jury trials allow democratic input into how we apply the law in difficult cases. Laws are written in broad, crude terms. They need someone with judgment to apply them. Trials make sure that the public has a role in those decisions.

* * * *

Even when defendants are guilty, our current system sacrifices too much in allowing plea bargaining to substitute for a system of criminal trials. A system that avoids trials makes it more difficult for voters to discover what our public officials are doing and to make them tell us why they've made the decisions that they have. Instead, those officials can lie to us and can even make defendants lie. Those lies keep us from finding out not only what happened in specific cases but also how the system works as a whole.

A system that prizes the efficiency of plea bargains deprives defendants and victims of their day in court. Defendants lose not only their right to trial but also their ability to protect other constitutional rights, such as the right to be free from illegal searches. And while trials allow both defendants and victims to tell their stories and see the process that decides between those stories, plea bargains strip the criminal justice process of any moral messages—and sometimes make it impossible for victims or defendants to even understand what happened in their cases.

Put simply, a system designed to circumvent jury trials actually ends up circumventing other controls on the criminal justice system as well, including the public's sense of right and wrong. Not only is the public not able to understand what the officials are doing in their name, but they are removed as a check in individual cases.

CHAPTER NINE

POSSIBILITIES FOR CHANGE

"If you didn't do this, then we are going to fight it."

It was Liza Jones's first day in the Salt Lake County Justice Court. Her office, the Salt Lake Legal Defender Association, which represents people who are too poor to pay for their own lawyers, rotates their lawyers in and out of different courtrooms a few times a year. Liza had been working in the district court, handling felony cases and class A misdemeanors, but she had handed off most of those cases to other lawyers, and now she was trying to establish a relationship with clients who had, until that morning, been represented by one of her coworkers.

Liza's new client, Kevin, had been visibly upset when Liza first introduced herself to him. "Where is . . . where is . . . ?" He seemed to be having a hard time expressing himself.

"Where is Hillary?" Liza prompted him. "She still works in our office, but now she is going to be working in another courtroom. But she has told me all about your case."

Kevin wore his janitor's uniform and had a look somewhere between fear and confusion on his face. Liza looked decades younger than Kevin. But Liza spoke to Kevin in a clear, confident voice, telling him about the details of his case, as if to reassure him that, even though she had never met him before, she really did know everything that she needed to in order to represent him.

Kevin had been accused of assaulting a neighbor when she inserted herself in a conversation between him and another driver who had been involved in a fender bender. The neighbor told the police that she had recorded the entire incident on her cell phone, but Liza's office still hadn't received a copy of that cell phone recording.

Kevin tried to tell Liza some of the background of the case. But he had a learning disability that affected his ability to communicate. Nonetheless, he was able to tell Liza that he was worried about losing his job. In particular, he was convinced that his current employer wouldn't let him stay if he was convicted. And he was especially upset because, as he said, he didn't do anything.

Liza's message to Kevin—that if he hadn't done anything wrong, they would fight the charges—shouldn't be remarkable. But as the previous chapters of this book make clear, it is.

One major reason that Liza was able to tell Kevin with such confidence that they would fight the charges was the court that they were in: the Salt Lake County Justice Court. Utah's justice courts handle only class B and class C misdemeanors: shoplifting, prostitution, possession of marijuana, trespassing, and other low-level crimes. More serious crimes—felonies and class A misdemeanors—are sent to district court.

Justice courts are informal courts rather than formal courts of record. And so, if a defendant goes to trial in a justice court and loses, he can get a brand-new trial in the formal district courts. Some other states have similar informal courts. But the law and culture surrounding those courts differ from state to state.

When I first started writing this book, I flew to Utah and spent the day with some young attorneys at the Salt Lake Legal Defender Association (LDA). I knew that plea bargaining looked different in justice court because I'd heard about those courts when I had taught on the faculty at the University of Utah a couple years before. Some of my students got jobs with LDA after graduating from law school, and they would sometimes come back to campus to speak to my classes or just to say hello.

Because the LDA lawyers cycle between justice court and regular district court, they were able to give me data showing the difference between trial rates in the different courts. Those statistics—which are drawn from cases that LDA has in the courts—show a difference in the dismissal, trial, and guilty plea rates in the two courts:

	Justice Courts	Misdemeanors (District Courts)	Felonies (District Courts)
Guilty Pleas	52 percent	64 percent	73 percent
Dismissals	45.6 percent	35 percent	26 percent
Trials	2.3 percent	0.09 percent	1 percent

The trial rate is higher in justice court, and so is the dismissal rate—that is, the rate at which judges or prosecutors will dismiss charges rather than letting them proceed. Of all the cases that are filed in justice court, only 2.3 percent went to trial. But of the cases that were not dismissed, nearly 5 percent proceeded to trial. That's hardly a high number, but it is larger than the rates we see in other state courts. Data collected by the National Center for State Courts didn't have a single state with more than a 3 percent trial rate. And it is higher than the 2 percent trial rate for felony charges that are not dismissed in district court.

When I asked them about it, the young defense attorneys explained to me that there is a legitimate difference in culture and attitude in justice court. The judges and prosecutors know that there is a real chance that any given case could go to trial. And the public defenders themselves felt far more empowered to counsel their clients to proceed to trial.

Importantly, while the justice court model doesn't result in a large number of trials, it results in far fewer individuals being punished without a trial. That is because prosecutors dismiss a much higher percentage of cases. More than 45 percent of charges were dismissed in justice court, as compared to 35 percent of misdemeanors and 26 percent of felonies in the regular district courts.

* * * * *

After spending the morning with Liza at justice court, I joined her and several of her coworkers at the Salt Lake Legal Defender Association for lunch. For a roomful of attorneys, it was a remarkably young-looking crowd. The most experienced attorney had graduated from law school only six years before. And the majority had graduated within the last three years.

It was a fun, talkative crowd. They joked about which judges were better than others and offered to spell the name of one particularly disliked prosecutor in the hope that their stories of his bad behavior would be included in my book.

Many of the young lawyers had spent time both in justice court and in district court, and so they were able to appreciate the flexibility of the justice courts. They emphasized that the justice courts gave prosecutors far less power to pressure defendants into pleas. Several of the defenders recounted stories about how pretrial incarceration led their clients in district court to plead guilty even though they had strong defenses. That rarely happened in justice court because most of their clients were not held in custody pending trial.

Although they saw the benefits of justice court, the defenders were quick to point out some serious deficiencies in the system. For example, because the judges and prosecutors dealt only with low-level crimes, their reactions to the more serious of those crimes was sometimes overly harsh. One defender explained that a class B misdemeanor—the most serious charge handled in justice court—could draw a six-month jail sentence in justice court but only a week or two in district court.

The defenders were also critical of a side effect of the de novo trial system, which entitles all defendants a new trial: it didn't result in clear reversals when justice court judges made mistakes. For example, if a justice court judge made an unconstitutional ruling in a motion to suppress evidence, the defender couldn't seek an immediate appeal of that ruling. Instead, she had to finish litigating the case in justice court—either by going to trial or by pleading guilty—and then file an appeal for a new trial in district court. The district court would hear the same suppression motion, and usually rule in her favor. But the favorable ruling wouldn't make clear to the justice court judge that the suppression ruling was wrong. So some justice court judges continued to make the same legal errors over and over in their rulings.

The risk of legal error is even bigger outside of Salt Lake City and the other more populous areas of the state. One of the defenders, Grant Miller, who worked for a private defense attorney before joining LDA, spoke about justice courts in outlying counties where he'd worked. The judges in those counties were not required to have a law degree. And when he showed up to represent a client in one rural county, both the prosecutor and the judge were surprised to see him: neither of them could remember ever seeing a defense lawyer in their county's justice court before.

Even within Salt Lake City, some of the defenders saw institutional actors try to circumvent the better procedural protections that the informality of justice court provided. For example, a defendant usually doesn't have to begin serving a jail sentence if she files an appeal from a justice court conviction. The justice court sentence is "stayed," and the defendant will serve it only if she loses in district court as well. There is, however, an exception to this rule for defendants who pose a threat to public safety: if a justice court judge finds that a defendant poses a risk to public safety, then she can require the defendant to serve her jail sentence while the appeal in district court makes its way through the system. One defender, Samantha Dugan, reported that after she'd filed a large number of appeals to the district court, one justice court judge suddenly started saying that her clients posed public safety risks. Samantha took it as a signal from the judge that he had decided her clients should have to serve their sentences even if they eventually won in district court. In other words, the judge was exploiting a procedural loophole in order to avoid one of the protections for defendants.

But overall, the Salt Lake Legal Defender Association attorneys were proud of what they were able to accomplish in justice court. They boasted to me that one of their group, Hillary King, was undefeated in justice court. (Hillary quietly corrected them, telling me that she had lost one case.) They explained that their ability to get a new trial in district court allowed them to be more confident and gave them a way to deal with difficult clients who wanted to fight about strategy or who were unwilling to plead guilty in the face of overwhelming evidence against them.

The justice court model also provides an answer to those who defend our current plea bargaining system on efficiency grounds. Rather than doing away with trials altogether, it makes trials less expensive by making them less formal. While the justice court model is more expensive than plea bargaining alone, it has the added benefit of not forcing defendants to give up their constitutional rights.

Some historians think that the formal procedures of modern trials contributed to the rise of guilty pleas and plea bargaining. When trials were less formal, they could be conducted relatively quickly; a single judge could hold multiple trials in a single day. There are obviously downsides to less formal trials: for example, when those trials don't include a jury, then some of the benefits of trial are lost. But even informal trials have serious benefits. They force the parties to investigate and present evidence. As Scott Hechinger observed when we met in Brooklyn, he could tell that prosecutors often hadn't really looked closely at their cases until just before a trial was set to begin. Informal trials force prosecutors to present the evidence they have, giving defendants the chance to see that evidence, and allowing someone *other than* the prosecutors to assess the strength of the government's case. Perhaps most important, trials—even informal trials—highlight that the goal of the criminal justice system is to figure out what happened, not simply to process cases and punish defendants as efficiently as possible. And when prosecutors don't think that a conviction is worth the time and the expense of a trial, they simply dismiss the charges because pressuring the defendant into accepting a plea just isn't an option.

* * * * *

One of the lessons from justice court is that people are less likely to plead guilty if they aren't being detained in jail before trial. When defendants are not detained, they do not need to choose between freedom and a trial. And so one obvious way to improve the system is to change our pretrial detention policies.

There is appetite for that kind of change: Congress has introduced bail reform legislation, and in recent years hundreds of bail reform bills have been introduced in the states. But when I spoke with Shima Baradaran Baughman, she expressed concern that the sort of bail reform legislation that is being considered wouldn't be enough to make the kinds of changes that we need. Until and unless pretrial detention is seen as something that we use for only the small number of people accused of truly serious crimes and who pose a risk of committing other significant violent crimes if released, then we won't see real changes in the system.

"Bail reform has basically failed," Shima said. "The first generation of bail reform in the 1960s failed. The second generation of bail reform in the 1980s failed. We are in the third generation of bail reform. And I think it is going to fail unless we are going to set a clear standard or a goal or even—I hate to say it—a quota. Like we could say that we can only detain 10 percent of people." As Shima pointed out, having a clear numerical goal would force judges and prosecutors to be careful and identify only those people who are actually dangerous and then release everyone else.

Shima has done extensive research on risk and pretrial release, and so I take her seriously when she says that only a small fraction of defendants need to be detained before trial to prevent future violence. But I imagine that it would be a hard sell in state legislatures to adopt a quota for pretrial detention. And even if a legislature did adopt a quota, I imagine that law enforcement and prosecutors would push hard for its repeal the first time that a person on pretrial release committed a violent crime.

We have seen as much in New York, where police have repeatedly told the media that the state's new bail reform policy was responsible for a spike in shootings—even though law enforcement's own data showed that simply was not true. Nonetheless, police, prosecutors, and other tough-on-crime groups managed to roll back some of the state's 2019 bail reforms soon after they were adopted.

Even if quotas are unlikely to be adopted, there are other modest bail reforms that would reduce the pressure on defendants to plead guilty in order to be released. Specifically, Shima recommended that pretrial detention be abolished for misdemeanors. She noted that there could be small carve-outs for DUI charges—keeping defendants in jail until they sober up—and domestic violence charges—keeping defendants in jail if it isn't possible to relocate the victims right away. But otherwise pretrial detention just shouldn't be legally available in these low level cases. If detention had been prohibited in misdemeanor cases, then Michael Bloch's client José in chapter 4 never would have been detained and he wouldn't have pleaded guilty in order to get released from jail—a decision that he made against the advice of his attorney and that resulted in him spending another year in prison.

In addition to abolishing pretrial detention for misdemeanors, states could reduce pretrial detention rates for felonies by making it slightly more inconvenient for prosecutors and judges. For example, prosecutors could be required to submit written, individualized motions to request pretrial detention. Or judges could be required to explain in detail why a particular defendant is likely to commit a violent crime when released. While decisions to detain before trial would require an explanation, decisions to release would not require any filings from prosecutors or explanations from judges. Explanations would create a small administrative hassle for judges and prosecutors, taking time away from other cases and other tasks, and so they would not want to make them as a matter of course; they would save them only for those cases in which defendants really seem to pose a risk.

* * * * *

Another lesson from justice court is to change the stakes associated with going to trial. There is no downside to a defendant insisting on a trial in justice court. If he loses in justice court, then he'll get another bite at the apple in his district court trial. That's what let Liza Jones tell Kevin that she would fight the charges with him: even if they lost, they could try again.

Of course, no government is going to give all defendants a second trial if they lose. But we could certainly make the downside of losing at trial less dramatic. Judges should stop imposing higher sentences on defendants who won't plead guilty. And state legislatures should repeal any mandatory minimum sentences that they keep on the books primarily to give prosecutors leverage at plea bargaining.

More generally, we could significantly limit the pressure to plead guilty by eliminating extreme sentences. Extremely harsh sentences give prosecutors tremendous pressure over defendants, and it changes defendants' calculus about whether to plead guilty. For example, when Harry in chapter 3 was facing up to two hundred years in prison for fraud allegations, it basically forced him to accept a guilty plea to two years' imprisonment. Turning down a deal like that would have been irrational.

The Sentencing Project, the organization that Nazgol Ghandnoosh works for, has been advocating for an end to extreme sentences. Specifically, they're arguing that sentences should be capped at twenty years in prison except for the most egregious cases, like those involving serial killers. Eliminating extreme sentences would likely help to reduce sentencing disparity across the board. Research suggests that extremely high sentences create "upward pressure" on all sentences, making sentences for other crimes longer than they would otherwise be.

Extreme sentences include not just life imprisonment but also sentences that run for fifty, seventy-five, or even hundreds of years. Nazgol gave the example of a man who was sentenced to 1,000 years in prison, saying, "When we give people sentences in these biblical terms, then it makes it so that a sentence for a lower-level offense with a one-, five-, or ten-year sentence seem quite light, when it's actually quite serious to take away someone's freedom and hold them in jail for that period of time."

Eliminating extreme sentences wouldn't just reduce prosecutors' leverage in plea bargaining; it would also help address mass incarceration. The Sentencing Project's research shows that one out of every seven people who are in prison is serving a life sentence. In fact, the number of people serving life sentences now exceeds the number of all people who were in prison in 1970, before America embraced mass incarceration policies.

* * * * *

Of course, not all defendants plead guilty because they are facing lengthy sentences or because they are incarcerated pretrial. As chapter 6 recounted, the very process of a criminal case can seem like punishment to defendants who must return to court repeatedly for pretrial appearances. Because the process feels like punishment, some of them decide to plead guilty rather than incur the time and expense associated with having to fight their charges. But there is no reason to impose that inconvenience or expense on people. In fact, most of these appearances are little more than scheduling conferences, at which the lawyers and the judge don't do anything other than set a date for the next court appearance.

Unfortunately, Salt Lake City's justice courts did not eliminate this pressure on defendants to plead guilty. When I visited the justice court, one of the defendants I saw in the courtroom was in big trouble because she had missed her previous court date. The judge demanded to know why, and the defendant explained that she had to work that day and her boss wasn't willing to give her the time off. The judge made her promise that she wouldn't miss any more court dates no matter what her boss said.

In some ways the woman was lucky that the judge didn't punish her for missing the court date by making her post a bond or, even worse, make her stay in jail. Judges have been known to do that when defendants miss their court dates. But on the other hand, it was ridiculous that the woman had to miss work for a status conference. The prosecutor was supposed to turn over evidence to the defense attorney—evidence that the prosecutor *still* didn't have when the woman showed up to be yelled at by the judge. But there was zero acknowledgment that the woman was being terribly inconvenienced because the prosecutor had failed to disclose that evidence.

Defendants in criminal cases shouldn't be required to show up for all of these pretrial court appearances. Parties in civil lawsuits are routinely allowed to let their lawyers appear on their behalf at any scheduled status conference, coming to the courthouse only if they need to testify at a hearing or once a trial begins. Even in criminal cases, prosecutors are regularly allowed to cover each other's court appearances if they have a conflict or if they are otherwise unable to appear at the scheduled time. As long as there is a lawyer present to represent the government, judges permit prosecutors' offices flexibility. Giving defendants the same flexibility—that is, allowing them to be represented by their lawyers rather than having to come to court themselves—would not only level the playing field between prosecution and defense but would also allow defendants to move closer to trial without having to endure so much inconvenience and expense. As an added bonus, if defendants don't have to attend all of those court dates, it avoids the problem of defendants missing one of the dates and then having the judges issue warrants for their arrest.

I asked David Jaros about this when he and I spoke about his clients who pleaded guilty rather than having to come back to court. He agreed that there was no good reason why defendants were essentially always required to appear at court dates. "I had a judge one time—wait, it might have been a couple of times—where a case was set over for another date in order to have the case dismissed. In those cases they would waive the client's appearance so he wouldn't have to appear," David recalled. "But it was stunning how rare that was. There was absolutely no recognition by the actors in the system about the level of the inconvenience for the people who were caught up in the system."

The conversation with David was depressing. Here was a simple solution that could make a difference in the millions of misdemeanor cases every year. And yet it seemed like judges were unwilling to entertain the idea.

Then, one morning, I received a surprise phone call from Judge Philip Calabrese, a federal judge in the Northern District of Ohio. A few days before, I had participated in an event about criminal justice reform hosted by the National Constitution Center. During that event, the moderator had asked me about how to fix plea bargaining, and I recommended that we stop making defendants show up for pointless court dates. No one seemed very interested in the recommendation, and the conversation quickly moved on. But Judge Calabrese had heard me speak, and he called to let me know that he had already adopted exactly that policy when he first became a judge in state court. "From the day I took the bench, I put the word out, saying 'From now on, unless I say otherwise, the client doesn't have to appear in the courtroom.'" A defendant had to come to court if she wanted to plead guilty or if it was time for sentencing, but otherwise Judge Calabrese didn't want to disrupt the defendants' lives any more than necessary. Disrupting their jobs and their child care was just making it harder for them to get their lives back on track. Having a job and taking care of their children, he explained, "are the things we want them to be doing. We shouldn't make it harder for them."

Several of Judge Calabrese's colleagues asked him about his policy, and some seemed surprised. But it worked just fine in his courtroom, and it served him well when courthouses had to start limiting occupancy during the coronavirus.

If we could make these kinds of changes to the criminal justice system—less formal trials, elimination of pretrial detention in most cases, shorter sentences, and letting defendants skip pretrial conferences—it would reduce the pressure on defendants to plead guilty. But such systemic change can be hard to accomplish. Police and prosecutors will often lobby against criminal justice reform legislation. And some of the changes would require new laws—especially the creation of informal court systems, elimination of extreme sentences, and prohibition of pretrial detention except in special cases. But other changes can be adopted by individual judges. As Judge Calabrese proved, a judge need not wait for a new law or a change in court rules to allow defendants to skip pretrial conferences. A judge could make that decision on her own and even make it a policy in all of the cases she hears.

Indeed, there are other judges who have already made changes in their own courtrooms—changes that have made the system fairer.

* * * * *

Joseph Goodwin, a federal judge in West Virginia, caused a big stir when he declared that he would no longer go along with the ordinary plea bargaining process. In a series of opinions that he wrote in 2017 and 2018, Judge Goodwin explained that he would stop accepting charge bargains—specifically, plea bargains in which a defendant pleaded guilty to one or more criminal charges in return for having other charges dismissed—unless there was a case-specific reason to do so. The three cases in which Judge Goodwin wrote these opinions were similar: Each involved a defendant accused of dealing in drugs on multiple occasions; each defendant was indicted on multiple drug charges and also a gun charge; and in each case the defendant agreed to plead guilty to a single drug charge in return for the government dismissing all other charges.

Judges generally say a plea bargain is a matter to be resolved by the prosecution and the defense. But that isn't true. The rules that set the procedures for federal criminal cases say that a judge may either accept or reject a plea bargain. And while the rule itself doesn't explain what criteria a judge is supposed to use when deciding to accept or reject a plea bargain, the notes from the committee that wrote the rule make clear that the judge is free to choose his own criteria.

After years of watching these charge bargains, it became clear to Judge Goodwin that prosecutors were bringing lots of criminal charges in order

to get leverage in plea bargaining: they had no intention of actually bringing those cases to trial. "The more I thought about it, the more it offended
me," Judge Goodwin said when we spoke by phone in March 2019. I had
emailed a mutual acquaintance to see whether he might be willing to put
me in touch with the judge. Fifteen minutes after I sent that email, my office
phone rang; it was Judge Goodwin.

In telling me about his views on plea bargaining, Judge Goodwin
emphasized how much had changed since he began practicing law in the
early 1970s. At the time, there was no public defender's office in West
Virginia, and so judges would appoint local members of the bar to represent defendants who were too poor to pay for their own lawyers. Some plea
bargaining took place, but he remembered it being much less common: at
least half of all criminal cases went to trial.

Of course, plea bargaining became more common over time. And the
practice was quite common by the time Judge Goodwin was appointed to
the federal bench by President Clinton in the mid-1990s. At first he didn't
give much thought to plea bargains; they were just part of the job. But
when the federal prosecutors started requiring defendants to waive more
rights—"waive just about anything you could think of," as Judge Goodwin
put it—he started thinking about no longer just routinely accepting plea
bargains. He was particularly concerned when federal prosecutors started
making all defendants waive their right to appeal. "I take a lot of comfort in
appellate review," Judge Goodwin said. "If I got something wrong, I want
someone who could correct it."

What eventually convinced Judge Goodwin to stop routinely accepting plea bargains wasn't its effect on him; it was the effect they had on
members of the general public who participate in the criminal justice
system. Because plea bargains circumvent the trial process, it stops the
public from participating on a jury. But in the federal system, the public is
still asked to participate as grand jurors. A grand jury is a body of citizens
that decides whether to bring criminal charges against a defendant or not.
A prosecutor will present evidence to them, and the grand jurors will vote
on whether that evidence is sufficient to indict the defendant of a crime.
All of the criminal charges that the prosecutors were dismissing in plea
bargaining had been voted on by grand jurors—people who had to put their
busy lives on hold to hear evidence and vote on indictments. The prosecutors convinced those people that these crimes were important and these

charges were worth bringing, and then they were ignoring the grand jurors' decisions in bargaining most of those charges away.

Dismissing these charges that the grand jury voted on is usually justified by saying it's impractical to bring all of the charges before a jury for a trial. In fact, that's the major justification of plea bargaining: that we simply don't have the time or money to try cases, and so we reward defendants for pleading guilty by dropping charges. But Judge Goodwin isn't buying it.

In the first of his plea bargaining opinions, Judge Goodwin provided statistics—illustrated by charts—in which he seriously undermines the idea that we can't bring more criminal cases to trial. (I included one of those charts in chapter 2.) His charts showed that, as the number of prosecutors and judges went up, the number of trials went down. In 1973, there were an average of 8.06 criminal trials for each person employed by the federal prosecutors' offices and 21.65 trials for every federal judge. By 2016 that number plummeted to 0.29 trials per federal prosecutor employee and 2.79 trials per federal judge.

Looking at those statistics, Judge Goodwin had no doubt that both prosecutors and judges had the ability to try more cases. Neither was, as he put it in one of his opinions, "overburdened by trials." Instead, the prosecutors were dismissing these charges as part of a plea bargain only because of "expediency and an abiding desire to avoid going to trial."

More generally, Judge Goodwin was concerned that plea bargaining cuts the public out of the criminal justice system. It doesn't just eliminate juries and disregard the decisions of grand jurors; it also allows decisions about guilt and punishment to be made in secret. "Government shouldn't be conducted in secret," he declared in our call. "It makes people think that they aren't allowed in the courtroom. I've actually had people *ask* whether they are allowed to come into my courtroom." (As a constitutional matter, courtrooms have to be open to the public except in rare circumstances.)

I asked Judge Goodwin about how plea bargaining diminishes the role of judges. But it became clear that he doesn't really care about that. He knows that, with the exception of mandatory minimums, he has a lot of power to choose the sentence that a defendant will serve. And he dismissed the idea that this power made the plea bargaining okay. "The United States criminal justice system is about far more than just punishment, and it was never intended to place all the power of accuser, judge, and jury into the hands of the government," he wrote in one of his anti–charge bargaining opinions. "I do not see justice in the plea agreement proffered in this case. As with most plea bargains, it eliminates the people's participation entirely on the reasoning that the people have 'an interest in the efficient and effective adjudication of criminal cases,' and that is good enough. Plea bargains like this one perpetuate the ongoing metamorphosis of the criminal justice system into nothing more than an administrative system controlled entirely by bureaucrats, where judge and jury are merely stage props to convince the general public that the criminal justice system they see nightly on television is being busily played out in the big courtroom downtown."

Judge Goodwin thinks that cutting people out of the justice system tears at the very fabric of our constitutional democracy. During our conversation, he repeatedly brought up the need to have the public participate in the criminal justice system, specifically referencing famous legal phrases like "We the People" and *e pluribus unum* to support his point.

He isn't alone in this belief. He told me about a woman who approached his wife in the grocery store one day. Judge Goodwin's plea bargaining opinions had caused a stir in the community, and folks had been talking about them. This woman told the judge's wife that she had served on a grand jury, that she and the other grand jurors had worked hard in those cases, and that the prosecutors "just threw them away." The woman saw what Judge Goodwin was doing as giving important recognition to the work that she and her fellow grand jurors had done.

It also became clear that the nature of these cases played a role in Judge Goodwin's decisions. All were cases involving the sale of heroin and other opioids. The opioid epidemic was hitting West Virginia hard, and he thought that the voices of the people who sat on the grand juries deserved to be heard. In refusing to accept routine charge bargains, Judge Goodwin was able to stick by his principles and honor the hard work of the grand jury.

But did it matter?

To some extent, the answer is no. Prosecutors didn't start trying more cases in Judge Goodwin's courtroom, and they aren't bringing fewer charges against defendants. Instead, defendants are pleading guilty to a single count of their indictments, without a plea bargain, and then the prosecutors come back later to dismiss the other counts. When this happens, Judge Goodwin asks the defense attorneys and their clients if they have been promised anything in return for the guilty plea—and both deny it. But he assumes there is an implicit understanding that the prosecutors will dismiss the other charges. Otherwise there is no reason these defendants plead guilty.

So if the same thing is happening—prosecutors are still bringing the same charges and defendants are still just pleading guilty to one charge—then did Judge Goodwin's decision not to accept charge bargains make any difference? I think it did. For one thing, prosecutors couldn't make defendants waive all of those other rights, like their right to an appeal. Because there were no formal plea bargains, the prosecutors couldn't demand anything else in return for dismissing charges.

In addition, Judge Goodwin shone a light on what was happening and explained why it was wrong. There are plenty of academics who say that plea bargaining is problematic, but it's a much bigger deal when a judge does so. Judge Goodwin was also able to make the prosecutors publicly explain and defend the decisions that they were making. Those explanations weren't very good. And so maybe voters—like the woman who approached the judge's wife in the grocery store—will start to demand more from their public officials.

* * * * *

Judge Goodwin is not the only judge who has used his power to push back against the worst excesses of our current structure. Another federal judge, Emmet Sullivan, has also made important changes about discovery rights in criminal cases. He has ordered every prosecutor who appears before him to turn over any exculpatory evidence—that is, evidence that suggests the defendant might not be guilty—to the defendant. Judge Sullivan, who tries cases in Washington D.C., has ordered prosecutors to resolve any doubts about whether evidence is material in favor of turning over the evidence, and he has told them if they think evidence isn't important enough to submit, they need to show it to him first before making that decision. Judge Sullivan adopted this rule in order to make sure that he can punish any prosecutor who fails to turn over this evidence.

Judge Sullivan made the decision to demand this of prosecutors after he presided over the Ted Stevens case. Ted Stevens was a senator from Alaska who had been charged with corruption. He was found guilty just before Election Day, and then he lost his reelection bid. But after the trial, it came out that prosecutors from the Department of Justice had failed to disclose exculpatory evidence to Stevens's defense attorneys. Judge Sullivan was furious. He ordered an independent investigation, which found that prosecutors had violated Stevens's constitutional rights to have that material turned over before trial. Judge Sullivan decided not to punish any of the prosecutors: although they had violated Stevens's constitutional rights, they hadn't defied any specific orders in the trial itself. But that prompted Judge Sullivan's decision to issue what is called a standing order in all of his criminal cases.

Unfortunately, Ted Stevens didn't live to see Judge Sullivan's response to the Department of Justice's misconduct: he died before the investigation was concluded. Nonetheless, Judge Sullivan's standing order has had a lasting impact. In particular, the order sweeps beyond what the Supreme Court says that the Constitution requires. Judge Sullivan's order requires prosecutors to turn over evidence during plea negotiations, not just when a case is heading to trial. And the order isn't limited to exculpatory evidence—evidence that suggests the defendant is not guilty. It also requires prosecutors to disclose any evidence "that is favorable to defendant and material either to defendant's guilt or punishment."

Judge Sullivan's requirement that prosecutors to turn over favorable evidence during plea negotiations doesn't allow the parties to negotiate around that requirement. We can see that in the recent prosecution involving former national security adviser Michael Flynn. Flynn's case had originally been assigned to a different judge, and Flynn pleaded guilty before that judge. When the case was transferred to Judge Sullivan, he told the prosecutors that they still had to turn over favorable evidence to Flynn's defense attorneys.

The evidence that federal prosecutors gave to Flynn's lawyers was not flattering. While I don't think that evidence showed that Flynn wasn't actually guilty of a crime, Flynn's defense attorney used the evidence to argue that he was innocent. More important, the evidence made the government investigators look bad. Flynn's defense attorneys were able to use that evidence to wage a media campaign against his prosecution and in favor of a motion to withdraw his guilty plea. The Department of Justice eventually caved to that pressure and filed a motion to dismiss the charges against Flynn. President Trump pardoned Flynn before Judge Sullivan ruled on that motion.

Giving defendants access to favorable information won't usually result in a media storm like the one we saw in the Flynn case. Nor is the Department of Justice likely to withdraw charges against defendants who don't have the personal backing of the president, as Flynn did with President

Trump. But the standing order gives all defendants something that they don't have in many cases: a good look at evidence that could help inform their decision to plead guilty.

As I indicated in chapter 3, the whole theory behind plea bargaining is that it gives defendants a chance to estimate the likelihood that they will be convicted and then use that information to negotiate for a plea bargain that is better than their "expected punishment." But defendants aren't able to estimate their chances of conviction if the government can hide evidence from them. Judge Sullivan's order ensures that defendants have that opportunity.

Because the order comes from a judge, it stops prosecutors from bargaining around any discovery rules. When prosecutors refuse to give defendants favorable plea offers if they insist on their right to see evidence, then the rules that require prosecutors to disclose that evidence make no difference. That is what we saw in Phoenix, where prosecutors have circumvented defense-friendly discovery rules by doing most plea bargaining before formal charges are filed and those rules take effect. Judges can prevent prosecutors from flouting their rules by refusing to accept a defendant's guilty plea until and unless prosecutors first turn over favorable evidence to the defendant.

In fact, because judges have to accept a guilty plea, they can refuse to sign off on plea bargains that seem unjust. For example, if a judge says that she will not accept a guilty plea that includes a waiver of the right to appeal, the prosecutor cannot insist that the defendant waive that right. To be clear, a prosecutor could insist that he will bring the defendant to trial if that term isn't included in the bargain. But while that sort of bullying is likely to work with a defendant—who has basically no power in the criminal justice system—it's unlikely to work with a judge, who has a lot of power. After all, prosecutors can't convict people on their own: as a legal matter, they need a judge to sign off on the decision and enter the judgment of conviction.

As I interviewed people for this book, I was often reminded that judges have the power to change how the modern criminal justice system operates in their own courtrooms. Even if they are not going to reject guilty pleas, judges can still help make certain that plea bargains are more just. Katie Gipson-McLean told me about a judge in Phoenix who pushes back against prosecutors when they've refused to give defendants a reasonable offer in plea negotiations. The judge will pause the proceeding and ask the prosecutor to call his or her supervisor to see whether the office would accept a less punitive plea bargain.

"Does it work?" I asked.

"Oh, yes," she replied. "The supervisor always agrees to the new plea bargain."

When judges decide to take a more active role at plea bargaining, it can make a real difference in how the other actors behave. For example, as I described in chapter 7, Judge Donnelly made significant changes to his courtroom in Ohio, refusing to let prosecutors take one position in private and another in public, as well as refusing to accept pleas when there were no facts to support them.

Judge Donnelly related a story about a young man who was accused of having sex with an underage girl. The victim was the defendant's girlfriend. She was fifteen years old and he was nineteen. But because he was more than four years older than she was, when they had sex, he committed a felony. If he was convicted of that felony, the defendant would have been required to spend at least twenty-five years on the sex offender registry.

The prosecutor and the defense attorney came up with a plea bargain that would allow the defendant to avoid a felony conviction and avoid being placed on the sex offender registry: They wanted the defendant to plead guilty to a misdemeanor, a crime that prohibited sexual conduct with a minor by someone who is *less* than four years older than the minor. The defense attorney and the prosecutor brought this agreement to Judge Donnelly. "I don't understand," he told the lawyers. "Is the defendant four years older than the victim or not?"

The prosecutor assured the judge that the defendant was, in fact, more than four years older than the victim. But the prosecutor agreed that it wasn't necessary—or maybe even just—to convict the defendant of a felony and put him on the sex offender registry. The sexual relationship was entirely consensual. The victim kept saying that she was in love with the defendant, and the only reason that the prosecutor's office had brought charges was because the victim's stepfather was angry that the defendant had been sneaking the victim out of her house to have sex, and the stepfather wanted the defendant to stay away from his stepdaughter.

Judge Donnelly told the prosecutor that he wouldn't accept a plea in a case that was based on false facts. He encouraged the prosecutor to try and come up with an agreement that wasn't built on a lie. The prosecutor eventually dismissed the charges.

When forced to decide whether it was actually just and appropriate to enforce the law as written in that case, the prosecutor used her discretion not to prosecute. That seems like a pretty good outcome. Prosecutors shouldn't be casting about to see whether there are *any* criminal charges that they can bring that match up with their own sense of how much punishment a defendant should receive. They should instead decide whether enforcing the law as written would be a good use of their power. And if it isn't, then they should just dismiss the charges.

My examples of how judges can change plea bargaining have focused on changes that individual judges can make. But judges don't just set the rules in their own courtrooms. They can also write rules that apply to all judges. This was the power that Judge Donnelly sought in his campaign to serve as a justice on the Ohio Supreme Court: the power to write a new state court rule that would require plea-bargained convictions be based on the facts of the defendant's crime.

Many states have court rules that regulate plea bargaining. For example, more than a dozen states allow judges to reject plea bargains that they think are inappropriate. Judges could write court rules that limit prosecutors' powers when plea bargaining—rules that tell judges not to accept plea bargains that require defendants to waive their right to appeal, or rules that require prosecutors to turn over evidence to defendants before judges will accept guilty pleas. These rules could help to regulate the plea bargaining process and make it fairer for everyone.

* * * * *

Of course, judges are not the only individuals within that system who can bring about change. Prosecutors have a lot of power, and their leverage is one of the major reasons we have the system that we do. They don't need to wait for judges to prompt them to turn over evidence, make fairer plea offers, or dismiss cases that aren't worth pursuing. Prosecutors can decide to do those things on their own.

That's exactly what Parisa Dehghani-Tafti has done. In 2019, Dehghani-Tafti defeated the incumbent prosecutor in Arlington County, Virginia. She ran on a platform that included ending cash bail and refusing to prosecute low-level marijuana cases. She was one of several reform prosecutors elected in Northern Virginia that year, and since her election, Dehghani-Tafti has captured headlines by filing a lawsuit against the judges in her jurisdiction. The judges had demanded that any decision Dehghani-Tafti makes to dismiss a case or reduce charges be accompanied by a written motion explaining the precise facts supporting her decision—a demand that Dehghani-Tafti says exceeds the judges' authority.

When I interviewed people for this book, I often began by asking them what made them become lawyers or choose their professional paths. Dehghani-Tafti's answer to that question was striking: When she was in college, a friend of hers was accused of raping a fourteen-year-old girl. As Dehghani-Tafti watched his trial unfold, it was clear to her that her friend was innocent and that the prosecutor in the case was engaged in serious misconduct. But because of the prosecutorial misconduct, her friend was convicted, and he spent five years in San Quentin before he was exonerated and his conviction was overturned.

Watching that injustice unfold, Dehghani-Tafti felt that she had to do something about it. She was raised in the Baha'i faith, a religion that teaches its adherents to do what they can to bring about a more peaceful and fairer world. And so, while she had originally been planning to pursue a PhD in philosophy, her friend's wrongful conviction prompted her to go to law school instead. After law school she worked as a public defender and then later joined the Mid-Atlantic Innocence Project, where she worked to exonerate innocent people convicted of crimes.

In light of her background, I was eager to ask Dehghani-Tafti how she views her role as a prosecutor. Her time working for an innocence project had clearly taught her that the criminal justice system isn't always very good at sorting the innocent from the guilty or getting at the truth of what happened. And so I wanted to know how that knowledge shaped her approach as a prosecutor.

"Well, there are two things that I think about," she said. "I think about sorting the people who are innocent from the people who are guilty. But the system also has a problem sorting out what things should be punished from those things that should not."

Dehghani-Tafti sees a deep connection between these problems, characterizing both of them as issues about truth.

"I care about truth in both the narrow sense and the broad sense. There is the truth of whether this person did something. But there is another truth about whether we should be putting someone in prison for simple marijuana possession," she observed. "I know that the system is really bad at sorting out the innocent and the guilty, particularly for lower-level crimes. And it is also bad at determining what is just and what isn't, particularly for lower-level crimes. And so that's why I decided to run for office: so that I would have a measure of influence, at least in my own backyard."

I was struck by Dehghani-Tafti's focus on less serious crimes because that's not the sort of crime that she worked on as an innocence lawyer. Exoneration can take years, and so only people who have been convicted of more serious crimes and received very long sentences end up being represented by people like her. But it seems as though the painstaking work that she did on those exoneration cases made Dehghani-Tafti even more skeptical of the pressure to plead guilty to low-level offenses.

"When someone is held without bail—or with cash bail that they can't pay—what happens is that they sit in jail, sometimes for up to three months. Then they get a deal that's going to let them walk out of jail that day. That deal looks really attractive. But if that person is safe enough to walk out of jail that day on a plea, then why is that person not safe enough to be out of jail while their case is pending? Why are we using somebody's financial status as leverage to get them to plead to something that they may or may not have done?" she asked, adding that, when a defendant is charged with a low-level crime, he isn't going to insist on his innocence when that would prevent him from being able to go home.

Dehghani-Tafti campaigned on ending cash bail, and so I asked whether she believed that prosecutors use pretrial detention as leverage to get people to plead guilty. "The *result* is leverage for plea bargaining," she replied. "Does anyone actually have the conscious thought of 'Well, let's impose cash bail so that we will have leverage'? I don't know that anyone actually goes through that thought process. But it almost doesn't matter because we see the result. And we should know better."

Since taking office at the beginning of 2020, Dehghani-Tafti has instructed the prosecutors in her office never to ask for cash bail. If they think that someone poses a danger or is a flight risk—"a *real* flight risk," she emphasized, not just someone who might forget a court date—then she instructs them to make that case to the judge and to argue why the defendant should be held without bail.

Sometimes the judges ask her prosecutors why they aren't seeking cash bail. They explain that it is against their office policy. They will sometimes ask for other, nonfinancial conditions to be placed on the defendant while he is waiting for trial. For some defendants that means home detention, electronic monitoring, or participation in some sort of mental health program. But other defendants they say can be released without any restrictions because they don't pose a danger and they will show up for their court dates.

As for how successful the new policy is, Dehghani-Tafti was quick to remind me that judges make the ultimate decision about bail and pretrial detention and that "judges will do what they will do." But she also pointed to the partnership that she had formed with the sheriff's and the public defender's offices in the early days of the coronavirus outbreak. Her office and the sheriff's identified all of the people who had been in jail for more than a few days and who had cash bail set that was under $10,000—basically, those people who couldn't pay the cash bail that judges had set and who her office thought should have been released anyway. Her office would call their defense attorneys, encourage them to file motions to reconsider the orders setting cash bail, and promise that their office wouldn't oppose the motions. The partnership proved to be very successful in reducing the jail population, thus better protecting people in jail—including the corrections officers—from exposure to the virus. "The population went down like 30 or 20 percent in just three weeks," she said.

Ending cash bail wasn't the only major policy change that Dehghani-Tafti campaigned on. She also promised that, if elected, she wouldn't prosecute marijuana possession cases. The decision of prosecutors not to prosecute certain crimes has drawn a lot of criticism. But Dehghani-Tafti sees it as part of why we elect our prosecutors: so that local communities will have a say in how the law is enforced against them and their neighbors.

That prosecutorial role is not new, she pointed out. She told a story about the prosecutor who had held her job during the 1960s civil rights movement. "One of the original Freedom Riders, Joan Trumpauer Mulholland, was working to integrate lunch counters in Virginia," she began. Mulholland decided to start her integration efforts in Arlington because that's where she was from. She purchased food from a lunch counter and gave it to her friends, who were African American. This was illegal under state law at the time: Mulholland, her friends, and the lunch counter were all violating the law.

"And so the police are, like, 'What are we supposed to do?' And the commonwealth attorney at the time said, 'We are not going to prosecute these laws.' He made that decision by simply saying that it wasn't an enforcement priority," Dehghani-Tafti continued. "And I don't mean to say that he had some grand vision about civil rights because I don't know; I just don't know that he did or he didn't. But he made the decision that it wasn't where he wanted to put our resources. Maybe he just thought it would look bad. Maybe it was because he felt sympathy for the civil rights movement. Maybe he thought it was an unconstitutional law. Maybe he just saw the effect of the law and thought that he shouldn't enforce it.

"Whatever the reason, that decision had a domino effect, and it made the rest of Virginia integrate. Because then Fairfax said, 'We are not going to prosecute these cases.' And then Alexandria was, like, 'Well, if Arlington and Fairfax aren't doing it, we're not going to do it.' And so people just stopped prosecuting those cases."

Dehghani-Tafti is quick to point out that there are major differences between the South's race-based segregation and the drug laws: laws legalizing segregation and discrimination are much more corrosive and indefensible than drug laws. Nonetheless, she sees parallels between the War on Drugs and segregation. "When you look at the origin story of why marijuana was criminalized to begin with and then you look at the disproportionate impact," then the parallels are "undeniable," she said. Some academics have attributed the initial decisions to criminalize marijuana to racism, and Dehghani-Tafti emphasized that our country is perfectly capable of regulating harmful substances like tobacco smoke and alcohol without criminalizing it. "If anything, alcohol is far more dangerous than marijuana," she observed, pointing to a higher correlation between alcohol and violence than for marijuana.

Dehghani-Tafti questioned not only the decision to criminalize marijuana but also how those criminal laws are enforced. "You are eight times more likely to be arrested if you are Black and have marijuana than if you are White," she said. "Whatever is happening there is morally wrong. As so that's why I took the position that I took. It's not a grand decision, like the sort of decision that is going to cause integration. But it is morally wrong to keep prosecuting something that has such a disproportionate impact and has such little public safety value in its enforcement."

Refusing to seek cash bail and to prosecute marijuana cases are not the only reforms that Dehghani-Tafti has instituted since taking office. As a former innocence lawyer, she has taken steps aimed specifically at ensuring that her office does not convict innocent people. "We give discovery very early so that defense attorneys can do their jobs. And we encourage defense attorneys to bring their facts to us—whether they are facts about innocence or facts about mitigation. And then we look at our own cases very critically ourselves and try to avoid tunnel vision."

Dehghani-Tafti repeatedly emphasized the need for her prosecutors to maintain a professional distance from their work and to view their cases with a critical eye. It's something that she seeks to reinforce by telling them that they shouldn't take anything for granted and that they should not continue to pursue charges if it turns out that the case just isn't all that strong. In those situations she encourages her prosecutors to seek alternative dispositions rather than just trying to get convictions.

Dehghani-Tafti's approach—one that doesn't just focus on getting convictions—is a stark contrast to the approach by her predecessor, Theo Stamos, whom Dehghani-Tafti defeated in the Democratic primary. During the election, more than one hundred attorneys signed an open letter to Stamos, criticizing her for securing 98 percent of her convictions from plea bargains rather than trials—a rate that was much higher than neighboring counties.

Some of those pleas appear to have come from questionable prosecutorial tactics. Dehghani-Tafti described one case involving a homeless man who had been accused of taking another person's iPad. The man was arrested and detained pretrial for six weeks. "During that six weeks, the owner of the iPad recanted, saying he'd found his iPad and that it was not in fact stolen. In my office, that case would have been dismissed the second we found out that the individual said he found it. Like, there would be no question. There would be no debate," she declared.

But rather than dismissing the charges, Stamos's office offered the man a plea to a lesser charge. "I think it was, instead of stealing, possession of stolen property," Dehghani-Tafti said. "And he took it because he didn't know how else to get out of jail."

Dehghani-Tafti's campaign used the case as an example of why Stamos needed to be replaced. "The response of Stamos in the press was 'Well, just because he found his iPad doesn't mean that it wasn't in fact stolen,'" Dehghani-Tafti said, her voice incredulous. She wasn't the only one who didn't find that explanation plausible. The homeless man brought a civil rights lawsuit, and he ultimately received a $250,000 settlement.

Dehghani-Tafti tells this story as an example of how her predecessor seemed to care only about convictions and not about fair and just outcomes. It wasn't her only example. She also believes that the attorneys in the office were sent the message that they would be evaluated based on their record in securing convictions. "I look at the personnel reviews of folks that were in the office, and the comments were 'You are not enough of an advocate' in the files of those prosecutors who were trying to dismiss a case that wasn't very strong," she said.

Dehghani-Tafti has adopted very different performance standards: "Our performance measure is not 'How many convictions did you get?' It's not 'How harsh were you?' It's 'Did you identify the problematic issues and make sure that you acted in a fair way? Did you come up with a creative solution for someone who shouldn't be criminalized?' Those are our performance measures."

But, she emphasized, one of the most important things her office does is to take some cases out of the system: "We've been dismissing cases that we think are not strong—cases where it is clear to us that the search was not good; cases where an officer's version of events is very different from the police report version, or where a video shows a different version. We just aren't trying to squeeze everything that we can out of every single case."

It's this commitment to dismissing weak cases—weak because the facts aren't strong or because the circumstances make punishment seem unfair—that has defined Dehghani-Tafti's first year in office. When local judges questioned her power to dismiss cases, Dehghani-Tafti filed a lawsuit against them, wrote an op-ed in the *Washington Post* defending her power, and inspired lawmakers to introduce a bill in the state legislature that would guarantee prosecutors the power even if judges object.

* * * * *

Like Parisa Dehghani-Tafti, Rachael Rollins had to fight with judges in order to dismiss cases. Rollins, the elected prosecutor in Boston, decided to drop the charges against some protesters who had been arrested at a rally, but a judge wouldn't allow her to do so. Rollins appealed that decision, and the appeals court confirmed that the trial judge had overstepped his authority. Under Massachusetts law, Rollins had the authority to decide not to pursue a case.

That is not the only opposition that Rollins has faced from judges since she was elected in 2018. She's also experienced pushback from judges about her bail policies, which I described in chapter 4. Nonetheless, she has persisted in making changes to how crimes are prosecuted in Boston. In addition to dismissing low-level cases and seeking bail less often, Rollins has said that she wants to have her office turn over more evidence before defendants plea bargain.

One major change that Rollins instituted was the creation of the Integrity Review Bureau. Several prosecutors have created "conviction integrity units"—special divisions that investigate claims that people convicted by their office were factually innocent. But, as Rollins pointed out, her Integrity Review Bureau does more than simply review claims of factual innocence. "We are taking it to the next level," she informed me. The bureau includes four different programs: a conviction integrity unit, a case integrity unit, a sentencing integrity unit, and a database about law enforcement misconduct.

The bureau was the brainchild of Donna Patalano, Rollins's general counsel and a veteran prosecutor whose appetite for reform had gone unfulfilled under previous chief prosecutors. But Rollins—who speaks glowingly about Patalano—has listened closely to suggestions for reform and implemented many of Patalano's suggestions. One suggestion was to make the conviction integrity unit in Boston more willing and able to revisit past convictions. The unit doesn't just examine cases of factual innocence; it also looks at questions of legal innocence, such as whether a defendant's behavior fell squarely within the language of the criminal law. The unit examines claims of innocence regardless of whether the defendant was convicted after a jury trial or pleaded guilty. Most important, the unit looks at all claims with fresh eyes rather than a presumption that the conviction was valid. As a result, the defendant doesn't need to satisfy a high burden of proof to get a review.

The case integrity unit, Patalano explained, grew out of an existing program in the district attorney's office—a unit that was tasked with deciding whether to appeal adverse decisions. Under the previous program, the unit would decide only whether to, for example, file an appeal if the office had lost a suppression motion. But in reviewing a case to decide whether to file an appeal, they sometimes found that the adverse decisions were the result of mistakes that were being made by some of their prosecutors. So Patalano suggested that they start reviewing cases not only to decide whether to appeal but also to figure out what went wrong.

Patalano compared this approach to the investigations conducted by the National Transportation Safety Board after a plane crash: the goal is to determine whether mistakes were made and, more important, how to make improvements that would result in positive change going forward. So, in addition to decide whether to appeal, the unit would look to see if there was a pattern of mistakes that suggested a need for further training within the office. If, for example, the office was getting negative rulings in forensic evidence cases, and if the review of those cases showed that line prosecutors weren't laying the proper foundation for the credentials of their expert witnesses, then they would schedule an office training session on how to do that properly.

The case integrity unit doesn't just look for possible mistakes by prosecutors; it also looks for mistakes by police and by judges. If the office finds those mistakes, then they might have a conversation with their law enforcement partners, or they might decide to prioritize appeals from a particular judge. Patalano told me that their office handles a large number of cases, and most of the mistakes they see are caused by sheer volume. "It's not about laying blame," she maintained. "I mean, if there is misconduct, then we will investigate and take that seriously. But this is really about what went wrong and how to fix it."

The case integrity unit helps ensure that supervisors within the office get a closer look at some fraction of their line prosecutors' cases. Whenever a career prosecutor gets an adverse decision—that is, whenever a grand jury won't indict, whenever evidence is suppressed, whenever a judge enters a verdict of not guilty or dismisses charges, or whenever a judge rules that prosecutors failed to turn over information that was constitutionally required—then the prosecutor has to fill out a form about that decision and provide supporting documentation. That form is sent up the chain of command, allowing office leadership to make decisions about appeals, training, and other ways to improve the office.

Rachael Rollins sees the case integrity unit as a way to lessen the chances that her office will convict innocent people. For example, if a prosecutor presents a case to a grand jury and the grand jury refuses to indict, then the case will be reviewed. As Rollins sees it, her prosecutors have no business pursuing a criminal case if they can't convince a grand jury that there is enough evidence for an indictment. "If they can't prove that there was probable cause," Rollins said, referring to the lower standard of proof that's required for an indictment, "then how are they going to prove it beyond a reasonable doubt?" When that case is reviewed, it will allow supervisors the opportunity to determine whether the line prosecutor is being too aggressive in the charges that she brings.

The other two components of the Integrity Review Bureau—the law enforcement database and the sentencing integrity unit—also have the potential to mitigate some problems with plea bargaining. The law enforcement database allows the office to track those police officers who have engaged in misconduct. When an assistant district attorney receives a police report, she has to type into the database the names of the officers involved. If the officer's name appears in the database, then the ADA must immediately notify the defense attorney of that misconduct. That misconduct could be embarrassing and damage an officer's credibility with the jury. And so the defense attorney might be more willing than usual to threaten to go to trial.

The sentencing integrity unit—which is still a pilot program—looks at cases in which defendants are serving incredibly long sentences to decide whether the office should try to work to shorten the sentences. In one recent case, the office discovered that two brothers who had been charged with first-degree murder were serving dramatically different sentences. One brother shot someone while the other brother stood by. The shooter fled, while the other brother was arrested and went to trial. Even though he hadn't pulled the trigger, the state's felony murder law allowed the jury to convict the brother who didn't shoot of first-degree murder. He received a sentence of life imprisonment. Two years after his conviction, his brother was arrested. When he stood trial, he testified that he'd shot the victim because the victim had assaulted him twice before and he was afraid of further violence. The jury believed him and convicted him of second degree murder rather than first-degree. As a result, the brother who actually shot the victim has been out of prison for more than a decade, while the other brother remains incarcerated.

The sentencing difference seems so unfair that Rollins wants to revisit it. But although the sentence seems unfair, it is still legal. And so the office is trying to figure out how, if at all, it can get the sentence modified.

The unit had success in a similar case earlier this year. An aging mobster who was suffering from dementia and who could no longer walk was not eligible to get released from prison under the state's very restrictive medical parole law. But the office was able to help secure a compassionate release for him by joining the defense's motion for a new trial. Once a judge granted that motion, they let the defendant plead to second-degree murder. This removed the mobster's mandatory life sentence, and he was sent home to live out the remaining months of his life outside of prison, where he could receive better medical care.

The sentencing integrity unit may hold the most promise for mitigating the problems associated with plea bargains. That is because it could be used to reduce the trial penalty. Many defendants plead guilty because they will face a much larger penalty if they are convicted at trial, as explained earlier. Prosecutors can reduce the pressure to plead and the unfairness by refusing to increase charges on those defendants who won't plead guilty and by recommending that judges impose lower sentences that are similar to bargained sentences after trial. And they can help undo some of the damage from past cases by reviewing old cases, joining motions for new trials where there were egregious trial penalties, and then offering new plea deals once those motions are granted.

* * * * *

Rollins and Dehghani-Tafti have inspiring stories to tell about the changes that they have made in their offices. But it's striking that their reforms—even if fully implemented—won't necessarily lead to more trials.

When I asked Dehghani-Tafti to tell me more about the creative solutions that her office uses to resolve cases, she never mentioned a trial. Instead, she talked about programs to get juvenile defendants into rehabilitation programs rather than filing charges against them, a pilot program on restorative justice, and a few other initiatives. "We are open to basically anything that will get at the root cause of a problem," she said.

As Dehghani-Tafti was listing these creative solutions, I was struck by the fact that they were not alternatives to plea bargaining. On the contrary: most of these actions depended heavily on the institution of plea bargaining in order to work. The incumbent whom Dehghani-Tafti defeated was criticized for obtaining 98 percent of her convictions through plea bargaining. But I didn't see how the new approach would reduce that number.

I mentioned this to Dehghani-Tafti, and she conceded that her approach might not reduce the rate of plea bargaining. But she insisted that her approach and her intentions were still very different from her predecessor's. "The office was charging to the hilt and then using those charges as leverage to get compliance. Our perspective is that you have to charge with accuracy and restraint. Then you offer better deals and you offer alternatives."

Dehghani-Tafti makes a compelling case that whether a system is fair or just can't simply be measured by the number of trials that it holds. To the extent it can be measured, that measurement has to include the rate at which cases are dismissed. "What I think we are going to see is that our dismissal rate is going to be really high," she said. "It is going to exceed what other jurisdictions see on a normal basis because what we are trying to do is to work something out, and we may not even end up with a conviction."

Dehghani-Tafti's remark about using dismissals as a measure of fairness reminded me of what I had seen in the Salt Lake County Justice Court. The defense attorneys and their clients felt empowered to bring cases to trials, and prosecutors did not have much leverage to pressure them into a plea bargain. Nonetheless, the trial rate was still quite low. The dismissal rate, on the other hand, was much higher. It was if *prosecutors* rather than defendants were eager to avoid trials.

A dismissal is also what happened when Judge Donnelly wouldn't let prosecutors design a fictional plea in his courtroom. He told the prosecutor and the defense attorney that he would only accept a plea from a defendant that was actually supported by the facts. And rather than enforcing a law that was too harsh considering the circumstances, the prosecutor decided to dismiss the case altogether.

Data about dismissals can be hard to find—certainly harder than conviction data. And even if we know what percentage of cases are dismissed, that doesn't tell us *why* a case was dismissed. A prosecutor might dismiss a case because she doesn't have enough evidence that a defendant is factually guilty. She might dismiss it because she thinks that the defendant's behavior, though illegal, isn't serious enough to deserve a criminal conviction. She might dismiss it because she entered into a deferred prosecution agreement with a defendant, and the defendant has held up his end of the bargain. She might dismiss it because the defendant has agreed to cooperate against other defendants. Or she might dismiss it because federal prosecutors have decided to bring charges instead.

Those are very different reasons for dismissal. Knowing more about dismissals would give people a better sense of how prosecutors are using their powers. Sometimes prosecutors might be dismissing cases for sketchy reasons. Dehghani-Tafti told me that her predecessor would sometimes dismiss a case because she didn't yet have a laboratory report and because the defendant had speedy trial rights that would prevent her from delaying that case any longer. But if the lab report came back positive, she would simply charge the defendant again, which would start a new speedy trial clock. That practice distorted the dismissal rate because some of those dismissed cases were actually prosecuted just a bit later.

* * * * *

A fair criminal justice system that does not have a lot of trials will almost certainly need a lot of dismissals. It will also need fairer plea bargaining. It is hard to measure when plea bargaining becomes more equitable. But that doesn't mean people aren't trying.

Several community groups in Chicago conducted a study in an attempt to see how plea bargaining had changed under Kim Foxx, a reform prosecutor who was elected in 2016. A report that the groups released explained that, because plea bargaining is all done verbally, and because there are no records kept of those negotiations, the report could not include any statistical information. This is a real problem because, like most places, more than 90 percent of convictions in Chicago are the result of plea bargains.

But rather than simply throw up their hands, the groups decided to study plea bargaining by conducting detailed interviews with defense attorneys in the city. They asked the defense attorneys a series of questions about how plea bargaining changed when Foxx took office compared to when the office was run by her predecessor, Anita Alvarez. The report documented important changes in plea bargaining practices. Prosecutors were more likely to offer alternatives to incarceration as part of a plea bargain. They were more likely to offer charge bargains that reduced low-level felonies to misdemeanors. And in cases involving small amounts of drugs, they were more likely to either immediately divert the case to a program that only required defendants to take a low-cost or free education class on drug use or just dismiss the case entirely.

When prosecutors work with defense attorneys to achieve fair outcomes, and when defendants are given a meaningful choice whether to accept those outcomes or proceed to trial, then it is hard to criticize plea bargaining. In those circumstances, plea bargaining looks like a cooperative and fair way to address criminal activity.

But unfortunately that often *isn't* what plea bargaining looks like. And we need to do more to change that. Because if plea bargaining is here to stay, then we need to start talking about how to have plea bargains that reach fair and accurate outcomes.

CHAPTER TEN

CONCLUSION

As I wrapped up my interview with Damian Mills—the man whose story I described at the very beginning of this book—I had one major question left to ask: I wanted to know whether Damian regretted his decision to plead guilty to a murder he didn't commit.

This question was jotted down in a notebook I had brought with me to the interview. I assumed that Damian would spontaneously tell me that he regretted the decision during the course of the interview, but I had written it down just in case. I knew that I wanted to start the book with Damian's story, and I thought a quote from Damian about how he regretted his decision would make for a good transition to talk about the pressure that defendants feel to plea bargain. But Damian didn't raise the subject himself. So I asked him.

Damian's answer surprised me.

His only regret, Damian told me, was not getting a better plea deal from the prosecutors. He didn't regret pleading guilty, he said, because he thought he would have been convicted at trial.

I was shocked, and so I pressed Damian for more information. He was innocent, so why did he assume that he was going to be convicted at trial? One big reason, he told me, was his attorney. Damian couldn't afford to hire his own lawyer, and so the state appointed one for him. Damian was convinced that there was zero chance that the lawyer he'd been appointed would get him acquitted.

There are a number of dedicated, talented lawyers who work as public defenders or court-appointed lawyers. I've profiled some of them in this book. But not all lawyers are the same. There are some who are overworked, who are jaded by the system, and who approach their job as a cog in the machine of criminal justice rather than as a champion for their clients.

Damian did not get a lawyer like the ones I have profiled in this book. The first time he met his attorney, the lawyer told him that he'd tried three cases just like his and he had always lost. To be fair to that lawyer, he might have thought that a plea bargain was the best choice for Damian. If so, then he probably told Damian about those losses to help convince him to accept a plea deal. But the message that Damian heard was that he had gotten a bad lawyer.

I was a little relieved when I heard Damian's concerns about his lawyer. It made sense that Damian wouldn't have wanted to go to trial with a bad lawyer. But if he'd had a different lawyer, then he would have made a different decision, right?

I could tell that Damian didn't really like this question when I asked it. Rather than answering, he told me that he tries to put the time he spent in prison behind him and not second-guess his decisions. But I really wanted that quote for my book, so I asked again.

And Damian told me that, even with a better lawyer, he thinks he probably would have been convicted anyway.

I tried not to let the shock show on my face. We finished the interview, and I thanked Damian and his lawyer Frank for all of the time that they'd given me. Then I drove away.

But weeks later Damian's answer still haunted me. I was writing a book about the problems with plea bargaining. An innocent person who pleaded guilty to a murder he didn't commit is basically the best example in the world of plea bargaining's problems. How could Damian *not* regret the decision to plead guilty?

Eventually I realized that Damian had already given me the answer to my question. However bad plea bargaining is, sometimes it is actually the best option. Don't get me wrong: plea bargaining is a *huge* problem that has distorted the very foundation of our criminal justice system. But it isn't the *only* problem.

Damian was right to be worried about a trial. When we see them on television, juries always convict the guilty and let the innocent walk free. But that's not what happens in real life. In reality, juries sometimes acquit guilty defendants, and other times they convict the innocent. Hundreds of people who were found guilty at trial have since been exonerated by DNA evidence. They told their juries that they were innocent, but the jurors didn't believe them.

In those cases where DNA evidence later exonerated people, we can see what went wrong. Duke University law professor Brandon Garrett studied trials that convicted innocent people, and he was able to identify a number of problems contributed to those false convictions. He found that law enforcement used eyewitness identification procedures that are overly suggestive and lead to false identifications. He found defendants who were pressured to give false confessions during coercive interrogations. He found unsound and unreliable forensic evidence and shoddy investigative practices. In other words, a lot of innocent people are convicted because of problems with law enforcement tactics and practices rather than just jurors getting it wrong.

But not much has been done to change those law enforcement tactics. For years, experts have said that eyewitness identification procedures that police use are unreliable. The Department of Justice even published national guidelines in 1999, telling states how they could change their procedures to reduce the number of mistaken identifications. But only ten states have made reforms. We see the same thing with police interrogations. We know that police sometimes use the power of suggestion—or even coercion—to trick innocent people into confessing to crimes. But very little has been done to change interrogation tactics. Most states don't even require police to videotape their interrogations.

If we want innocent people like Damian to insist on a trial rather than plead guilty, then, at a minimum, we need to fix the problems with law enforcement that we know lead to the conviction of innocent people. We also need to fully fund our public defenders and make sure that prosecutors don't rely on false or misleading evidence from law enforcement. We can't ask juries to tell us whether people are innocent or guilty unless we give them the evidence that they need to make better decisions.

* * * * *

The possibility of juries convicting innocent people isn't the only problem that leads to plea bargaining. The harsh sentencing laws that we have in this country give prosecutors a lot of leverage to pressure defendants into pleading guilty. Some of those sentences were adopted *precisely because* they give prosecutors plea bargaining leverage. But that's not the only reason those harsh sentencing laws were passed: they were also passed because we have convinced ourselves that the best way to deal with crime is to lock people in jail for extremely long periods of time. Some policy makers helped to feed the public desire for punitive laws in order to help avoid trials. But others did it to look tough on crime and win reelection. Whatever the reason, a lot of people now think that really long sentences are a good idea, and so legislatures keep making sentences harsher.

If we got rid of plea bargaining without changing those sentencing laws, then we would not fix the criminal justice system. In fact, we would probably make it worse. Right now only some defendants—usually the defendants who insist on going to trial—serve the extremely long sentences that we have adopted. Without plea bargaining, *everyone* who is convicted will serve those sentences. And while I would like to see more people be able to use their right to a jury trial, all of those extra years of punishment strike me as too high of a price to pay.

As Scott Hechinger noted as we sat in the Brooklyn courtroom, he needs plea bargaining: in many cases it is the only way that he can secure any leniency for his clients. That's why he doesn't support getting rid of plea bargaining. Plea bargaining, he believed, is "relatively good for my clients." (He said "relatively" because, as he emphasized, what would be best for his clients is if they weren't mired in poverty or if they had access to better social services before they were ever brought into the system.) "When they get an offer that is better than what they'd otherwise be facing, that's great. But that's really bad for the system," he acknowledged,

Prosecutors also rely on plea bargaining. Some prosecutors rely on it because they want to punish defendants without the hassle of trials. But other prosecutors rely on plea bargaining because they are trying to help defendants, not just punish them. For example, Parisa Dehghani-Tafti depends on plea bargaining to help deal with her juvenile offender cases.

"We've been reaching out to the families before charges are filed—because they are serious cases—and we try to get the kids into services before we even bring charges," she explained. After the kids have been placed in services—services that can help them deal with issues that might have caused them to break the law in the first place—her office can see whether they are responding well. If they are, then negotiations begin.

"We can agree on what the charge is going to be—like, maybe we can agree on a misdemeanor that they would eventually be able to expunge from their records, as opposed to a felony."

A defendant's desire for leniency and a prosecutor's desire for flexibility are what led to plea bargaining in the first place. And it is also why any attempt to prohibit plea bargaining is almost certainly destined to fail.

Alaska tried to ban plea bargaining. The attorney general, who oversees all criminal cases in the state, announced the ban in 1975. Initially, the number of trials increased and bargaining appeared to be mostly limited to a small number of cases that were specifically approved by the attorney general or his top staff. But when a study of the state's criminal justice system was undertaken in 1990, it found that plea bargaining had become just as widespread as before the ban. Some attorneys who were interviewed for the study didn't even realize that a plea bargaining ban was even in effect! Eventually, Alaska began to look like other states. A study of Alaska's criminal cases during the years 2005 to 2012 found that 97 percent of defendants who were convicted of a felony had pleaded guilty.

Although Alaska was the only state to ban plea bargaining, there have been a few instances of local bans. For example, El Paso, Texas, banned plea bargaining in felony cases beginning in December 1975. That plea bargaining ban grew out of a dispute between the local district attorney and the judges handling criminal cases. The district attorney refused to recommend probation for any defendant convicted of burglary—even young first-time offenders with no history of violence. The judges wanted to give some first-time offenders probation, but they didn't want to be accused of being "soft" on crime by going against the prosecutors' recommendations.

So the judges announced that they were no longer going to accept *any* sentencing recommendations that were the result of plea negotiations. Instead, the judges would make their own decisions using a point system based on the facts of the crime and the defendants' prior convictions. The district attorney responded by telling defense attorneys that they would no longer plea bargain in felony cases.

Just like in Alaska, the number of trials in El Paso increased. The trial rate jumped from 21 percent to more than 40 percent. But plea bargaining never actually stopped. Even under the official ban, the district attorney permitted plea bargaining in death penalty cases, sexual assault cases, and cases in which defendants agreed to cooperate against others. More important, individual prosecutors routinely defied office policy and plea bargained other cases, sometimes with a judge's approval. These plea bargains occurred in secret because the district attorney had threatened to fire any prosecutors who negotiated a plea in violation of office policy.

When judges (rather than prosecutors) have tried to ban plea bargaining, they haven't fared much better. Judge Joseph Goodwin acknowledged that, despite his refusal to allow charge bargaining in his courtroom, attorneys appear to be bargaining around those limits. The defense attorneys know that prosecutors are willing to dismiss some of the charges in return for a guilty plea on others—after all, that's what the prosecutors are doing in all of the other courtrooms—so they still convince their clients to plead guilty.

The bans in Alaska and El Paso were eventually lifted. And Judge Goodwin appears to accept that he can't stop the prosecution and defense from reaching implicit bargains. These stories show that there will always be some people who want to plea bargain. If we tell them that they can't, they will figure out some underhanded way to do it anyway.

Even though prosecutors and judges haven't been able to ban plea bargaining, their attempts to do so were still important. Those attempts pushed back on the conventional wisdom that plea bargaining is a good thing. They forced people who want to keep plea bargaining to mount a defense, and that defense rings pretty hollow. The major reason to have plea bargaining is that we don't want to take the time and effort to actually prove who is guilty. That's a hard position to defend, and it may cause people to rethink whether we want to give prosecutors more tools—like harsh mandatory minimum sentences—that make plea bargaining even easier for them.

And even though efforts to ban plea bargaining might have ultimately failed, they still made a real difference. By changing the expectations around plea bargaining, these bans also changed other practices. For example, in both Alaska and El Paso, prosecutors made significant changes to their charging practices. Prior to the plea bargaining ban, police were allowed to make charging decisions in Alaska. When the attorney general announced the ban, he also announced that prosecutors would begin deciding what charges to file and that they would use a higher standard than the police had used. This change not only resulted in weaker cases never being filed but also required police to perform better investigations than before—improvements that were widely celebrated.

In El Paso, prosecutors had always been responsible for charging decisions, and the plea bargaining ban wasn't accompanied by any formal changes to charging policies. Nonetheless, charging practices changed. In particular, the ban made overcharging—that is, including charges that were probably more serious than what the evidence supported—less frequent. As one prosecutor explained, he became more conservative in his charging decisions—making sure not to overcharge—because the ban made it more likely that a case would go to trial. If a case was overcharged, then a jury was more likely to acquit, which would be embarrassing for the office.

As these examples show, changing *expectations* about plea bargaining can change how the system is run more generally, even in cases where a defendant still pleads guilty. The threat of a jury trial makes prosecutors think about whether they can actually win at trial. If everyone *expects* a case to plea bargain, then prosecutors tend to make those decisions less carefully.

* * * * *

Some plea bargaining may be inevitable. But that doesn't mean we should just accept it without complaint. More important, that does not mean that the criminal justice system itself should be designed around plea bargaining or that we should adopt policies that make it easier for plea bargaining to take place. If anything, we should change the system to decrease prosecutors' leverage and to make sure that the bargains they strike are fair.

In order for these changes to implemented, we need to acknowledge how the widespread acceptance of plea bargaining has fundamentally warped our criminal justice system. It has caused lawmakers to make sentences longer and allowed prosecutors to evade all sorts of rights and protections for defendants. Perhaps most important, it has made it far too easy to punish people, and because it is so easy to do that, our jails and prisons are bursting at the seams.

People within the system can—and should—push back.

Judges should make prosecutors explain *in public* that they brought extra criminal charges just to force defendants to plead guilty. They should give defendants the right to see the evidence against them before accepting guilty pleas, and they should refuse to accept any plea bargains that require them to waive their right to the effective assistance of counsel, appeal, or other important nontrial rights. Judges should also refuse to play along with plea bargains that make a mockery of justice by requiring discussions about a case to happen in open court and by refusing to accept fictional pleas.

Prosecutors should use their power to reach bargains that are more just. And they should dismiss charges when there seem to be things that are wrong with their cases rather than just offering defendants better deals. In addition, prosecutors should criticize their colleagues when they fail to do the same.

Defense attorneys have much less power than judges and prosecutors to change the system. But they can tell their clients' stories and let the public know about the injustices that are being done in their name.

Actually, *all of us* should let people know about the injustices of our system—that we have created a system that is designed to impose punishment without trial. Letting people know was the reason I wrote this book. I want people to know what actually happens in our criminal justice system. I want them to know that people plead guilty because the system has been designed to pressure everyone—the guilty and the innocent alike—into giving up their constitutional right to a trial. I want people to know that our system has given up on finding the truth in criminal cases. Instead, it just tries to be efficient.

Plea bargaining didn't cause all of the problems with the criminal justice system. Juries convicted innocent people and sentences were often too harsh even before plea bargains were widely accepted. But plea bargaining has introduced new problems and made some of those old problems worse.

Convictions no longer tell us what a defendant actually did; they simply represent the end of a negotiation between lawyers. A defendant who pleads guilty to a low-level assault in Ohio may have committed that assault, he may have committed a rape, or he may be innocent of any crime. We do not know, and widespread acceptance of plea bargaining seems to tell us that we should not care.

Plea bargaining also stops us from making other parts of the criminal justice system better. Plea bargaining doesn't make society face the consequences of all of the crimes we've added to the books or the sentences that we've repeatedly lengthened. Instead, of having to give everyone who is swept up in the system a fair chance to show they are innocent, we cycle them through the courtrooms quickly, promising to knock months, years, or even decades off sentences that were much longer than they needed to be.

Plea bargaining also doesn't prompt us to make our system more accurate. If a jury mistakenly convicts an innocent person after a trial, we can go back and look at the witnesses who testified and try to figure out what went wrong. But when we discover that an innocent person has pleaded guilty, we can't do the same analysis. Plea bargains don't give us a fully developed factual record, nor do we know whether the jury would have convicted the defendant. Neither police, nor prosecutors, nor judges, nor anyone else in the criminal justice system has to take responsibility for falsely convicting the defendant; instead they can lay the blame at the feet of the defendant because she made the "choice" to plead guilty.

* * * * *

We need to stop seeing our current system as normal. It shouldn't be easy to punish people. It should be hard. We should be able to punish people only if we are willing to spend time, money, and effort to do so. If we aren't willing to endure expense and inconvenience to punish someone, then maybe we don't care that much about the crime that they committed. If we do care enough about a crime to punish someone, then we should make that decision openly, as a community, using procedures that protect the person we think committed a crime.

After all, it shouldn't be easy for the government to punish its citizens. It should be a trial.

ACKNOWLEDGMENTS

This book never would have been written if not for the help and encouragement of many people.

I am indebted to the men and women who allowed me to interview them. Although only snippets of what they said made it into print, their stories deeply influenced how the book was written.

In addition to individual stories, this book includes insights from academic articles, news media reporting, and data. I had a lot of help gathering those materials. Nicole Downing, Melissa Hyland, Aaron Kirschenfeld, and the rest of the staff at UNC's Katherine R. Everett Law Library were absolute wizards when it came to tracking down difficult-to-locate sources. Aaron was especially helpful in helping me find the data I needed, as were Jeff Asher and John Pfaff. I was also lucky to have a series of hardworking UNC Law student research assistants: Andrew Coyle, Zachary Gorelick, Alexandra Lawson, and Logan Rigsbee.

When I first sat down to write this book, I struggled with how to make all my ideas fit together. And so I'm thankful to Sheldon Gilbert, Clark Neilly, and Scott Greenfield for early conversations that helped shape the book. Once I started writing, I often worried whether I said something wrong. Luckily, I was able to get incredibly helpful feedback from fellow law professors Shima Baradaran Baughman, Thea Johnson, Andrew Kent, and Will Ortman, who read drafts of various chapters.

I never would have been able to write this book without the support of the University of North Carolina School of Law. Dean Martin Brinkley gave me the time and resources that I needed to write this book, and so many of my colleagues gave me their encouragement and support, especially Andrew Chin, Joe Kennedy, Eric Muller, and Rick Su. Melissa Jacoby and Max Eichner gave me fantastic advice about how to turn ideas into a book, and they also inspire me to work harder every day.

Some of the data on state legislation and prosecutor lobbying that I mention in this book comes from a research project funded by a generous gift from the Charles Koch Foundation. Many UNC Law students, Amy Ullrick, and Jessica Pishko have worked tirelessly to gather and analyze that data.

I especially have to thank Toby Stock, whose only somewhat-joking question "Do you ever worry that the stuff you write doesn't make a difference?" inspired me to tell him about a book on plea bargaining that I wanted to write someday. Lucky for me, Toby asked that question in front of Margy Slattery, who was kind enough to tell me about a literary agent she'd just met. She offered to introduce me to him, and that is how I met the indefatigable Matt Carlini at Javelin.

Matt is everything I could have hoped for in an agent, and then more. He helped me translate my sometimes archaic and often rambling abstract thoughts about the criminal justice system into a series of stories—stories that I hope will change the way that people think about criminal justice. And most important, he convinced the good people at Abrams Press that they should take a chance on a first-time author from North Carolina.

More than anyone, Andy Hessick made this book a reality. He is the smartest person I know, the love of my life, and my best friend. He makes me think, reads my drafts, and keeps our family fed and on schedule. I never could have written a book if it weren't for his constant support.

NOTES

Chapter 1

2 **an Alford plea, a special type of guilty plea that allows a defendant to be convicted without admitting that he'd actually committed the crime:** *North Carolina v. Alford*, 400 U.S. 25 (1970).

4 **Annie Dookhan, a chemist with the Massachusetts state drug lab, admitted that she had contaminated samples and faked test results:** Katie Mettler, "How a lab chemist went from 'superwoman' to disgraced saboteur of more than 20,000 drug cases," *Washington Post* (Apr. 21, 2017), washingtonpost .com/news/morning-mix/wp/2017/04/21/how-a-lab-chemist-went-from -superwoman-to-disgraced-saboteur-of-more-than-20000-drug-cases/

4 **many served time in jail and prison before that happened:** Patrick G. Lee, "Thousands of Potentially Wrongful Convictions; Years of Delayed Action," *ProPublica* (Nov. 10, 2016).

4 **San Francisco:** Associated Press, "San Francisco crime lab scandal strains justice system," *Deseret News* (Apr. 3, 2010).

4 **Houston:** Brian Rogers, "Scores of cases affected after HPD crime lab analyst ousted," *Houston Chronicle* (Jun. 18, 2014).

4 **Oklahoma City:** Lois Romano, "Police Chemist's Missteps Cause Okla. Scandal," *Washington Post* (Nov. 26, 2001).

4 **and St. Paul:** Madeleine Baran, "Troubled St. Paul crime lab problems even worse than first thought, probe reveals," MPR News (Feb. 14, 2013), mprnews .org/story/2013/02/14/troubled-st-paul-crime-lab-problems-even-worse -than-first-thought-probe-reveals.

4 **Police departments across the country use these tests:** Ryan Gabrielson & Topher Sanders, "Busted," *ProPublica* (Jul. 7, 2016).

4 **But it also turns blue for more than eighty other substances, including some acne medications and common household cleaning materials:** Ryan Gabrielson & Topher Sanders, "Busted," *ProPublica* (Jul, 7, 2016). Additional information can be found at documentcloud.org/documents/2801460-Spot -Tests-a-Color-Chart-Reference-for-Forensic.html#document/p2/a305872.

5 **police departments often fail to train their officers to use them correctly:** Topher Sanders & Ryan Gabrielson, "Confusion Over Drug Tests Highlights Lack of Training for Florida Officers," *ProPublica* (Nov. 22, 2016).

7 **there is no single "system" of criminal justice in our country:** Ames Grewart, "How to Fix the Federal Criminal Justice System (in Part)," Brennan Center (Jan. 2, 2020), brennancenter.org/our-work/research-reports/how -fix-federal-criminal-justice-system-part ("People often talk about reforming 'the criminal justice system.' But there is no single such system in the United States. When counting state and local jurisdictions, there are really thousands of 'systems,' all with their own distinct challenges.").

9 **prosecuted by attorneys who are White:** David A. Graham, "Most States Elect No Black Prosecutors," *Atlantic* (Jul. 7, 2015).

9   **sentenced by judges who are White:** Malia Reddick, Michael J. Nelson, and Rachel Paine Caufield, "Racial and Gender Diversity on State Courts," 48 *Judges' Journal* 28 (2009), judicialselection.us/uploads/documents/Racial_and_Gender_Diversity_on_Stat_8F60B84D96CC2.pdf.

9   **written by people who are overwhelmingly White:** Teresa Wiltz, "Why State Legislatures Are Still Pretty White," *Governing* (Dec. 9, 2015), governing .com/topics/politics/legislative-boundaries-lack-of-connections-lead-to-few -minority-lawmakers.html.

9   **the mountain of studies that show how Black and Brown Americans are disproportionately affected by the criminal justice system:** Elizabeth Hinton, LeShae Henderson, and Cindy Reed, "An Unjust Burden: The Disparate Treatment of Black Americans in the Criminal Justice System," *Vera Evidence Brief* (May 2018), vera.org/downloads/publications/for-the-record-unjust -burden-racial-disparities.pdf (collecting studies).

9   **developed a national reputation for refusing to convict defendants, even in the face of overwhelming evidence:** John Kifner, "Bronx Juries: a Defense Dream, a Prosecution Nightmare," *New York Times* (Dec. 5, 1988).

9   **writing powerful opinions:** *Blakely v. Washington*, 542 U.S. 296, 306 (2004).

10   **he accepted plea bargaining "as a necessary evil" because "without it our long and expensive process of criminal trial could not sustain the burden imposed on it, and our system of criminal justice would grind to a halt.":** *Lafler v. Cooper*, 566 U.S. 156, 185 (2012) (Scalia, J. dissenting).

Chapter 2

11   **He immigrated to the colony of New York with his family in 1710, while he was still a boy:** Arthur E. Sutherland, review of *A Brief Narrative of the Case and Trial of John Peter Zenger*, by James Alexander, ed. Stanley Nider Katz (Cambridge, Massachusetts: Belknap Press, 1963), in 77 *Harvard Law Review* 787, 787 (1964).

11   **After his father died, John served as an apprentice to William Bradford, the first printer in New York:** H.V. Kaltenborn, foreword to *The Trial of Peter Zenger*, ed. Vincent Buranelli (New York University Press, 1957); William Lowell Putnam, *John Peter Zenger and the Fundamental Freedom* 11 (Jefferson, North Carolina: McFarland & Company, 1997).

11   **The *New-York Weekly Journal* reported on these stories, accusing Cosby of tyranny and violating the colonists' rights.:** Introduction to *The Trial of Peter Zenger*, 24–30; William Lowell Putnam, 57–59.

11   **That criticism often took the form of satire and lampoons:** William Lowell Putnam, 19.

11   **So he decided to shut down the *Journal* by arresting John:** William Lowell Putnam, 59–63.

11   **Because there was no real dispute that John had published the *Journal* and that the *Journal* had criticized Governor Cosby, it looked like John was going to be convicted:** Arthur E. Sutherland, 787–88.

12   **he told the jury that they should consider whether the statements in the newspaper were true:** *The Trial of Peter Zenger*, 109–112.

12   **the case wasn't just about "one poor printer." It was a case that "may in its consequence affect every free man that lives under a British government on the main of America. It is the best cause. It is the cause of liberty.":** *The Trial of Peter Zenger*, 131.

12   **After a brief deliberation, the jury returned a verdict of not guilty:** The *Trial of Peter Zenger*, 132.

12   **People often point to the Zenger case as convincing the public about the necessity of a free press:** H.V. Kaltenborn, foreword to *The Trial of Peter Zenger*.

12   **colonial juries routinely refused to convict their peers of violating unfair laws, like the Stamp Act:** Nino C. Monea, "Bulwark of Equality: The Jury in America," 122 *West Virginia Law Review* 513, 527–28 (2019).

12   **The British government responded by allowing these cases to be tried by judges without any juries:** Nino C. Monea, 513, 528–29.

12   **One of the specific complaints against King George III in the Declaration of Independence was that he deprived the colonists of trial by jury:** *Duncan v. Louisiana*, 391 U.S. 145, 151–53 (1968).

12   **A big portion of that constitution is devoted to protecting the rights of people accused of crimes:** Carissa Byrne Hessick & Joseph E. Kennedy, "Criminal Clear Statement Rules," 97 *Washington University Law Review* 351, 382–83 (2019).

13   **Their commitment to this principle was embodied by one of the most famous legal sayings of all time: "It is better that ten guilty persons escape than that one innocent suffer.":** William Blackstone, *Commentaries on the Laws of England: Book the Fourth* 352 (Oxford: Clarendon Press, 1765–1770). For a discussion of the importance of this saying and this concept, see Alexander Volokh, "*n* Guilty Men," 146 *University of Pennsylvania Law Review* 173, 174–77 (1997).

13   **the jury trial is arguably the most important:** *Blakely v. Washington*, 542 U.S. 296, 305–306 (2004) (describing the jury as "no mere procedural formality, but a fundamental reservation of power in our constitutional structure. Just as suffrage ensures the people's ultimate control in the legislative and executive branches, jury trial is meant to ensure their control in the judiciary."); Jamal Greene, "Foreword: Rights as Trumps?," 132 *Harvard Law Review* 28, 112 (2018) (citing John Adams).

13   **All of the state constitutions also protect the right to a jury trial in criminal cases:** *Duncan v. Louisiana*, 391 U.S. 145, 153–54 (1968).

14   **"Criminal justice today is for the most part a system of pleas, not a system of trials.":** *Lafler v. Cooper*, 566 U.S. 156, 170 (2012).

14   **The Revolutionary War was fought, in large part, as a resistance to this conspiracy:** Bernard Bailyn, *Ideological Origins of the American Revolution* (Cambridge, Massachusetts: Harvard University Press, 1968).

14   **evidence of guilty pleas dating back at least to the late sixteenth century.** J.S. Cockburn, "Trial by the Book? Fact and Theory in the Criminal Process, 1558–1625," in *Legal Records and the Historian*, ed. J.H. Baker, 60, 73 (1978).

14   **guilty pleas were relatively rare; most defendants pleaded not guilty and went to trial:** Albert W. Alschuler, "Plea Bargaining and Its History," 13 *Law and Society Review* 211, 214 (1979).

14   **trial judges would resist accepting the plea and encourage the defendant to go to trial:** John H. Langbein, "On the Myth of Written Constitutions: The Disappearance of Criminal Jury Trial," 15 *Harvard Journal of Law and Public Policy* 119, 120 (1992); Albert W. Alschuler, "Plea Bargaining and Its History," 13 *Law and Society Review* 211, 214–15 (1979); Albert W. Alschuler, "Plea Bargaining and Its History," 79 *Columbia Law Review* 1, 9–11 (1979).

14   **only 15 percent of people convicted of felonies pleaded guilty in 1839:** Raymond Moley, *Politics and Criminal Prosecution* (New York: Minton, Balch & Company, 1929).

14   **Even in Boston, which some say was an early adopter of plea bargaining:** Mary E. Vogel, *Coercion to Compromise: Plea Bargaining, the Courts, and the Making of Political Authority* 5 (Oxford: Oxford University Press, 2007).

14   **only 35 percent of convictions were the result of guilty pleas at that time:** Mary E. Vogel, 344n8.

15   **It was because trials were such an important part of early American society that some judges were hesitant to accept guilty pleas:** Mary E. Vogel, 91; John H. Langbein, "Understanding the Short History of Plea Bargaining," 13 *Law and Society Review* 261, 264–65 (1979) (citing Matthew Hale).

15   **Judges would refuse to accept guilty pleas until defendants had time to reconsider, and judges would sometimes appoint lawyers to advise defendants or make sure that the defendants weren't suffering from mental illness:** Albert W. Alschuler, "Plea Bargaining and Its History," 13 *Law & Society Review*. 211, 215–17 (1979).

15   **But even before judges gained the power to tailor punishment to individual defendants, they had some limited ability to recommend mercy:** John H. Langbein, "The Criminal Trial before the Lawyers," 45 *University of Chicago Law Review* 263, 297 (1978) (discussing judicial recommendations for pardon and commutation); Albert W. Alschuler, "Plea Bargaining and Its History," 13 *Law & Society Review*. 211, 217 (1979) ("In practice, therefore, judges did exercise substantial sentencing discretion through their recommendations of executive clemency, but this exercise of discretion apparently did not lead to the exchange of leniency for pleas of guilty.").

15   **then we have a plea bargain:** Some people have defined plea bargaining differently, which causes confusion. For example, historian Mary Vogel defines a plea bargain as "a defendant's entry of a guilty plea in anticipation of concessions from the prosecutor or judge." Mary E. Vogel, 91. But that's not a very good definition. The word "bargain" suggests two sides negotiating, not one party doing something in the hope that someone else will do something in return.

16   **The history of this shift from guilty pleas to plea bargains and trial penalties is murky:** Lawrence M. Friedman, "Plea Bargaining in Historical Perspective," 13 *Law and Society Review* 247, 247 (1979) (describing plea bargaining as "a fairly blank chapter in the history of criminal justice").

16   **it mostly occurred in secret:** Mary E. Vogel, 91–92 (noting that bargains only rarely appeared in court records, but they can be identified through "indirect clues" like reduction in charge or sentence when the guilty plea is entered).

16   **(A no contest plea is a way for a defendant to plead guilty without having to admit that he is, in fact, guilty.):** George Fisher, *Plea Bargaining's Triumph: A History of Plea Bargaining in America* 21–22 (Palo Alto, California: Stanford University Press, 2003).

16   **the best method to "attain the just end of all punishment"—namely, preventing crime and reforming defendants:** George Fisher, 30–31.

16   **plea bargained even more cases than Huntington:** George Fisher, 32.

16   **many state courts refused to uphold guilty pleas when the defendants had pleaded guilty because of pressure from prosecutors or trial judges:** Albert W. Alschuler, "Plea Bargaining and Its History," 13 *Law and Society Review* 211, 224–26 (1979) (collecting and describing cases).

16   **The Michigan court called this behavior by the trial judge a "great impropriety," adding that that "no sort of pressure can be permitted to bring the party to forego any right or advantage however slight.":** *O'Hara v. People*, 41 Mich. 623, 624 (1879).

17   **prosecutors had no authority to enter into that agreement with the defendants, and so the seizure could go forward:** *The Whiskey Cases*, 99 U.S. 594 (1878).

17   **increased steadily during the mid- and late nineteenth century:** Albert W. Alschuler, "Plea Bargaining and Its History," 13 *Law and Society Review* 211, 223 (1979).

17   **plea bargaining increased significantly beginning in the 1870s:** George Fisher, 112–13.

17   **it is fair to assume at least some of those guilty pleas were the result of under-the-table bargaining between prosecutors and defense attorneys:** Lawrence M. Friedman, 247, 249–51.

17   **many thought that the Constitution did not allow prosecutors to incentivize (or to pressure) defendants to give up their right to trial:** As one Georgia appellate court put it: "A 'plea of guilty,' being but a confession of guilt in open court, ought to be received with care and scanned with caution. It ought never to be received unless freely and voluntarily made, and if entered under a misapprehension as to its legal effect or the consequences which are to follow, honestly entertained because of representations made or inducements held out either by the court or by counsel for the state, the prisoner ought to be allowed to withdraw the plea, even after sentence, if he moves promptly upon discovering that he has been misled." *Griffin v. State*, 12 Ga. App. 615, 77 S.E. 1080, 1081 (1913).

17   **And when rumors of the practice reached the public, it was condemned as corrupt:** William Ortman, "When Plea Bargaining Became Normal," 100 *Boston University Law Review* 1435, 1446n62 (2020) (describing press accounts).

17   **And when bar associations and academics set out to study the criminal courts in the 1920s, they were surprised and shocked to discover that**

plea bargaining wasn't just a one-off occurrence: it was pervasive: Mark H. Haller, "Plea Bargaining: The Nineteenth Century Context," 13 *Law and Society Review* 273, 276 (1979); William Ortman, 1435, 1448–59.

18   the crime commission movement of the early twentieth century—a series of criminal justice surveys conducted in the 1920s and 1930s by public bodies, universities, and private civic associations in different cities and states: William Ortman, 1435, 1448.

18   "Criminal Justice in Cleveland," was prompted by two issues: rising crime in the city and the dramatic acquittal of a local judge for murder based on perjured testimony: William Ortman, 1435, 1449–50.

18   The study was led to two very prominent men: Roscoe Pound, who was the dean of Harvard Law School, and Felix Frankfurter, who was also on the faculty at Harvard and who would later go on to serve as a justice on the U.S. Supreme Court: William Ortman, 1435, 1449–53.

18   But even those defendants who were convicted often received only suspended sentences: William Ortman, 1435, 1453.

18   "With all these avenues of escape open," the report said, "it is not surprising that Cleveland has had extreme difficulty in punishing its criminals or in restraining crime by swift and certain justice": William Ortman, 1435, 1454 (quoting report).

18   they also discovered that those guilty pleas were the result of compromises between prosecutors and defendants: William Ortman, 1435, 1457–63.

19   Some called plea bargaining corrupt: William Ortman, 1435, 1463.

19   Others criticized prosecutors for using plea bargaining to inflate their conviction statistics to help them during reelection: William Ortman, 1435, 1462.

19   according to the commissions, caused distrust and disrespect for the law: William Ortman, 1435, 1460–62.

19   only after a committee of appellate judges conducted an inquiry and concluded that prosecutors rather than the judges were responsible for the plea bargains: Albert W. Alschuler, "Plea Bargaining and Its History," 13 *Law and Society Review* 211, 232 (1979); William Ortman, 1435, 1460–61.

19   one half of them were allowed to plead guilty to a lesser crime and escape the life sentence: William Ortman, 1435, 1461.

19   those on the crime commissions wanted to create a more efficient criminal justice system: William Ortman, 1435, 1463–66.

20   as Professor Ortman argues, one example of a larger shift in legal theory: William Ortman, 1435, 1472–85.

20   Guilty Pleas as a % of Adjudicated Cases table is based on data in the statistical appendices to Ronald F. Wright, "Trial Distortion and the End of Innocence in Federal Criminal Justice," 154 *University of Pennsylvania Law Review* 79 (2005), which are available at http://ssrn.com/abstract=809124.

20   did the U.S. Supreme Court make clear that plea bargaining was, in fact, constitutional: The Supreme Court had suggested that it would permit plea

bargaining in some cases during the 1960s, but the question was definitively answered only in *Santobello v. New York*, 404 U.S. 257 (1971).

21   **it "made the risk of death the price of a jury trial.":** *Brady v. United States*, 397 U.S. 742, 745–46 (1970) (describing the outcome of *United States v. Jackson*, 390 U.S. 570 (1968)).

21   **that "there is little to differentiate Brady" from a defendant who pleaded guilty because his lawyer told him that "the judge is normally more lenient with defendants who pleaded guilty rather than with those who go to trial":** *Brady v. United States*, 397 U.S. 742, 751 (1970).

22   **"No sort of pressure can be permitted to bring the party to forego any right or advantage however slight,":** *O'Hara v. People*, 41 Mich. 623, 624 (1879)

22   **they said plea bargaining "is to be encouraged.":** *Santobello v. New York*, 404 U.S. 257, 260 (1971)

22   **that plea bargaining was "highly desirable":** *Santobello v. New York*, 404 U.S. 257, 261 (1971).

22   **and "an essential component of the administration of justice.":** *Santobello v. New York*, 404 U.S. 257, 260 (1971).

22   **The *Brady* opinion explained "that at present well over three-fourths of the criminal convictions in this country rest on pleas of guilty, a great many of them no doubt motivated at least in part by the hope or assurance of a lesser penalty than might be imposed if there were a guilty verdict after a trial to judge or jury.":** *Brady v. United States*, 397 U.S. 742, 751–52 (1970).

23   **the *Santobello* opinion said, "the States and the Federal Government would need to multiply by many times the number of judges and court facilities.":** *Santobello v. New York*, 404 U.S. 257, 260 (1970).

23   **he added that the number would have to triple if only 70 percent of defendants pleaded guilty:** Chief Justice Warren Burger, "State of the Judiciary 1970," 56 *American Bar Association Journal* 929, 931 (1970).

23   **as prosecutions increased almost 70 percent in the final decades of the twentieth century, judicial staffing increased by only 11 percent and public defense lawyer staffing increased by only 4 percent:** Donald A. Dripps, "Charging as Sentencing," working paper available at https://papers. ssrn.com/sol3/papers.cfm?abstract_id=3427333, page 3 (collecting figures showing that the United States "made a major investment in policing and corrections" during the final decades of the twentieth century and that "[r]esources devoted to adjudication did not keep up").

24   **the formal procedures of modern trials contributed to the rise of guilty pleas and plea bargaining:** John H. Langbein, "Understanding the Short History of Plea Bargaining," 261.

24   **a single judge could hold multiple trials in a single day:** John H. Langbein, "The Criminal Trial Before the Lawyers," 263.

24   **increased from three and a half days to more than seven days during the 1960s:** Albert W. Alshuler, "Plea Bargaining and Its History," 79 *Columbia Law Review* 1, 38 (1979).

24   **In 1970, 81 percent of convictions in federal court were the result of guilty pleas:** The Bureau of Justice Statistics make this data available on its website, bjs.gov.

24   **it is difficult to obtain reliable data about what happens in state courts:** Stephen B. Burbank, "Keeping Our Ambition Under Control: The Limits of Data and Inference in Search for the Causes and Consequences of Vanishing Trials in Federal Court," 1 *Journal of Empirical Legal Studies* 571, 577 (2004).

24   **the rate of criminal trials dropped from 8.5 percent in 1976 to 3.3 percent in 2002:** Marc Galanter, "The Vanishing Trial: An Examination of Trials and Related Matters in Federal and State Courts," 1 *Journal of Empirical Legal Studies* 459, 510 (2004).

24   **New York had 2.91 percent of criminal cases proceed to trial, Michigan had 2.12 percent of cases go to trial, and Texas had fewer than 1 percent of cases go to trial:** John Gamlich, "Only 2% of federal criminal defendants go to trial, and most who do are found guilty," *Pew Research Center* (Jun. 11, 2019) pewresearch.org/fact-tank/2019/06/11/only-2-of-federal-criminal-defendants-go-to-trial-and-most-who-do-are-found-guilty/.

25   **some states have even passed laws charging defendants fees if they require the state to seat a jury and hold a trial:** T. Ward Frampton, "The Uneven Bulwark: How (and Why) Criminal Jury Rates Vary by State, 100 *California Law Review* 183, 207–214 (2012).

25   **charging people fees to vote *is* unconstitutional:** *Harper v. Virginia Board of Elections*, 383 U.S. 663 (1966).

25   **the number of trials has actually gone down:** Marc Galanter, 459, 493, 510.

25   **the number of trials has fallen even as the number of people employed in federal prosecutors' offices has increased:** *United States v. Walker*, 423 F.Supp.3d 281, 294 (S.D.W. Va. 2017).

26   **By 2016 that number plummeted to 2.79 trials per year:** *United States v. Walker*, 423 F.Supp.3d 281, 295 (S.D.W. Va. 2017).

26   **a prominent study found "no noticeable increase in the length of federal criminal trials" during that time period:** Marc Galanter, 459, 497.

26   **Those new institutions combined expertise and efficiency:** James Landis, *The Administrative Process* (New Haven, Connecticut: Yale University Press, 1938).

26   **many prominent lawyers and government officials began to criticize the jury trial as an institution:** Andrew Kent, "The Jury and Empire: The Insular Cases and the Anti-Jury Movement in the Gilded Age and Progressive Era," 91 *Southern California Law Review* 375, 398–406 (2018).

26   **Taft called the criminal justice system "a disgrace to our civilization":** Taft, "Delays and Defects in the Enforcement of Law in This Country," 187 *North American Review* 851, 857 (1908).

26   **Taft successfully argued against expanding the jury trial right to new American territories:** Taft, "The Administration of Criminal Law," 15 *Yale Law Journal* 1 (1905).

27   **the "science" of modern law should focus more on preventing crime and protecting the community:** Taft, "The Administration of Criminal Law," 1.

27   **criticized the criminal justice system as too protective of individual rights and not concerned enough with convicting guilty people and protecting the community:** Andrew Kent, 395–96 (collecting sources).

27   **The jury trial was criticized as "an intolerable burden":** Alfred C. Coxe, "Trials of Jury Trials," 1 *Columbia Law Review* 286, 289 (1901).

27   **that was "destroying the certainty of punishment.":** Hal W. Greer, "Should Trial by Jury Be Abolished?," 42 *American Law Review* 192, 197 (1908).

27   **characterized as "lawlessness.":** Thomas J. Kernan, "The Jurisprudence of Lawlessness," 29 *Annual Report of the American Bar Association* 450 (1906).

27   **Americans had "no reason to fear oppression of the people by those in authority.":** M. Romero, "Anglo-Saxon and Roman Systems of Criminal Jurisprudence," 8 *The Green Bag* 410, 411 (1896).

27   **they argued, the jury trials were no longer necessary to protect individual liberty:** Hal W. Greer, 192, 194.

27   **"The evils of our jury system are so glaring, and so promotive of crime, that it is surprising that neither the judiciary nor the bar have before now made any effort to reform it":** "Our Jury System," *Nation* (May 9, 1895): 357.

27   **characterizing jurors as either corrupt or ignorant:** F.J. Cabot, "Is Trial by Jury, in Criminal Cases, a Failure?", in 33 *Arena*, ed. B.O. Flower, 510, 511 (1905).

27   **though certainly not all:** Andrew Kent, 408–11 (identifying some people who opposed the anti-jury sentiment of the late-nineteenth and early twentieth century).

28   **a potential reason that plea bargaining increased in the late nineteenth and early twentieth century:** Lawrence M. Friedman and Robert V. Percival, *The Roots of Justice: Crime and Punishment in Alameda County, California, 1870–1910* (Chapel Hill: University of North Carolina Press, 1981).

28   **During that time police became more professional, district attorneys became full-time public employees, and the system grew to include other experts, such as probation officers and parole boards:** Lawrence M. Friedman and Robert V. Percival, 311.

28   **"Plea bargaining," they explain, "was part of the new system; it was part of a more 'rational,' 'professional' process.":** Lawrence M. Friedman and Robert V. Percival, 195.

28   **justified their deference to prosecutors' decisions because prosecutors are in a much better position to make decisions about policy priorities and resources:** *Wayte v. United States*, 470 U.S. 598, 607 (1985).

28   **the Supreme Court declared that the jury trial is a "fundamental right" and no state can punish a defendant for more than six months in jail without giving him the right to a jury:** *Duncan v. Louisiana*, 391 U.S. 145 (1968).

28   **judges have often given speeches and written opinions talking about the importance of the jury:** Judge Randy Wilson, "What do judges

say about the jury system?," *Texas Bar Blog* (May 2, 2017), https://blog
.texasbar.com/2017/05/articles/jury/guest-blog-what-do-judges-say
-about-the-jury-system/; Layne Smith, Ask Judge Smith: "My patriotic,
flag-waving jury service speech," *Tallahassee Democrat* (Oct. 26, 2019),
tallahassee.com/story/life/2019/10/26/my-patriotic-flag-waving-jury
-service-speech/2453814001/; "Judge William G. Young Speech at Judicial
Luncheon The Florida Bar's Annual Convention in Orlando," *Florida Bar
News & Journal* (Jul. 15, 2007), floridabar.org/the-florida-bar-news/judge
-william-g-youngs-speech-at-annual-convention/.

29   **it has been roundly criticized:** Kate Stith & José A. Cabranes, *Fear of Judging:
Sentencing Guidelines in the Federal Courts* 60–61 (Chicago: University of
Chicago Press, 1998); Bernard E. Harcourt, "From the Ne'er-Do-Well to the
Criminal History Category: The Refinement of the Actuarial Model in Criminal
Law," 66 *Law & Contemporary. Problems* 99, 123–26 (2003).

29   **the Sentencing Commission hasn't been required to justify its decisions,
which are shielded from judicial review:** Kate Stith & José A. Cabranes,
40, 208–09n20.

29   **they adapt to the system and start plea bargaining like everyone else:**
Milton Heumann, *Plea Bargaining: The Experiences of Prosecutors, Judges, and
Defense Attorneys* (Chicago: University of Chicago Press, 1981).

29   **as Professor Ortman put it, "normal.":** William Ortman, 1435.

30   **The cultural expectations shifted, and so did most people's behavior:**
Diana Crane, *Fashion and Its Social Agendas: Class, Gender, and Identity in
Clothing* (Chicago: University of Chicago Press, 2000).

30   **"enables the assistant district attorney and the defense lawyer to
bargain on the middle ground of what experience has shown to be 'justice' without the defense running the risk of the occasional [murder]
conviction which carries a mandatory minimum of life imprisonment
and without the Commonwealth tying up a jury room for 3 to 5 days
and running the risk of acquittal.":** Arlen Specter, review of *Conviction:
The Determination of Guilt or Innocence Without Trial,* by Donald J. Newman
(Boston: Little, Brown & Co., 1966), in 76 *Yale Law Journal* 604, 606–07 (1967).

31   **his office was less likely to plea bargain than others:** Arlen Specter, 604,
605–06.

32   **The United States has the highest incarceration rate in the Western
world:** Sintia Radu, "Countries with the Highest Incarceration Rates," *U.S.
News & World Report* (May 13, 2019), usnews.com/news/best-countries/
articles/2019–05–13/10-countries-with-the-highest-incarceration-rates (citing data from the World Prison Brief, an online database hosted by the Institute
for Criminal Policy Research at the University of London).

32   **We have increased our prison populations even as crime has been falling:** John F. Pfaff, *Locked In: The True Causes of Mass Incarceration and How
to Achieve Real Reform* 2, figure 1 (New York: Basic Books, 2017).

32   **In the federal system, for example, although the percentage of pleas
would rise and fall, they never fell below 50 percent:** Statistical

appendices to Ronald F. Wright, 79, available at http://ssrn.com/abstract
=809124.

33   **Guilty Pleas and Mass Incarceration table**: The table was created based
on data drawn from the Bureau of Justice Statistics Prisoners Series, the
Administrative Office of the Courts Criminal Justice Sourcebook, and statistical appendices to Ronald F. Wright, 79, which are available at http://ssrn.com/
abstract=809124.

33   **But our incarceration rate continued to rise even as crime rate
went down:** John F. Pfaff, 9, figure 3; charts are based on Bureau of Justice
Statistics data.

33   **"even as the number of arrests declined, the number of felony cases
filed in state courts rose sharply.":** John F. Pfaff, 127.

33   **By the time that the increase in incarceration per crime began to level
out—or at least not increase as dramatically—"the probability that
a prosecutor would file felony charges against an arrestee basically
doubled . . ."** John F. Pfaff, 127.

Chapter 3

36   **federal law allows judges to give you a higher sentence if they think
you probably committed other crimes:** *United States v. Watts*, 519 U.S. 148
(1997).

37   **We can do this by calculating what economists call the "expected punishment.":** John F. Pfaff, *Sentencing Law and Policy* 38–39 (Foundation Press,
2016) (using the term "expected penalty").

38   **That's actually what everyone thought about Joseph Tigano:** *United
States v. Tigano*, 880 F.3d 602 (2d Cir. 2018).

39   **"some other psychological problem that's going to prevent him from
understanding the difference between what he potentially looks at as
far as a conviction as well as what's being offered by way of this plea.":**
United States v. Tigano, 880 F.3d 602, 609 (2d Cir. 2018).

39   **At that point, both he and Joseph had sat in jail for four years:** Alan
Feuer, "Court Clears Man Who Waited 7 Years for Trial on Pot Charges," *New
York Times* (Jan. 23, 2018).

40   **As a result, the two major political parties have sometimes tried
to outdo each other to see who can be the harshest when it comes
to crime:** William J. Stuntz, "Unequal Justice," 121 *Harvard Law Review*
1969, 1998 (2008) (characterizing this as a "bidding war" between the
parties).

40   **political bidding war between Republicans and Democrats, who were
both trying to win the votes of people who were afraid of America's
growing drug problem:** Elise Viebeck, "How an early Biden crime bill created
the sentencing disparity for crack and cocaine trafficking," *Washington Post*
(Jul. 28, 2019).

40   **numerous examples of the Department of Justice and the National
Association of Assistant U.S. Attorneys, a lobbying group of federal**

prosecutors, opposing federal criminal justice reform: Shon Hopwood, "The Misplaced Trust in DOJ's Expertise on Criminal Justice Policy," 118 *Michigan Law Review* 1181 (2020).

40   **a federal law that would have reduced mandatory minimum sentences for certain nonviolent drug defendants:** "Sentencing Reform and Corrections Act of 2017," Senate Bill 1917, 115th Congress (2017–2018).

40   **claiming that this law would "make it more difficult for law enforcement to pursue the most culpable drug dealers and secure their cooperation to pursue others . . .":** Shon Hopwood, 1181, 1191 (quoting Letter from Lawrence Leiser, National Association of Assistant U.S. Attorneys, et al. to Charles E. Grassley, Chair, Committee on the Judiciary, U.S. Senate, and Dianne Feinstein, Ranking Member, Committee on the Judiciary, U.S. Senate (Nov. 2, 2017)).

41   **precisely because they *want* to give prosecutors this sort of leverage:** William J. Stuntz, "The Pathological Politics of Criminal Law," 100 *Michigan Law Review* 505 (2001).

41   **So now a person who sells 28 grams of crack cocaine (instead of just 5 grams) will receive the same five-year mandatory minimum sentence as a person who sells 500 grams of powder cocaine:** 21 U.S.C. § 841(b)(1)(B).

41   **But legislation to change the mandatory minimum sentences themselves didn't pass:** For example, the Sentencing Reform and Corrections Act of 2017 did not pass.

41   **"That is an intended goal of current Federal sentencing policy, to put pressure on defendants to cooperate in exchange for a lower sentence so evidence against more responsible criminals can be attained.":** 161 Congressional Record S955-02, S963 (daily ed. Feb. 12, 2015) (statement of Sen. Grassley).

43   **Indeed, many times when a legislator introduces a bill for a new criminal law, that law covers behavior that is already illegal:** Erik Luna, "The Overcriminalization Phenomenon," 54 *American Criminal Law Review* 703, 708 (2005).

43   **a law making it a crime to make false statements to federal officials:** 18 U.S.C. §1001.

43   **A 1998 study found that there were 642 separate sections in the federal criminal code about crimes involving false statements to government officials:** Ronald L. Gainer, "Federal Criminal Code Reform: Past and Future," 2 *Buffalo Criminal Law Review* 45, 62 (1998).

45   **"as an unwritten but nevertheless strictly enforced threat by judges to intimidate defendants" into pleading guilty:** Malcolm M. Feeley, *The Process Is the Punishment: Handling Cases in a Lower Criminal Court* 196 (New York: Russell Sage Foundation, 1979).

45   **The minimum term will be twenty years in the penitentiary.":** Albert W. Alschuler, "The Trial Judge's Role in Plea Bargaining, Part I," 76 *Columbia Law Review* 1059, 1089 (1976).

45   **Judges resent these defendants for making everyone—including the judges themselves—go through the time and effort of a trial:** Malcolm M. Feeley, 196–197.

46   **their average sentence was more than twelve years:** National Association of Criminal Defense Lawyers, *The Trial Penalty: The Sixth Amendment Right to Trial on the Verge of Extinction and How to Save It* 20, figure 1 (2018), nacdl.org/getattachment/95b7f0f5–90df-4f9f-9115–520b3f58036a/the-trial-penalty -the-sixth-amendment-right-to-trial-on-the-verge-of-extinction-and-how -to-save-it.pdf.

46   **even back in the 1970s the average defendant who insisted on a jury trial received a sentence that was three times longer than those of the defendants who pleaded guilty:** Albert W. Alschuler, "The Trial Judge's Role in Plea Bargaining, Part I," 76 *Columbia Law Review* 1059, 1082–83 (1976) (describing data from the Administrative Office of the United States Courts).

46   **Some people say that the trial penalty doesn't punish people for exercising their right to a trial; it just grants a benefit (a shorter sentence) to those who are willing to plead guilty:** Ben Grunwald, "Distinguishing Plea Discounts and Trial Penalties," 37 *Georgia State University Law Review* 261, 276–81 (2021) (explaining whether to describe the difference in sentences as trial penalty or a plea discount is a question of baselines).

46   **The courts don't usually let government officials force you to waive your constitutional rights even if they give you something in return:** Rachel Elise Barkow, *Prisoners of Politics: Breaking the Cycle of Mass Incarceration* 187–88 (Cambridge, Massachusetts: Belknap Press, 2019).

46   **But judges haven't extended their unconstitutional conditions cases to plea bargaining:** Jason Mazzone, "The Waiver Paradox," 97 *Northwestern University Law Review* 801 (2003).

47   **The Supreme Court admitted as much in a 1978 U.S. Supreme Court case, *Bordenkircher v. Hayes*:** Bordenkircher v. Hayes, 434 U.S. 357 (1978).

47   **The Supreme Court reaffirmed that it is "patently unconstitutional" for a government official to penalize people for exercising their "legal rights.":** *Bordenkircher v. Hayes*, 434 U.S. 357, 363 (1978).

47   **a "give-and-take negotiation" that occurs "between the prosecution and defense, which arguably possess relatively equal bargaining power.":** *Bordenkircher v. Hayes*, 434 U.S. 357, 362 (1978) (quoting *Parker v. North Carolina*, 397 U.S. 790, 809 (1970) (opinion of Brennan, J.).

47   **the prosecutor's interest at the bargaining table is to persuade the defendant to forgo his right to plead not guilty.":** *Bordenkircher v. Hayes*, 434 U.S. 357, 364 (1978).

47   **implies rejection of any notion that a guilty plea is involuntary in a constitutional sense . . .":** *Bordenkircher v. Hayes*, 434 U.S. 357, 363 (1978).

48   **Those attempts to justify plea bargaining describe a plea bargain as a contract between the prosecution and the defendant:** Robert E. Scott & William J. Stuntz, "Plea Bargaining as Contract," 101 *Yale Law Journal* 1909 (1992).

48   **"The defendant will trade the right to plead not guilty and force a trial for the prosecutor's right to seek the maximum sentence.":** Robert E. Scott & William J. Stuntz, 1914.

48   **the assumption is that they do not have the ability to try more than just a few cases, and so any threat by a defendant to take a case to trial has to be taken seriously:** Robert E. Scott & William J. Stuntz, 1924, 1941.

48   **a criminal defendant should be able to demand a shorter sentence in return for giving up a higher likelihood of acquittal at trial:** Stephanos Bibas, "Plea Bargaining Outside the Shadow of Trial," 117 *Harvard Law Review* 2463, 2465 (2004) (explaining [and ultimately critiquing] the "the classic shadow-of-trial model" of plea bargaining which "predicts that the likelihood of conviction at trial and the likely post-trial sentence largely determine plea bargains").

48   **People who defend plea bargains speak about these different plea bargains as "different prices.":** Robert E. Scott & William J. Stuntz, 1942.

48   **Any problems with innocent people who plead guilty as part of a plea bargain are recast as problems with trials, not plea bargains:** Frank H. Easterbrook, "Plea Bargaining as Compromise," 101 *Yale Law Journal* 1969 (1992).

48   **Similarly, they dismiss arguments about how the trial penalty and harsh sentences create too much pressure on defendants to plead guilty as criticisms of sentencing laws rather than plea bargaining:** Robert E. Scott & William J. Stuntz, 1920.

50   **many judges impose whatever sentence the prosecutor recommends:** Albert W. Alschuler, "The Trial Judge's Role in Plea Bargaining, Part I," 76 *Columbia Law Review* 1059, 1065–66 at n.25 (1976) (collecting sources).

51   **a judge who was "considered a maverick by prosecutors and defense attorneys alike"—followed the prosecutor's recommendation in approximately 90 percent of cases.** Albert W. Alschuler, "The Trial Judge's Role in Plea Bargaining, Part I," 76 *Columbia Law Review* 1059, 1063–64 (1976).

51   **a judge's options are limited to either imposing that sentence or rejecting the plea bargain altogether:** Federal Rule of Criminal Procedure 11(c)(1)(C).

51   **then it seems like the defendant got a raw deal:** Albert W. Alschuler, "The Trial Judge's Role in Plea Bargaining, Part I," 76 *Columbia Law Review* 1059, 1068–1073 (1976).

51   **Sentencing is one of the traditional powers of judges:** *Ex parte United States*, 242 U.S. 27, 41 (1916).

52   **the country responded by reducing their leverage:** "'Common Sense' Legislation: The Birth of Neoclassical Tort Reform," 109 *Harvard Law Review* 1765 (1996).

52   **laws that cap money damages or make it easy for companies to avoid courtrooms and send civil claims to arbitration:** Conn. Gen. Stat. 52–240b (capping punitive damages in products liability cases); Idaho Code Ann. § 6–1603(1) (capping non-economic damages); Article 75, New York Civil Procedure Practice and Rules (arbitration rules); Oh. Rev. Code § 2315.18

(capping non-economic damages); Virginia Code § 8.01–581.15 (capping damages in medical malpractice cases); 9 U.S.C. Section 1 et seq. (Federal Arbitration Act).

52 **a number of other constitutional rights, in addition to their right to a jury trial, in order to get a plea deal:** Susan R. Klein, et al., "Waiving the Criminal Justice System: An Empirical and Constitutional Analysis," 52 *American Criminal Law Review* 73 (2015).

53 **On November 30, 2001:** These facts are drawn from *Buffey v. Ballard*, 782 S.E.2d 204 (W.Va. 2015).

54 **Joseph served more than thirteen years in prison for a crime he didn't commit:** Joseph was finally released in 2015, following a decision by the West Virginia Supreme Court. *Buffey v. Ballard*, 782 S.E.2d 204 (W.Va. 2015).

54 **the famous Supreme Court case *Brady v. Maryland*:** *Brady v. Maryland*, 373 U.S. 83 (1963).

54 **The Supreme Court dismissed the argument in a unanimous decision:** *United States v. Ruiz*, 536 U.S. 622 (2002).

54 **if prosecutors did not continue to plea bargain "in a vast number" of cases, that would be a "radical" change—a change that they didn't think was justified "in order to achieve so comparatively small a constitutional benefit" as discovery for the defendant:** *United States v. Ruiz*, 536 U.S. 622, 632 (2002).

57 **The Arizona Supreme Court has said that a defendant can have her conviction reversed if a defense attorney fails to accurately explain the relative merits of the plea offer as compared to the expected sentence after trial and then the defendant goes to trial based on that bad legal advice:** *State v. Donald*, 198 Ariz. 406 (2000).

59 **It's actually a violation of the legal ethics rules, which specifically tell prosecutors not to ask people who don't have a lawyer for a "waiver of important pretrial rights.":** American Bar Association Model Rule of Professional Conduct 3.8(c); Pennsylvania Rule of Professional Conduct 3.8(c).

59 **almost never result in any discipline or other consequences:** Fred C. Zacharias, "The Professional Discipline of Prosecutors," 79 *North Carolina Law Review* 721 (2001).

60 **"should no longer seek in plea agreements to have a defendant waive claims of ineffective assistance of counsel . . .":** James Cole, Memorandum, Department Policy on Waivers of Claims of Ineffective Assistance of Counsel (Oct. 14, 2014), justice.gov/file/70111/download.

Chapter 4

63 **Some of those people prey on the others, inflicting horrific violence or acts of sexual abuse:** "Justice Department Finds Alabama Prison Conditions Unconstitutional," Equal Justice Initiative (Apr. 3, 2019), https://eji.org/news/justice-department-finds-alabama-prison-conditions-unconstitutional/.

63 **More than half of incarcerated prisoners suffer from mental illness:** Bureau of Justice Statistics, *Mental Health Problems of Prison and Jail Inmates* (Sept. 2006).

63   **can be so overwhelming that people in jail sometimes take their own lives:** Ryan J. Reilly, "Jeffrey Epstein Death Shines Light on Understaffed, Unaccountable Federal Prison System," *Huffington Post* (Aug. 15, 2019).

63   **The suicide rate in jail is much higher than the rate for people who are not incarcerated:** National Institute of Corrections, *National Study of Jail Suicide 20 Years Later* (April 2010).

63   **That's what happened to Jerome Hayes:** The facts of Jerome's case are taken from Topher Sanders's reporting: Topher Sanders, "Was locking up a man for 589 days only to dismiss the charges an injustice?," *Florida Times-Union* (Aug. 1, 2015); Topher Sanders, "T-U Investigation: Public Defender considers filing complaint over handling of Jerome Hayes case," *Florida Times-Union* (Aug. 3, 2015).

65   **a legal obligation to turn over evidence to defendants before trial—especially evidence that is helpful to a defendant's case:** *Giglio v. United States*, 405 U.S. 150 (1972); *Brady v. Maryland*, 373 U.S. 83 (1963); American Bar Association Model Rules of Professional Responsibility 3.8(d).

65   **And they are not allowed to lie about what evidence they do have:** American Bar Association Model Rules of Professional Responsibility 4.1(a).

66   **investigated by the Florida state bar for withholding evidence in Jerome's case:** Sebastian Kitchen, "Panel reviewing complaints against Jacksonville prosecutors," *Florida Times-Union* (Dec. 29, 2015).

66   **another case in which an innocent man was kept in jail for more than three years on murder and arson charges before prosecutors dismissed the charges.:** Andrew Pantazi, "A man spent 1,140 days in jail, then the prosecutor called the murder case 'weak,'" *Florida Times-Union* (Apr. 19, 2017).

67   **could not have been detained before trial:** Shima Baradaran Baughman, "The History of Misdemeanor Bail," 98 *Boston University Law Review* 837, 858–61 (2018).

68   **People who were charged with capital crimes were denied the right to bail:** Shima Baradaran Baughman, *The Bail Book: A Comprehensive Look at Bail in America's Criminal Justice System* 20 (Cambridge, UK: Cambridge University Press, 2018).

68   **Congress passed a law when it first met in 1789 that ensured all defendants were entitled to release pretrial except for those facing the death penalty:** Shima Baradaran Baughman, *The Bail Book: A Comprehensive Look at Bail in America's Criminal Justice System*, 20.

68   **Instead, the rule told judges to consider the crime the defendant was charged with, the strength of the evidence against him, the defendant's financial situation, and his character in setting the financial guarantee:** Shima Baradaran Baughman, *The Bail Book: A Comprehensive Look at Bail in America's Criminal Justice System*, 21–22.

68   **It passed a law trying to make sure that judges didn't set bail amounts too high and that judges didn't use pretrial detention to keep defendants from committing new crimes while awaiting trial.** H.R. Rep. No. 89–1541 (1966); Shima Baradaran Baughman, *The Bail Book: A Comprehensive Look at Bail in America's Criminal Justice System* 165–66.

69   **In 1984, Congress passed a new bail law:** The Bail Reform Act of 1984, 18 U.S.C. §§ 3141–3156.

69   **federal laws aimed at cracking down on crime, which had surged in the 1960s and 1970s:** William J. Stuntz, *The Collapse of American Criminal Justice* 227–243 (Cambridge, Massachusetts: Belknap Press, 2011) (describing the rise in crime and the political backlash).

69   **And it also blessed Congress's decision to make "dangerousness" part of the bail decision:** *United States v. Salerno*, 481 U.S. 739 (1987).

69   **But two hundred years later Congress and the courts had largely abandoned the view of pretrial detention as an exception rather than the rule:** Shima Baradaran Baughman, *The Bail Book: A Comprehensive Look at Bail in America's Criminal Justice System*, 18–27; Shima Baradaran, "Restoring the Presumption of Innocence," 72 *Ohio State Law Journal* 723 (2011).

69   **Then—remarkably—things got even worse:** These figures come from Shima Baradaran Baughman, *The Bail Book: A Comprehensive Look at Bail in America's Criminal Justice System*, 163–164.

70   **Even misdemeanor defendants are sometimes required to pay bail amounts of up to $20,000 to be released before trial:** Shima Baradaran Baughman, "Dividing Bail Reform," 105 *Iowa Law Review* 947, 1006–07 (2020).

70   **Nearly half a million people sit in jail every day in the United States because they cannot make bail:** Partick Liu, et al., Hamilton Project, *The Economics of Bail and Pretrial Detention* 13 (Dec. 2018), hamiltonproject.org/assets/files/BailFineReform_EA_121818_6PM.pdf.

70   **more than 80 percent of defendants charged with low-level crimes were unable to make bail that was set at less than $500:** New York City Comptroller, *The Public Cost of Private Bail: A Proposal to Ban Bail Bonds in NYC* 12 (Jan. 2018), https://comptroller.nyc.gov/wp-content/uploads/documents/The_Public_Cost_of_Private_Bail.pdf.

71   **One of those groups—Civil Rights Corps, an organization devoted to challenging systemic injustice in the American legal system—had a big win in Houston, Texas:** *ODonnell et al. v. Harris County, Texas*, 251 F.Supp.3d 1052 (S.D. Tex. 2017).

72   **The Supreme Court has said that poor people can't be sent to jail as punishment simply because they are unable to pay their fines:** *Bearden v. Georgia*, 461 U.S. 660 (1983).

72   **State courts and lower federal courts are split on the issue:** Congressional Research Service, *U.S. Constitutional Limits on State Money-Bail Practices for Criminal Defendants* 9–10 (Feb. 26, 2019), https://fas.org/sgp/crs/misc/R45533.pdf.

73   **the 2021 bail schedule in Los Angeles suggests that judges set bail at $25,000 for bribery and $50,000 for campaign finance violations:** Superior Court of California County of Los Angeles, 2021 Felony Bail Schedule 5, lacourt.org/division/criminal/pdf/felony.pdf.

73   **It has a population of more than 4.5 million people:** This figure is based on U.S. Census Population estimates, Jul. 1, 2019.

74   **Robert Ryan Ford was arrested for shoplifting from Walmart:** These facts are drawn from the Amended Complaint in *ODonnell et al. v. Harris County, Texas,* 251 F.Supp.3d 1052 (S.D. Tex. 2017), which can be found here: https://cdn.buttercms.com/R5BRcSFSvWo57Kr2Net1.

74   **After the hearing, the federal judge granted them something called a preliminary injunction:** *ODonnell et al. v. Harris County, Texas,* 251 F.Supp.3d 1052 (S.D. Tex. 2017).

75   **a judge has to find that a plaintiff (the person who brought the lawsuit) is likely to win at trial and that there will be irreparable damage or injury if the judge waits until trial to address the conduct underlying the lawsuit:** *Winter v. National Resources Defense Council,* 555 U.S. 7, 20 (2008).

75   **They appealed and managed to get some of the important parts of the judge's decision overruled:** *ODonnell v. Harris County, Texas,* 892 F.3d 147 (5th Cir. 2018).

75   **The November 2018 elections gave Democrats a majority of county commissioners, and all of the Republican judges lost their reelection campaigns in 2018:** Brian Rogers, "Republican judges swept out by voters in Harris County election," *Houston Chronicle* (Nov. 8, 2018), chron.com/news/houston-texas/houston/article/GOP-Free-Zone-Republican-judges-swept-out-by-13376806.php.

75   **a result that some saw as a "reckoning" for what they had done in the bail system:** Maura Ewing, "Harris County Judges May Face a Reckoning Over Bail on Election Day," *The Appeal* (Nov. 4, 2018), https://theappeal.org/harris-county-judges-may-face-a-reckoning-over-bail-on-election-day/.

75   **sweeping changes to the misdemeanor bail system in Houston:** Gabrielle Banks, "Federal judge gives final approval to Harris County bail deal," *Houston Chronicle* (Nov. 21, 2019).

77   **Studies also show that both Black and Hispanic defendants, as a group, have to pay higher bail amounts to be released than White defendants charged with the same crimes:** Shima Baradaran Baughman, *The Bail Book: A Comprehensive Look at Bail in America's Criminal Justice System,* 93.

77   **Shima and the economist concluded that judges could safely release many more people without increasing crime in those communities:** Shima Baradaran & Frank L. McIntyre, "Predicting Violence," 90 *Texas Law Review* 497 (2012).

78   **bail companies will cover the fee for defendants in return for a fee—usually 10 to 15 percent of the bail amount:** Shima Baradaran Baughman, *The Bail Book: A Comprehensive Look at Bail in America's Criminal Justice System,* 163–164; Andrew Davis, "How bail keeps people locked up for being poor, and led to a $2 billion private industry," CNBC (Nov. 14, 2019), cnbc.com/2019/11/14/who-makes-money-from-bail.html.

79   **For example, a number of people insist that the problems of mass incarceration are attributable to private prisons:** American Civil Liberties Union, *Banking on Bondage: Private Prisons and Mass Incarceration* 8 (Nov. 2011) ("The private prison industry helped to create the mass incarceration crisis and feeds off of this social ill."), aclu.org/files/assets/

bankingonbondage_20111102.pdf; Michael Cohen, "How for-profit prisons have become the biggest lobby no one is talking about," *Washington Post* (Apr. 28, 2015) ("CCA states that the company doesn't lobby on policies that affect 'the basis for or duration of an individual's incarceration or detention.' Still, several reports have documented instances when private-prison companies have indirectly supported policies that put more Americans and immigrants behind bars."); Chris Kirkham, "Prison Quotas Push Lawmakers To Fill Beds, Derail Reform," *Huffington Post* (Sept. 19, 2013) (noting that "contractually obligated promise to fill prison beds is a common provision in a majority of America's private prison contracts" and that "such requirements create an incentive for policymakers to focus on filling empty prison beds, as opposed to pursuing long-term policy changes, such as sentencing reform, that could significantly reduce prison populations").

79 **don't appear to be growing any faster than states without them:** John Pfaff, "Five myths about prisons," *Washington Post* (May 17, 2019).

79 **But the bail bond industry has repeatedly blocked attempts at bail reform:** Alex Vitale, "Bail Bond Industry Fights Back Against Reform," *The Appeal* (Jul. 27, 2017), https://theappeal.org/bail-bond-industry-fights-back-against-reform-b4bacb510140/.

80 **spending millions of dollars in campaign contributions and to lobby state lawmakers:** Ciara O'Neill, "Bail Bond Businesses Buck for Bookings," FollowTheMoney.org (Jun. 7, 2018), followthemoney.org/research/institute-reports/bail-bond-businesses-buck-for-bookings#section_3.

81 **His crime was minor, there was no reason to think that he wouldn't appear at his court dates, and he was getting treatment for his substance abuse problem:** Andrea Estes and Shelley Murphy, "Stopping injustice or putting the public at risk? Suffolk DA Rachael Rollins's tactics spur pushback," *Boston Globe* (Jul. 6, 2019).

81 **To be sure, some judges have said that it is unconstitutional to keep someone in jail because they are too poor to post bail:** *Pierce v. City of Velda City*, No. 4:15-cv-570, 2015 WL 10013006 (E.D. Mo. Jun. 3, 2015); *Walker v. City of Calhoun*, 4:15–CV–0170, 2016 WL 361612 (N.D. Ga. Jan. 28, 2016), reversed by 901 F.3d 1245 (11th Cir. 2018).

81 **And some appellate judges have refused to reverse those decisions:** United *States v. McConnell*, 842 F.2d 105 (5th Cir. 1988); United States ex rel. *Fitzgerald v. Jordan*, 747 F.2d 1120 (7th Cir. 1984).

81 **Sometimes judges are just doing what the prosecutors ask for:** Aurelie Ouss and Megan Stevenson, "Bail, Jail, and Pretrial Misconduct: The Influence of Prosecutors," working paper available at https://papers.ssrn.com/sol3/papers.cfm?abstract_id=3335138 (presenting empirical findings that suggest judges often follow prosecutor recommendations about bail and pretrial release).

82 **Like many judges across the country, trial judges in Florida are elected:** Florida Statutes § 105.011.

82 **The inescapable reality is that no judge can predict the future with certainty or guarantee that a person will appear in court or refrain from**

committing future crimes: *State v. Brown*, 2014-NMSC-038, ¶ 54, 338 P.3d 1276, 1292–93.

83   **There are many examples of criminal justice decisions in favor of defendants being used as a wedge issue in judicial elections:** Jed Handlesman Shugerman, *The People's Courts: Pursuing Judicial Independence in America* 1–3 (Cambridge, Massachusetts: Harvard University Press, 2012) (collecting recent incidents); Judith S. Kaye, "State Courts at the Dawn of a New Century: Common Law Courts Reading Statutes and Constitutions," 70 *New York University Law Review* 1, 14n74 (1995) (collecting incidents from the 1980s and 1990s).

83   **they may be refusing to release defendants because they've already made up their minds that those defendants are guilty:** Shaila Dewan, "When Bail Is Out of Defendant's Reach, Other Costs Mount," *New York Times* (Jun. 10, 2015) ("Baltimore public defenders say, judges here assume the defendant is guilty when setting bail.").

83   **'Go get the belt. You get three licks.'":** Gabrielle Banks and Zach Despart, "Harris County Reaches Landmark Settlement Over 'Unconstitutional' Bail System," *Houston Chronicle*, Jul. 26, 2019.

83   **Police would do this by initially setting a high bail, requiring the defendant to come up with a large amount of money in order to be released, and then reduce the amount of bail eight or twelve hours later:** Malcolm M. Feeley, 204.

84   **A recent study by researchers at the University of Pennsylvania's law school found that people charged with misdemeanors were 25 percent more likely to plead guilty if they were detained pretrial than if they were released:** Paul Heaton, Sandra Mayson & Megan Stevenson, "The Downstream Consequences of Misdemeanor Pretrial Detention," 69 *Stanford Law Review* 711, 747 (2017).

Chapter 5

92   **In 2013 the *New Yorker* magazine published an exposé on Tenaha:** Sarah Stillman, "Taken," *New Yorker* (Aug. 5, 2013).

93   **The *Post* had previously published an extensive exposé on roadside seizures and forfeitures that analyzed years of data:** Michael Sallah, Robert O'Harrow Jr., Steven Rich, and Gabe Silverman, "Stop and Seize," *Washington Post* (Sept. 6, 2014).

93   **The story had been published just before the hearing took place—and it did not make Muskogee look good:** Christopher Ingraham, "How police took $53,000 from a Christian band, an orphanage and a church," *Washington Post* (Apr. 25, 2016).

94   **Across the country, there are hundreds of police departments that receive as much as 20 percent of their total budgets from forfeitures:** Robert O'Harrow Jr., Steven Rich, Shelly Tan, "Asset seizures fuel police spending," *Washington Post* (Oct. 11. 2014).

94   **And there are counties in Texas where nearly 40 percent of the police budget comes from forfeiture money:** Sarah Stillman, "Taken."

94   **For example, in 1990 the attorney general of the United States distrib-
      uted a memo to federal prosecutors encouraging them to "significantly
      increase" their forfeiture efforts "in order to meet the Department
      of Justice's annual budget target.":** The Supreme Court quoted this
      memo in *United States v. James Daniel Good Real Property*, 510 U.S. 43,
      56 n.2 (1993).

95   **But instead they made ten times as many stops on the westbound lanes,
      making clear that their priority was to seize money rather than drugs:**
      Institute for Justice, "Policing for Profit: The Abuse of Civil Asset Forfeiture,"
      2nd edition, 16 (2015), http://ij.org/wp-content/uploads/2015/11/policing
      -for-profit-2nd-edition.pdf.

95   **Nationally, criminal charges are never filed in 80 percent of civil forfei-
      ture cases:** Rep. Henry Hyde, *Forfeiting our property rights: Is your property
      safe from seizure?* 6 (Washington, D.C.: Cato Institute, 1995).

95   **The town even confiscated a simple gold cross from around a woman's
      neck when she was stopped for a minor traffic violation:** Sarah Stillman,
      "Taken."

95   **In Philadelphia, half of the forfeitures between 2011 and 2013 involved
      less than $193:** Institute for Justice, "Policing for Profit: The Abuse of Civil
      Asset Forfeiture."

96   **it only has to satisfy the lesser standard of proof that applies in civil
      cases:** *United States v. One Assortment of 89 Firearms*, 465 U.S. 354 (1984).

96   **it appears that some criminal procedure protections applied and that
      the sort of property that could be seized was much more limited:** *Leonard
      v. Texas*, 137 S. Ct. 847, 848–50 (2017) (Thomas, J., dissenting from denial
      of cert.)

96   **As Michelle Alexander explained in *The New Jim Crow: Mass
      Incarceration in the Age of Colorblindness*, the War on Drugs played
      a prominent role in the rise of civil forfeiture:** Michelle Alexander, *The
      New Jim Crow: Mass Incarceration in the Age of Colorblindness*, revised edition,
      78–84 (New York: New Press, 2012).

96   **That profit-sharing program prompted law enforcement across the
      country to begin seizing cash, cars, and other property if they thought it
      might be connected to drug crimes:** Alan Nicgorski, "The Continuing Saga
      of Civil Forfeiture, the 'War on Drugs,' and the Constitution: Determining the
      Constitutional Excessiveness of Civil Forfeitures," 91 *Northwestern University
      Law Review* 374, 375–77 (1996).

96   **And a 2017 inspector general's report that examined a subset of fed-
      eral forfeitures found that federal officials could verify only that less
      than half of those forfeitures were even related to a criminal inves-
      tigation:** Office of the Inspector General, Department of Justice, *Review of
      the Department's Oversight of Cash Seizure and Forfeiture Activities* 16–21
      (March 2017) https://oig.justice.gov/reports/2017/e1702.pdf.

97   **They have even admitted that one reason for civil forfeiture is to pun-
      ish people for committing crimes:** *Austin v. United States*, 509 U.S. 602
      (1993).

97   **Only Justice Clarence Thomas appears to have doubts about the consti-
      tutionality of this practice:** *Leonard v. Texas*, 137 S. Ct. 847, 848–50 (2017)
      (Thomas, J., dissenting from denial of cert.).

97   **You would think that their work would be relatively easy, since 84 per-
      cent of Americans don't think that people should lose their property
      without first being convicted of a crime:** Emily Ekins, "84% of Americans
      Oppose Civil Asset Forfeiture," *Cato at Liberty Blog* (Dec. 13, 2016), cato.org/
      blog/84-americans-oppose-civil-asset-forfeiture.

98   **That team has analyzed forfeiture laws in all fifty states:** Institute for
      Justice, *Policing for Profit: The Abuse of Civil Asset Forfeiture*.

99   **In fact, the FBI says on its own website says that it uses forfeiture to
      "punish criminals.":** The website says:
      Why does the FBI Use Asset Forfeiture?
      • To punish criminals
      • To deter illegal activity
      • To disrupt criminal organizations
      • To remove the tools of the trade from criminals
      • To return assets to victims
      • To protect communities
      fbi.gov/investigate/white-collar-crime/asset-forfeiture.

99   **the profit motive seems to drive these fees:** Michael Makowsky, Hamilton
      Project, *A Proposal to End Regressive Taxation through Law Enforcement*
      9–14 (Mar. 2019), hamiltonproject.org/assets/files/Makowsky_PP_20190314
      .pdf.

99   **A person who is found guilty of a traffic violation in California and
      has to pay a $100 fine as punishment also has to pay an additional
      $490 in costs and fees:** Alex Bender, et al., *Not Just a Ferguson Problem:
      How Traffic Courts Drive Inequality in California* 9–10, https://lccrsf
      .org/wp-content/uploads/Not-Just-a-Ferguson-Problem-How-Traffic
      -Courts-Drive-Inequality-in-California-4.20.15.pdf?_ga=2.213658068
      .1149551463.1599070314–766609329.1596834045.

100   **A study by the Brennan Center for Justice found that, in many states,
      defendants routinely have to pay hundreds if not thousands of dol-
      lars in fees:** Alicia Bannon, Mitali Nagrecha, and Rebekah Diller, Brennan
      Center, *Criminal Justice Debt: A Barrier to Reentry* (2010), brennancenter.org/
      our-work/research-reports/criminal-justice-debt-barrier-reentry.

100   **Many states impose "jury fees" or "jury taxes" on defendants who insist
      on their right to trial:** T. Ward Frampton, 207–214.

100   **states began to pass on to defendants the costs associated with trials:**
      T. Ward Frampton, 210.

100   **When the Montana legislature passed a law in 2009 designed to offset
      the costs of providing appointed attorneys to poor defendants, they
      adopted different payment amounts for defendants who insisted on
      a jury trial and those who pleaded guilty or allowed themselves to be
      tried by a judge without a jury:** S.B. 263, 61st Leg., Reg. Sess. (Mont. 2009);
      Mont. Code Ann. § 46–8–113 (2009).

100   He also said that he was exempting bench trials—trials before judges without juries—from the higher fees because "a bench trial to me is like pleading guilty slowly.": T. Ward Frampton, 209.

100   Some local governments have decided to impose their own booking fees even without state law authorization: Wayne A. Logan and Ronald F. Wright, "Mercenary Criminal Justice," 2014 *University of Illinois Law Review* 1175, 1186.

100   But some governments put the burden on people who aren't convicted to seek a refund: "Booking fees and the Supreme Court: Our view," editorial, *USA Today* (Jan. 8, 2017).

101   the Court said "this smacks of administrative detail and of procedure.": *Schilb v. Kuebel*, 404 U.S. 357, 365 (1971).

101   If something is a fee, then the Constitution's prohibition on excessive fines doesn't apply: Beth A. Colgan, "Reviving the Excessive Fines Clause," 102 *California Law Review* 277, 285–90, 298–300 (2014).

101   For centuries, criminal prosecutions in England were usually brought by a victim or a victim's family to recover "bot" or "wergild"—money from the defendant to compensate for the harm done: Wayne A. Logan and Ronald F. Wright, "Mercenary Criminal Justice," 1179–80.

101   Even judges were sometimes paid for each affirmative action that they took, such as each time they signed a search warrant, and they didn't get paid if they didn't authorize the search: Wayne A. Logan and Ronald F. Wright, "Mercenary Criminal Justice," 1180–85.

102   For example, in the late 1920s, the Supreme Court overturned the conviction of Ed Tumey, who had been fined $100 for unlawfully possessing intoxicating liquor during Prohibition: *Tumey v. Ohio*, 273 U.S. 510 (1927).

102   Soon after the Tumey case, the Supreme Court refused to reverse a conviction by a local court where the judge served as mayor and the mayor's town profited from convictions: *Dugan v. Ohio*, 277 U.S. 61 (1928).

102   But several years later it did reverse such a conviction: *Ward v. Village of Monroeville*, 409 U.S. 57 (1972).

102   (These two cases appear to have come out differently because of obscure differences between the precise powers that the mayors had over the town's finances.): Wayne A. Logan and Ronald F. Wright, "Mercenary Criminal Justice," 1198.

102   the Supreme Court has not required the same neutrality from police and prosecutors as it has from judges: *Marshall v. Jerrico Inc.*, 446 U.S. 238 (1980); Wayne A. Logan and Ronald F. Wright, "Mercenary Criminal Justice," 1199.

102   rejected a constitutional challenge to a Mississippi law that paid constables $10 per charging decision that results in a conviction: *Brown v. Edwards*, 721 F.2d 1442 (5th Cir. 1984).

103   Washington, D.C., has a similar program in which people can have their charges dismissed if they agree to "forfeit" a small amount of money: Wayne A. Logan and Ronald F. Wright, "Mercenary Criminal Justice," 1188.

104   **The company running the program made millions of dollars, and so did the local prosecutor's office, which received a kickback of $600 for every defendant enrolled in the program:** Lauren Castle, "County to make diversion affordable," *Arizona Republic* (Jan, 13, 2020).

104   **The Civil Rights Corps—the same organization that challenged the bail practices in Houston—brought a lawsuit against Phoenix officials, arguing that the program violated the constitutional rights of defendants who couldn't pay the fees:** *Briggs v. Montgomery*, No. CV-18–02684, 2019 WL 2515950 (D. Ariz. Jun. 18, 2019).

104   **Since then, Phoenix prosecutors have changed their program to provide better screening for those who can't pay and to make the overall costs lower:** Lauren Castle, "County to make diversion affordable."

105   **Only a civil rights lawsuit stopped the practice:** *Caliste v. Cantrell*, 937 F.3d 525 (5th Cir. 2019).

105   **public defenders in several states actively sought to have a new fee added in order to help fund their offices:** Ronald F. Wright & Wayne A. Logan, "The Political Economy of Application Fees for Indigent Criminal Defense," 47 *William and Mary Law Review* 2045, 2055–68 (2006).

105   **City officials routinely urged the police chief to generate more revenue by arresting more people, and the municipal court served as essentially a collection agency for the city:** Department of Justice, Civil Rights Division, *Investigation of the Ferguson Police Department* (Mar. 4, 2015).

105   **a former state trooper told city officials that they could pay the town's expenses if they began stopping cars on the local highway:** Sarah Stillman, "Taken."

Chapter 6

108   **two theories of criminal courts: the due process model and the plea bargain model:** Malcolm M. Feeley, 25–28.

109   **The negotiation takes place in the "shadow of a trial":** Stephanos Bibas, "Plea Bargaining Outside the Shadow of Trial," 2464–65 (explaining and ultimately critiquing this theory).

109   **Feeley did not find a single trial in his yearlong study of more than 1,600 cases in a Connecticut courtroom:** Malcolm M. Feeley, 9.

109   **They also bargained over issues that were irrelevant to whether the defendant would have prevailed at trial, like the relationship between the defendant and the victim before or after the crime was committed:** Malcolm M. Feeley, 159, 162–63.

110   **Or a defense attorney would argue in favor of a dismissal by noting that he hadn't asked the prosecutor for anything yet that day:** Malcolm M. Feeley, 159, 161, 193.

110   **Invoking the process that they were entitled to would often prolong the defendants' interactions with the criminal justice system, and so defendants readily give up their ability to test the prosecution's evidence or even secure a lawyer because those rights meant more time and effort for the defendant.** Malcolm M. Feeley, 199–243.

110   **"Cases in which there was no trial, no witnesses, no formal motions, no pretrial involvement from the bench, and no presentence investigation still required as many as eight or ten different appearances spread over six months.":** Malcolm M. Feeley, 10.

110   **As a result, defendants with complex cases would plead guilty at arraignment rather than trying to wait and convince the prosecutor to give them a better deal:** Malcolm M. Feeley, 10.

111   **answer further questions by judges or other court personnel who might be skeptical of their claim that they can't afford to pay for a lawyer:** Malcolm M. Feeley, 220–221.

112   **He saw prosecutors tell defendants to plead guilty at arraignment— including a defendant a with complex case that could have benefited from further investigation and negotiations—on the theory that they should "be smart and get it over with today."** Malcolm M. Feeley, 10.

112   **"Officials are often willing to drop minor charges, feeling that the arrestees have learned their lesson by spending a night in jail.":** Malcolm M. Feeley, 25.

115   **So the objective in substance abuse courts is to treat the substance abuse problem and use the threat of criminal punishment to get defendants to comply with the terms of the treatment program:** Bureau of Justice Assistance, *Defining Drug Courts: The Key Components* 6–10, 13–14 (Jan. 1997), ncjrs.gov/pdffiles1/bja/205621.pdf.

117   **Stevenson ended up winning the case, resulting in a landmark ruling that the Eighth Amendment forbids mandatory life-without-parole sentences for juveniles.** *Miller v. Alabama*, 567 U.S. 460 (2012).

117   **The judges appear to have complained to the county commissioners, who fired the defenders:** Radley Balko, opinion, "A Pennsylvania county fired its two top public defenders for doing their jobs," *Washington Post* (Mar. 2, 2020).

118   **We met at an academic conference organized by NYU:** The conference "Plea Bargaining: Reforming An (Un)Necessary Evil?" was organized by NYU's Center on the Administration of Criminal Law, and it took place on Apr. 8, 2019.

118   **_Teen Vogue_ did a profile of him:** Allegra Kirkland, "Scott Hechinger: A Day in the Life of a Brooklyn Public Defender," *Teen Vogue* (Jan. 2, 2020).

119   **Scott's tweet about the man was retweeted more than 6,000 times:** https://twitter.com/ScottHech/status/1275549616033992704.

119   **One day later, the local prosecutor issued a statement saying that the man was being released:** https://twitter.com/ScottHech/status/1276261069913276421.

122   **More than 3,000 of the Clean Halls buildings were in the Bronx, which resulted in thousands of arrests:** Larry Neumeister, "Judge: NYPD must halt suspicion-less Bronx stops," Associated Press Wire: New York (Jan. 9, 2013).

123   **A 2013 study by New York City's Civilian Complaint Review Board found that 40 percent of fully investigated complaints by people who had been caught up in of Operation Clean Halls were "substantiated.":** Civilian Complaint Review Board Memorandum, *Follow-up Report on Criminal*

Trespass Related Complaints in Patrolled Housing 2 (May 31, 2013), https://www1.nyc.gov/assets/ccrb/downloads/pdf/policy_pdf/issue_based/20130513_patrolled_housing_memo.pdf.

123 **As the report noted, this rate was twice as high as the rate for complaints against officers outside of Clean Halls buildings:** Civilian Complaint Review Board Memorandum.

123 **The settlement also required police to keep records about everyone whom they stop or frisk near a Clean Halls buildings—something that will allow more scrutiny of police behavior in the future:** New York Civil Liberties Union, *Settlement will end unconstitutional NYPD stops, frisks, and arrests in clean halls buildings* (Feb. 2, 2017), nyclu.org/en/press-releases/settlement-will-end-unconstitutional-nypd-stops-frisks-and-arrests-clean-halls.

124 **But more than 60 percent of Clean Halls arrests ended either in a guilty plea or another unfavorable disposition for the person arrested:** Alexandra Natapoff, *Punishment Without Crime: How Our Massive Misdemeanor System Traps the Innocent and Makes America More Unequal* 98–100 (New York: Basic Books, 2018).

124 **We don't know how many of the thousands of people arrested in Operation Clean Halls were innocent or how many of those innocent people pleaded guilty.** Jessica S. Henry, "Smoke but No Fire: When Innocent People Are Wrongly Convicted of Crimes That Never Happened," 55 *American Criminal Law Review* 665, 672–73 (2018).

124 **there are approximately 13 million misdemeanor cases filed every year:** Alexandra Natapoff, 13.

124 **Those cases can range from serious criminal behavior like domestic violence to trivial misconduct like littering:** Alexandra Natapoff, 45–50.

126 **It can even result in a person who is not a U.S. citizen being deported:** Jason A. Cade, "The Plea-Bargain Crisis for Noncitizens in Misdemeanor Court," 34 *Cardozo Law Review* 1751, 1758–60 (2013) (collecting misdemeanors that subject defendants to removal).

126 **As law professor Eisha Jain has explained:** Eisha Jain, "Arrests As Regulation," 67 *Stanford Law Review* 809 (2015).

128 **I did some poking around and found the rule against reading on the Brooklyn criminal court website:** The rule is available here: http://ww2.nycourts.gov/COURTS/2jd/KINGS/CRIMINAL/GeneralInformation.shtml

128 **several studies showing that those people who end up in prison have very high rates of illiteracy:** National Center for Education Statistics, *Literacy Behand Bars: Results From the 2003 National Assessment of Adult Literacy Prison Survey* (May 2007), https://nces.ed.gov/pubs2007/2007473.pdf; National Center for Education Statistics, *Literacy Behind Prison Walls: Profiles of the Prison Population From the National Adult Education Survey* (Oct. 1994), https://nces.ed.gov/pubs94/94102.pdf.

128 **That's what Noor Ahmad thought:** Reuven Blau, "Read away! Teen defendants can now take books from courthouse mini library bookshelf," *New York Daily News* (Dec. 26, 2018).

129   **Ahmad's employer, Legal Aid, even has plans to expand the program to juvenile courtrooms across New York City in a partnership with publisher Penguin Random House:** Rob Abruzzese, "Legal Aid Campaign Brings Books to Kids in Court," *Queens Daily Eagle* (Dec. 27, 2018).

Chapter 7

132   **President Trump publicly thanked him for his efforts and asked Shon to speak at a White House event celebrating the legislation:** Karen Sloan, "Bank-Robber-Turned-Law-Prof Lands a Starring Role in Criminal Justice Reform," *National Law Journal* (Apr. 2, 2019).

132   **Charles Kushner served more than a year in federal prison for those crimes.):** Ted Sherman, "Trump pardons Jared Kushner's father. N.J. developer went to prison in lurid tax fraud, sex case," *NJ.com* (Dec. 23, 2020), nj.com/politics/2020/12/trump-pardons-jared-kushners-father-nj-developer-went-to-prison-in-lurid-tax-fraud-sex-case.html.

132   **Shon had written a book about his redemption story that was published in 2012:** Shon Hopwood, *Law Man: My Story of Robbing Banks, Winning Supreme Court Cases, and Finding Redemption* (New York: Crown Publishing Group, 2012).

135   **He speaks movingly in his book about his father's cancer diagnosis and death while he was in prison:** Shon Hopwood, *Law Man: My Story of Robbing Banks, Winning Supreme Court Cases, and Finding Redemption* 198–200, 214–215, 230–235.

135   **Shon first told that story publicly because he was asked to write something that he knew was going to be sent to federal judges:** Shon R. Hopwood, "Improving Federal Sentencing," 87 *UMKC Law Review* 79 (2018).

136   **For years the conventional wisdom was that voters were afraid of crime and that anyone who was "soft on crime" would lose an election:** Rachel Elise Barkow, *Prisoners of Politics: Breaking the Cycle of Mass Incarceration,* 6–9; Jonathan Simon, "Megan's Law: Crime and Democracy in Late Modern America," 25 *Law and Social Inquiry* 1111, 1120–21 (2000); Eli Lehrer, op-ed., "It's Hard to Be Soft on Crime," *National Review* (Dec. 14, 2009).

136   **Some of those stories focus on district attorney elections in which the winning candidates ran on criminal justice reform platforms and won:** Del Quentin Wilber, "Once tough-on-crime prosecutors now push progressive reforms," *Los Angeles Times* (Aug. 5, 2019); Daniel A. Medina, "The progressive prosecutors blazing a new path for the US justice system," *Guardian* (Jul. 23, 2019), theguardian.com/us-news/2019/jul/23/us-justice-system-progressive-prosecutors-mass-incarceration-death-penalty.

136   **These successes, we are told, are a sign that the era of tough-on-crime politics is coming to an end:** Jody D. Armour, "How being 'tough on crime' became a political liability," *Conversation* (Dec. 20, 2019), https://theconversation.com/how-being-tough-on-crime-became-a-political-liability-128515.

136   **They highlight new reform efforts in red states like Texas and Mississippi:** Shane Bauer, "How Conservatives Learned to Love Prison

Reform," *Mother Jones* (Mar./Apr. 2014); David Dagan and Steven M. Teles, "Conservatives and Criminal Justice," 47 *National Affairs* 118 (Spring 2021).

136   **January 2017 inaugural address appealed to law and order while decrying "American carnage":** "President Trump's Inaugural Address," *Washington Week* (Jan. 20, 2017), pbs.org/weta/washingtonweek/web-video/president-trumps-inaugural-address.

137   **Trump's speech at the Republican National Convention railed against violence in the streets and insisted on the need to restore law and order:** "Full text: Donald Trump 2016 RNC draft speech transcript," *Politico* (Jul. 21, 2016), politico.com/story/2016/07/full-transcript-donald-trump-nomination-acceptance-speech-at-rnc-225974.

137   **Ogg's victory marked the first time in nearly forty years that a Democrat would serve as the district attorney in that county:** Jordan Smith, "Overzealous Prosecutors Ousted Across the Country, Showing There Is Still Hope for Reform," *The Intercept* (Nov. 10, 2016), https://theintercept.com/2016/11/10/overzealous-prosecutors-ousted-across-the-country-showing-there-is-still-hope-for-reform/.

137   **Alvarez didn't file criminal charges until after the video of the shooting was released by court order:** Monica Davey, "Prosecutor Criticized Over Laquan McDonald Case Is Defeated in Primary," *New York Times* (Mar. 16, 2016).

138   **Reform candidates also won in Denver, Jacksonville, St. Louis, Santa Fe, Tampa, and a few other races in counties without large cities:** Jordan Smith, "Overzealous Prosecutors Ousted Across the Country, Showing There Is Still Hope for Reform."

138   **Many of these victories were supported by significant campaign spending by billionaire activist George Soros:** Frances Robles, "5 Prosecutors With a Fresh Approach," *New York Times* (Mar. 30, 2017).

138   **"These results signify that overzealous prosecutors that resort to draconian sentences and pursue convictions with a win-at-all-costs mentality will soon see themselves being replaced with leaders who have rejected these failed policies of the 1980s and 90s, and are truly committed to reforming the justice system with proven, evidence-based, equitable solutions that increase public safety.":** Jordan Smith, "Overzealous Prosecutors Ousted Across the Country, Showing There is Still Hope for Reform."

138   **running on his record as a criminal defense attorney and civil rights lawyer who had filed dozens of lawsuits against the Philadelphia police for violating citizens' constitutional rights:** Jennifer Gonnerman, "Larry Krasner's Campaign to End Mass Incarceration," *New Yorker* (Oct. 22, 2018).

138   **after publicly releasing a list of low-level crimes that she vowed not to prosecute:** Maria Cramer, "DA candidate Rachael Rollins hailed nationally, but locally her plan not to prosecute petty crimes alarms some," *Boston Globe* (Sept. 12, 2018).

138   **(Boudin's parents, who were members of the radical group the Weather Underground, were arrested and convicted of participating in an armored car robbery when Boudin was a toddler.):** Tim Arango, "Dad's

in Prison, Mom Was on Parole. Their Son Is Now Running for D.A.," *New York Times* (May 24, 2019).

138   **a progressive primary challenger who had received financial support from George Soros and other progressive groups:** Marcos Bretton, opinion, "Sacramento's DA race is done: Why progressives never should have backed Noah Phillips," *Sacramento Bee* (Jun. 15, 2018).

138   **hundreds of thousands of dollars spent by law enforcement groups who did not want a reformer elected:** Shaun King, "Law Enforcement Groups Gave $420,000 to DA Deciding Whether to Bring Charges Against Cops Who Killed Stephon Clark," *The Intercept* (Apr. 25, 2018), https://theintercept.com/ 2018/04/25/stephon-clark-police-shooting-district-attorney/.

138   **Stephan painted her challenger as "anti-prosecutor" and claimed that her "reform agenda endangered public safety.":** Greg Moran, "DA race: Stephan easily defeats challenger Jones-Wright, earns full term," *San Diego Union-Tribune* (Jun. 6, 2018).

139   **Adel had faced criticism for her failure to charge police who had shot and killed civilians, and Gunnigle ran on a platform of criminal justice reform:** Catherine Holland, "Julie Gunnigle concedes race for Maricopa County Attorney to Allister Adel," *AZFamily.com* (Nov. 9, 2020), azfamily .com/news/politics/election_headquarters/julie-gunnigle-concedes-race -for-maricopa-county-attorney-to-allister-adel/article_320750ca-1a1d-11eb -aa8f-4f29572c1807.html.

139   **decreased almost 45 percent during Kim Foxx's first term:** Chick Goudie and Barb Markoff, "Kim Foxx says progressive prosecution could result in safer neighborhoods," ABC7Chicago.com (Dec. 2019), https://abc7 chicago.com/kim-foxx-says-progressive-prosecution-could-result-in-safer -neighborhoods—/5763245/.

139   **reduced the jail population by more than 10 percent within the first six months of taking office in 2019:** Thomasi McDonald, "Six Months In, Satana Deberry Talks About How She's Changing Durham's Criminal Justice System," *IndyWeek* (Jul. 26, 2019), https://indyweek.com/news/durham/ satana-deberry-six-month-report/.

139   **changed his office's bail policy, reducing the number of people held on bail before trial more than 50 percent:** Eric Gonzalez, *Justice 2020: An Action Plan for Brooklyn* 16, brooklynda.org/wp-content/uploads/2019/03/ Justice2020-Report.pdf.

139   **significantly increased the number of juveniles diverted from the justice system:** Claire Goforth, "Jacksonville, Tampa Prosecutors Pursue Aggressive Reform Agendas with Public Support," *Juvenile Justice Information Exchange* (May 30, 2019), https://jjie.org/2019/05/30/jacksonville-tampa -prosecutors-pursue-aggressive-reform-agendas-with-public-support-few -setbacks-so-far/.

139   **have taken a "measured" approach to reform:** Claire Goforth, "Jacksonville, Tampa Prosecutors Pursue Aggressive Reform Agendas with Public Support."

140   **George Soros spent more than a million dollars to help elect Ayala, and she was the first African American to be elected prosecutor in the**

state of Florida: Yamiche Alcindor, "After High-Profile Shootings, Blacks Seek Prosecutor Seats," *New York Times* (Nov. 5, 2016).

140   **Ayala announced that she would not seek a second term:** Monivette Cordeiro and Jeff Weiner, "Aramis Ayala won't seek re-election as Orange-Osceola state attorney; Belvin Perry may enter race," *Orlando Sentinel* (May 28, 2019).

140   **One challenger announced his candidacy only days after Ayala's death penalty announcement:** Steven Lemongello, "Republican attorney announces 2020 run against State Attorney Aramis Ayala," *Orlando Sentinel* (Mar. 20, 2017).

140   **a prosecutor from within Ayala's own office—was endorsed by the police union:** Deirdra Funcheon, "Florida State Attorney Who Fought Death Penalty Won't Run Again; No Shortage of Challengers," *Juvenile Justice Information Exchange* (May 28, 2019).

141   **the incumbent prosecutor lost his primary election when he failed to secure an indictment in the police shooting of twelve-year-old Tamir Rice:** Leon Neyfakh, "Big Wins for Black Lives Matter," *Slate* (Mar. 16, 2016), https://slate.com/news-and-politics/2016/03/the-prosecutors-in-the-tamir -rice-and-laquan-mcdonald-cases-lose-their-primary-races.html.

141   **an outspoken progressive campaign that promised to increase prosecutions of corporate crime, crimes by landlords, and employers who failed to pay workers what they had earned:** Joey Fox and Ben Max, "20 Things Tiffany Cabán Promised to Do as Queens District Attorney," *Gotham Gazette* (Jun. 26, 2019), gothamgazette.com/city/8641–25-things-tiffany-caban-has -promised-to-do-as-queens-district-attorney.

141   **promise to investigate and prosecute constructions companies and real estate developers who failed to appropriately pay their employees or who didn't maintain safe work sites:** Christine Chung, "Developers Donate Big to Queens DA Candidate Who Vows Construction Crackdown," *City* (Apr. 7, 2019), thecity.nyc/2019/4/7/21211163/developers-donate-big-to-queens-da -candidate-who-vows-construction-crackdown.

141   **Cabán received endorsements from many prominent progressives, including Senator Elizabeth Warren:** Jeff Coltin, "The endorsements for Queens district attorney candidates," *City & State New York* (Jun. 25, 2019), cityandstateny.com/articles/politics/campaigns-elections/endorsements -queens-district-attorney-candidates.html.

141   **During her time in the Senate, Elizabeth Warren has also sought to increase corporate crime prosecutions:** Elizabeth Warren, *Rigged Justice: How Weak Enforcement Lets Corporate Offenders Off Easy* (Jan. 2016), warren .senate.gov/files/documents/Rigged_Justice_2016.pdf.

141   **Warren didn't seem to think that negligent executives actually deserved punishment; instead, she wanted to make it easier for prosecutors to win their cases:** Carissa Byrne Hessick and Benjamin Levin, "Elizabeth Warren's Proposal to Imprison More Corporate Executives Is a Bad Idea," *Slate* (Apr. 4, 2019), https://slate.com/news-and-politics/2019/04/elizabeth-warren -corporate-fraud-prison-negligence-mass-incarceration.html.

142   **successful in making animal cruelty a crime in states across the country and in getting people who abuse animals sent to jail:** Justin Marceau, *Beyond Cages: Animal Law and Criminal Punishment* (Cambridge, UK: Cambridge University Press, 2019).

142   **feminists have fought to increase prosecutions and lengthen sentences for domestic violence and rape:** Aya Gruber, *The Feminist War on Crime: The Unexpected Role of Women's Liberation in Mass Incarceration* (Berkeley: University of California Press, 2020).

142   **academics have coined a term for the phenomenon: "carceral progressivism.":** Savannah Shange, *Progressive Dystopia: Abolition, Antiblackness, and Schooling in San Francisco* (Durham, North Carolina: Duke University Press, 2019).

142   **someone in the audience posed this very question to some of the progressive prosecutors who appeared to speak:** law.nyu.edu/centers/ adminofcriminallaw/events/plea-bargaining "Whither the Prosecutor" panel at 1:14:00.

143   **The state increased the number of people in its prisons by 300 percent between 1985 and 2005:** Michael May and Laura Burke, "Freedom's Just a Word," *Texas Observer* (Mar. 3, 2011), texasobserver.org/freedoms-just-a-word/.

143   **The costs of adding those additional beds was estimated at more than $2 billion:** "Texas," *Right on Crime*, http://rightoncrime.com/category/ state-initiatives/texas/.

143   **fund more treatment programs and take steps to help released prisoners reintegrate into society so that they were less likely to commit new crimes and end up back in prison:** "Texas," *Right on Crime*.

143   **other states were sending their officials to Texas in order to try and mimic the state's criminal justice reforms:** Michael May and Laura Burke, "Freedom's Just a Word."

143   **In 2014 the Mississippi legislature passed a law allowing defendants convicted of nonviolent crimes to be released on parole after serving 25 percent of their sentences:** Pew Charitable Trusts, *Mississippi's 2014 Corrections and Criminal Justice Reform* (May 2014), pewtrusts.org/~/media/ assets/2014/09/pspp_mississippi_2014_corrections_justice_reform.pdf.

144   **But Republican governor Tate Reeves vetoed the bill:** Leah Willingham, "Mississippi governor vetoes criminal justice bills," *Associated Press* (Jul. 9, 2020).

144   **It also reduced other statutory maximum and minimum drug sentences as well as reducing the number of federal gun enhancement charges that could be brought in some cases:** Shon Hopwood, "The Effort to Reform the Federal Criminal Justice System," 128 *Yale Law Journal Forum* 791, 795–96 (2019).

144   **if the incarceration rate continued to grow, the state would have to spend hundreds of millions of dollars to build new prisons:** "Justice Reinvestment in Missouri," Justice Center, the Council of State Governments, https://csgjusticecenter.org/projects/justice-reinvestment/current-states/ missouri/.

145   **legislature passed a bill to make sentences longer and to create new crimes:** Crystal Thomas, "'A step in the wrong direction.' Parson urged to veto crime bill that harshens sentences," *Kansas City Star* (Jun. 10, 2020).

146   **And studies of bail and pretrial detention show that defendants who are released are less likely to plead guilty than those who are jailed pretrial:** Paul Heaton, Sandra Mayson & Megan Stevenson, "The Downstream Consequences of Misdemeanor Pretrial Detention," 69 *Stanford Law Review* 711, 747 (2017).

147   **Conservatives who believe in free markets and small governments have long tried to get rid of occupational licenses altogether:** Ryan Nunn, "The future of occupational licensing reform," *Brookings* (Jan. 30, 2017), brookings.edu/opinions/the-future-of-occupational-licensing-reform/.

148   **the liberal and conservative reform movements aren't necessarily fighting for the same things—or for the same reasons:** Benjamin Levin, "The Consensus Myth in Criminal Justice Reform," 117 *Michigan Law Review* 259 (2018).

148   **James Forman, a professor at Yale Law School, has written eloquently about this issue:** James Forman, Jr., *Locking Up Our Own: Crime and Punishment in Black America* (New York: Farrar, Straus and Giroux, 2017).

148   **there is no disputing that Blacks are drastically overrepresented in America's prisons.:** Bureau of Justice Statistics, *Prisoners in 2018* figure 1 (Apr 2020), bjs.gov/content/pub/pdf/p18.pdf.

148   **popularized by Michelle Alexander's *The New Jim Crow*:** Michelle Alexander, 205.

148   **When it comes to absolute numbers, there are nearly as many Whites in prison in this country as Blacks:** Bureau of Justice Statistics, *Prisoners in 2018* table 9 (April 2020), bjs.gov/content/pub/pdf/p18.pdf.

148   **As Forman says, "That's a lot of 'collateral damage.'":** James Forman, Jr., "Racial Critiques of Mass Incarceration: Beyond the New Jim Crow," 87 *New York University Law Review* 21, 58 (2012).

149   **people on the left have started to call for dramatic funding cuts to police departments:** J. Edward Moreno, "Ocasio-Cortez dismisses proposed $1B cut: 'Defunding police means defunding police,'" *The Hill* (Jun. 30, 2020).

149   **a progressive movement to abolish prisons and/or police departments and instead address crime and public safety through other means—has begun to gain traction in mainstream discussions:** Mariame Kaba, opinion, "Yes, We Mean Literally Abolish the Police," *New York Times* (Jun. 12, 2020).

149   **Congressional Democrats moved quickly to quash any talk about defunding the police:** Sarah Ferris, Marianne Levine, and Heather Caygle, "Hill Democrats quash liberal push to 'defund the police,'" *Politico* (Jun. 8, 2020), politico.com/news/2020/06/08/defund-police-democrats-307766.

149   **Joe Biden said that he was "totally opposed" to defunding the police:** Rachel Epstein, "What's at Stake for Police Reform in the 2020 Election," *Marie Claire* (Oct. 16, 2020).

149   **and his campaign platform actually called for more funding for law enforcement:** Chelsey Sanchez, "What Is Joe Biden's Position on Policing and Criminal Justice in America?," *Harper's Bazaar* (Jan. 19, 2021).

149   **A majority of the Minneapolis city council pledged to defund the city's police department in the wake of George Floyd's death, but many later backed away from the pledge:** Astead W. Herndon, "Minneapolis officials said they would defund the police. Some now regret that pledge.," *New York Times* (Sept. 26, 2020).

149   **By earnestly proposing a policy that seems radically unthinkable—getting rid of prisons—abolitionists may make other radical policies that stop short of abolition—like decriminalizing most misdemeanors—seem more reasonable:** Maggie Astor, "How the Politically Unthinkable Can Become Mainstream," *New York Times* (Feb. 26, 2019).

150   **Shon had even written an academic article encouraging people to have patience with modest, incremental reforms because those reforms were a step in the right direction:** Shon Hopwood, "The Effort to Reform the Federal Criminal Justice System," 128 *Yale Law Journal Forum* 791, 809–811 (2019).

151   **The two law professors who came up with this thought experiment—Rachel E. Barkow and Mark Osler—have explained at great length how the views of prosecutors dominate federal criminal justice policy:** Rachel E. Barkow & Mark Osler, "Designed to Fail: The President's Deference to the Department of Justice in Advancing Criminal Justice Reform," 59 *William & Mary Law Review* 387 (2017).

151   **When Congress passed the First Step Act, for example, it did so over the vocal objection of the DOJ:** Shon Hopwood, "The Misplaced Trust in the DOJ's Expertise on Criminal Justice Policy," 118 *Michigan Law Review* 1181, 1196–1201 (2020) (describing DOJ opposition).

152   **quitting in protest because the DOJ frustrated her efforts, denying her sufficient funding, reversing her favorable recommendations, and forbidding her from speaking to the White House to explain why she thought the prisoners actually deserved relief:** Gregory Korte, "Former administration pardon attorney suggests broken system in resignation letter," *USA Today* (Mar. 28, 2016).

152   **a letter to President Obama in which they told him that he shouldn't be granting clemency to nonviolent drug offenders who had already served decades in prison:** Shon Hopwood, "The Misplaced Trust in the DOJ's Expertise on Criminal Justice Policy."

152   **For example, during the years 2015 to 2018, the legislatures in Arizona, Oklahoma, and Pennsylvania did not pass a single bill that prosecutors opposed.:** The Prosecutors and Politics Project, *Prosecutor Lobbying in the States, 2015-2018* at 24, 224, 239 (June 2021), https://law.unc.edu/wp-content/uploads/2021/06/Prosecutor-Lobbying-in-the-States-2015-2018.pdf.

152   **When polled, many voters say that they think the criminal justice system isn't harsh enough—that sentences are too short and that judges are too lenient:** Stephanos Bibas, "Transparency and Participation in Criminal

Procedure," 81 *New York University Law Review* 911, 927 (2006) ("In polls, the public says in the abstract that it thinks that judges sentence too leniently."); Adriaan Lanni, note, "Jury Sentencing in Noncapital Cases: An Idea Whose Time Has Come (Again)?," 108 *Yale Law Journal* 1775, 1780–81 (1999) ("Public opinion polls and surveys designed to elicit general impressions of the criminal sentencing system have repeatedly found that respondents believe that courts are too lenient in their determinations of punishment."); Loretta J. Stalans & Arthur J. Lurigio, "Lay and Professionals' Beliefs About Crime and Criminal Sentencing: A Need for Theory, Perhaps Schema Theory," 17 *Criminal Justice and Behavior* 333, 344 (1990) (reporting that 72 percent of the lay subjects in the study said that judges are too lenient in sentencing burglary).

152   **"voters are relatively uninformed, both in general and specifically about criminal justice issues.":** Rachel Elise Barkow, *Prisoners of Politics: Breaking the Cycle of Mass Incarceration*, 106.

152   **suggested imposing sentences that were below the statutory minimum sentence:** Douglas R. Thomson & Anthony Ragona, "Popular Moderation Versus Governmental Authoritarianism: An Interactionist View of Public Sentiments Toward Criminal Sanctions," 33 *Crime & Delinquency* 337 (1987).

153   **most Americans can't name all three branches of government, and more than a third of Americans can't name a single right that is guaranteed by the First Amendment:** "Americans Are Poorly Informed About Basic Constitutional Provisions," *Annenberg Public Policy Center* (Sep. 12, 2017), annenbergpublicpolicycenter.org/americans-are-poorly-informed-about-basic-constitutional-provisions/.

153   **a sentence that seems about right isn't newsworthy, so there is no reason for the media to cover it:** Rachel Barkow, *Administering Crime*, 52 *UCLA Law Review* 715, 750 (2005).

153   **The lead story on local news outlets is either a crime story or an accident story 77% of the time, and 32% of all local television news stories are about crime.":** Rachel Elise Barkow, *Prisoners of Politics: Breaking the Cycle of Mass Incarceration*, 106.

153   **"Murder stories dominate the news whether overall homicide rates are up or down.":** Rachel Elise Barkow, *Prisoners of Politics: Breaking the Cycle of Mass Incarceration*, 107.

154   **2017 study that found that people who lived in conservative areas and watched a lot of local news had more punitive attitudes than people who lived in high-crime areas or had themselves been a victim of crime:** Rachel Elise Barkow, *Prisoners of Politics: Breaking the Cycle of Mass Incarceration*, 108.

154   **the public will resist, no matter what the overall benefits are:** Rachel Elise Barkow, *Prisoners of Politics: Breaking the Cycle of Mass Incarceration*, 6.

154   **A recent Gallup poll shows a smaller number of Americans who say that the criminal justice system is not tough enough and a larger number who say the system is too tough than in years past:** Megan Brenan, "Fewer Americans Call for Tougher Criminal Justice

System," Gallup (Nov. 16, 2020), https://news.gallup.com/poll/324164/fewer-americans-call-tougher-criminal-justice-system.aspx?utm_source witterbutton&utm_medium witter&utm_campaign=sharing.

Chapter 8

157   **His case largely escaped public notice until the *Miami Herald* published an exposé in the fall of 2018:** Julie K. Brown, "Cops worked to put serial sex abuser in prison. Prosecutors worked to cut him a break," *Miami Herald* (Nov. 28, 2018); Julie K. Brown, "Even from jail, sex abuser manipulated the system. His victims were kept in the dark," *Miami Herald* (Nov. 28, 2018).

157   **These sex party allegations were especially explosive because Epstein's social circle at the time included former President Bill Clinton, England's Prince Andrew, and Donald Trump:** Julie K. Brown, "Cops worked to put serial sex abuser in prison. Prosecutors worked to cut him a break," *Miami Herald* (Nov. 28, 2018); Aaron Albright and Julie K. Brown, "Sex abuser Jeffrey Epstein was surrounded by powerful people. Here's a sampling," *Miami Herald* (Nov. 28, 2018).

157   **After the *Herald*'s story was published, a 2002 quote from Trump surfaced in which he said that Epstein was "terrific" and that he "likes beautiful women as much as I do, and many of them are on the younger side."** David A. Fahrenthold, Beth Reinhard, and Kimberly Kindy, "Trump called Epstein a 'terrific guy' who enjoyed 'younger' women before denying relationship with him," *Washington Post* (Jul. 8, 2019).

158   **Acosta resigned two days later:** Annie Karni, Eileen Sullivan, and Noam Scheiber, "Acosta to Resign as Labor Secretary Over Jeffrey Epstein Plea Deal," *Washington Post* (Jul. 12, 2019).

158   **Epstein was arrested on sex trafficking charges in New York:** Patricia Mazzei and William K. Rashbaum, "Jeffrey Epstein, Financier Long Accused of Molesting Minors, Is Charged," *New York Times* (Jul. 6, 2019).

158   **Epstein was denied bail and awaiting trial in federal custody when he committed suicide in August 2019:** William K. Rashbaum, Benjamin Weiser, and Michael Gold, "Jeffrey Epstein Dead in Suicide at Jail, Spurring Inquiries," *New York Times* (Aug. 10, 2019).

159   **the criminal justice system treats wealthy people better than those without money:** Alexandra Natapoff, "The Penal Pyramid," in *The New Criminal Justice Thinking*, eds. Sharon Dolovich and Alexandra Natapoff (New York: NYU Press, 2017).

160   **Rape carries a mandatory sentence of three years in prison:** Office of the Butler County Prosecutor, "Rape Penalty Sentencing," supremecourt.ohio.gov/Boards/Sentencing/resources/judPractitioner/rapeChart2018.pdf.

160   **And other sex offenses carry mandatory minimum penalties of five, ten, or fifteen years:** Ohio Revised Statutes § 2971.03(A)(3)(e).

164   **He brought the rule to the Ohio Supreme Court—which is responsible for writing the court rules in the state—but the justices there rejected it:** Randy Ludlow, "State Supreme Court rejects truth-in-sentencing rule," *The Columbus Dispatch* (Jan. 15, 2016).

164   **As of January 2019, he sits on the Ohio Supreme Court:** "Justice Michael P. Donnelly: 'My Journey in the Field of Law,'" *Daily* (Oct. 5, 2020), https://thedaily.case.edu/justice-michael-p-donnelly-my-journey-in-the-field-of-law-2/.

164   **Sexual assaults are rarely reported:** Lynn Langton, Marcus Berzofsky, Christopher Krebs, and Hope Smiley-McDonald, Bureau of Justice Statistics, *Special report—National crime victimization survey: Victimizations not reported to the police, 2006–2010* (August 2012), bjs.gov/content/pub/pdf/vnrp0610.pdf.

164   **Police are less likely to believe victims of sexual assault than victims in other types of cases:** Christine Mitchell and Benjamin Peterson, Utah Commission on Criminal and Juvenile Justice, *Rape in Utah 2007: A survey of Utah women* 33 (May 14, 2008), https://justice.utah.gov/wp-content/uploads/RapeinUtah2007.pdf.

164   **prosecutors will often refuse to bring charges even when police have arrested a suspect:** J. Bouffard, "Predicting type of sexual assault case closure from victim, suspect, and case characteristics," 28 *Journal of Criminal Justice* 527 (2000); C. Spohn, D. Beichner, and E. Davis-Frenzel, "Prosecutorial justifications for sexual assault case rejection: Guarding the 'gateway to justice,'" 48 *Social Problems* 206 (2001).

164   **As a result, even when they are reported, sexual assault cases rarely result in convictions:** Rose Corrigan, *Up Against a Wall: Rape Reform and the Failure of Success* 65–116 (New York: New York University Press, 2013); Wayne A. Kerstetter, "Gateway to Justice: Police and Prosecutorial Response to Sexual Assaults Against Women," 81 *Journal of Criminal Law and Criminology* 267 (1990).

164   **This practice is so common in federal court that it has a name: "swallowing the gun.":** Kay A. Knapp and Denis J. Hauptly, "State and Federal Sentencing Guidelines: Apples and Oranges," 25 *U.C. Davis Law Review* 679, 686 (1992); Herbert Wechsler, "Sentencing, Correction, and the Model Penal Code," 109 *University of Pennsylvania Law Review* 465, 470 (1961).

164   **New York has a harsh law that requires a mandatory sentence of three and a half years in prison for people who possess a loaded gun without a license:** NY Penal Law 265.03.

165   **And then he went on to say, "I don't think that anybody should be exempt from that . . .":** Associated Press, "Bloomberg Urges Full Prosecution of Burress, YouTube.com (Dec. 1, 2008), youtube.com/watch?v=iJ_jAQMMD-E.

165   **Burress took that deal and ended up serving two years in prison:** "Burress begins sentence in gun case," ESPN.com (Sept. 22, 2009), espn.com/nfl/news/story?id=4493887.

165   **Because of that we got the state legislature to pass a law that if you carry a loaded handgun, you get an automatic three-and-a-half years in the slammer.":** Associated Press, "Bloomberg Urges Full Prosecution of Burress, YouTube.com (Dec. 1, 2008), youtube.com/watch?v=iJ_jAQMMD-E.

166   **calls these cases "fictional pleas.":** Thea Johnson, "Fictional Pleas," 94 *Indiana Law Journal* 855 (2019).

167   **Johnson points out that the U.S. Supreme Court endorsed the practice in a case called _Padilla v. Kentucky_:** Thea Johnson, 867–868 (discussing _Padilla v. Kentucky_, 559 U.S. 356 (2010)).

167   **A lawyer who knows the immigration consequences of different convictions, the Supreme Court tells us, can engage in "plea bargaining creatively with the prosecutor.":** _Padilla v. Kentucky_, 559 U.S. 356, 373 (2010).

167   **But when the facts don't allow for a creative solution, Professor Johnson wrote in an article about this topic, then defense attorneys must "turn to fiction.":** Thea Johnson, 858.

168   **because it wasn't a drug crime, it didn't make him eligible for deportation under federal immigration law:** Thea Johnson, 864–865.

169   **she used that new evidence and an affidavit from Flynn to argue that Flynn should be permitted to withdraw his guilty plea because he wasn't actually guilty:** David Jackson and Kristine Phillips, "Trump says new FBI notes exonerate Michael Flynn, analysts say that's not the case," _USA Today_ (Apr. 30, 2020).

169   **abruptly filed a motion to dismiss all of the charges against Flynn:** Michael Balsamo and Eric Tucker, "New twist in Trump-Russia investigation: DOJ drops Flynn case," _Christian Science Monitor_ (May 7, 2020).

169   **He just couldn't remember what he'd talked about with the Russian ambassador:** Tobias Hoonhout, "Michael Flynn Explains Guilty Plea Withdrawal in New Filing: 'I Never Lied . . . I Am Innocent,'" _National Review_ (Jan. 29, 2020).

169   **Perjury—lying under oath—is a crime:** Josh Gerstein and Kyle Cheney, "Federal judge mulls contempt charge against Michael Flynn," _Politico_ (May 13, 2020), politico.com/news/2020/05/13/judge-appoints -retired-judge-to-represent-flynn-prosecution-256509.

170   **contains many references to interviews with Michael Flynn:** 1 Special counsel Robert S. Mueller, III, _Report on the Investigation into Russian Interference in the 2016 Presidential Election_ 147, 167–173 (Mar. 2019).

170   **the system "finds something sacrosanct and inviolable—even magical—in the bottom-line accuracy of the defendant's admission that she behaved (in some fashion) illegally.":** Josh Bowers, "Punishing the Innocent," 156 _University of Pennsylvania Law Review_ 1117, 1171 (2008).

171   **say, if they search someone's house without a warrant—then people can often keep this evidence from being used against them at trial:** _Mapp v. Ohio_, 367 U.S. 643 (1961).

171   **or they may be able to sue the police and collect money damages:** 42 U.S.C. § 1983.

171   **allows prosecutors to insist on the waiver of additional constitutional rights as part of the bargain:** _Town of Newton v. Rumery_, 480 U.S. 386 (1987).

171   **some courts allow defendants who plead guilty to file a civil suit for money damages if the police search was illegal:** _Gonzalez v. Entress_, 133 F.3d 551, 553–54 (7th Cir. 1998); _Beck v. City of Muskogee Police Department_, 195 F.3d 553, 558–59 (10th Cir. 1999).

171   others will not allow those civil suits unless the defendant first gets the guilty plea withdrawn or the conviction overturned: *Harvey v. Waldron*, 210 F.3d 1008, 1015 (9th Cir. 2000); *Schilling v. White*, 58 F.3d 1081, 1085–86 (6th Cir. 1995).

172   reason to believe that they will find evidence of a crime before they can search your car, especially the trunk: *Arizona v. Gant*, 556 U.S. 332 (2009); *United States v. Ross*, 456 U.S. 798 (1982); *New York v. Belton*, 453 U.S. 454 (1981).

172   your consent makes an otherwise illegal search constitutional: *United States v. Drayton*, 536 U.S. 194 (2002); *Schneckloth v. Bustamonte*, 412 U.S. 218 (1973).

175   trials also teach moral lessons; in particular they teach defendants that their criminal behavior was unacceptable while reaffirming society's commitment to its criminal laws: Stephanos Bibas, *The Machinery of Criminal Justice* 69–72 (Oxford: Oxford University Press, 2012).

178   they also send messages to victims: Stephanos Bibas, *The Machinery of Criminal Justice*, 84–88.

178   They were outraged not only by the lenient way he was treated but also by the denial of an opportunity to speak out about what happened to them and to have that pain and violence acknowledged: Mattie Kahn, "'This Is Not Our Shame': Five Survivors of Jeffrey Epstein's Abuse on Trauma, Justice, and Sisterhood," *Glamour* (Dec. 10, 2019).

179   But a juror also has the ability to nullify—to refuse to punish a defendant even if that defendant is guilty: *Sparf v. United States*, 156 U.S. 51 (1895); *Georgia v. Brailsford*, 3 U.S. (3 Dall.) 1 (1794); Paul Butler, "Racially Based Jury Nullification: Black Power in the Criminal Justice System," 105 *Yale Law Journal* 677 (1995).

180   if he had to choose between democratic participation in the legislature and democratic participation in the judicial branch in the form of juries, he would choose juries: Letter from Thomas Jefferson to the Abbe Arnoux (Jul. 19, 1789), reprinted in 15 *Papers of Thomas Jefferson* 282, 283 (J. Boyd ed. 1958).

180   Similarly, John Adams said, "The common people, should have as complete a control . . . in every judgment of a court" as in the legislature: John Adams, Diary Entry (Feb. 12, 1771), reprinted in 2 *Works of John Adams* 252, 253 (C. Adams ed. 1850).

180   More recently, Justice Antonin Scalia—a modern proponent of interpreting the Constitution according to its original meaning—called the jury "a fundamental reservation of power in our constitutional structure.": *Blakely v. Washington*, 542 U.S. 296, 306 (2004).

180   Three juries acquitted him: Keith Schneider, "Dr. Jack Kevorkian Dies at 83; A Doctor Who Helped End Lives," *New York Times* (Jun. 3, 2011).

180   he was later convicted of second-degree murder by a jury that decided not to nullify: Dirk Johnson, "Kevorkian Sentenced to 10 to 25 Years in Prison," *New York Times* (Apr. 4, 1999).

180   **they have acquired a nationwide reputation for nullification:** John Kifner, "Bronx Juries: a Defense Dream, a Prosecution Nightmare," *New York Times* (Dec. 5, 1988).

180   **Bronx juries acquitted nearly half of all defendants, as compared to less than 20 percent in the rest of the city:** Dean Balsamini, "Bronx delivers fewest convictions and Staten Island locks up the most," *New York Post* (Feb. 29, 2020).

181   **So the defendant shot him:** Robert E. Tomasson, "Man in Courthouse Shooting Is Acquitted," *New York Times* (Jul. 26, 1991).

Chapter 9

184   **he can get a brand-new trial in the formal district courts:** Sam Newton, "Justice Court Appeals: The Good, the Bad, and the Unintended," *Utah Bar Journal* 22 (Jan./Feb. 2005).

184   **Some other states have similar informal courts:** Hon. Michael J. McDermott, "Jurisdiction of NYS Justice Courts to Adjudicate Issues of Law and Equity," 37 *Westchester Bar Journal* 42 (2010); Anne E. Nelson, "Fifty-Eight Years and Counting: The Elusive Quest to Reform Arizona's Justice of the Peace Courts," 52 *Arizona Law Review* 533 (2010).

184   **which are drawn from cases that LDA has in the courts:** I created this chart using data that was provided to me by the Salt Lake Legal Defender Association. It covers cases from 2017 to 2018 that their office handled.

187   **formal procedures of modern trials contributed to the rise of guilty pleas and plea bargaining:** John H. Langbein, "Understanding the Short History of Plea Bargaining," 261.

187   **when those trials don't include a jury, then some of the benefits of trial are lost:** T. Ward Frampton, 183.

188   **Shima has done extensive research on risk and pretrial release:** Shima Baradaran Baughman, "Costs of Pretrial Detention," 97 *Boston University Law Review* 1 (2017); Shima Baradaran & Frank L. McIntyre, 497.

189   **police have repeatedly told the media that the state's new bail reform policy was responsible for a spike in shootings—even though law enforcement's own data showed that simply was not true:** Craig McCarthy, Carol Campanile, and Aaron Feis, "NYPD's own stats debunk claims of bail reform leading to spike in gun violence," *New York Post* (Jul. 8, 2020).

189   **managed to roll back some of the state's 2019 bail reforms soon after they were adopted:** Jeff Coltin, "How New York changed its bail law," *City & State New York* (Apr. 4, 2020), cityandstateny.com/articles/policy/criminal-justice/how-new-york-changed-its-bail-law.html.

190   **sentences should be capped at twenty years in prison except for the most egregious cases, like those involving serial killers:** Ashley Nellis, The Sentencing Project, *No End in Sight: America's Enduring Reliance on Life Imprisonment* (Feb. 17, 2021), sentencingproject .org/publications/no-end-in-sight-americas-enduring-reliance-on -life-imprisonment/; Marc Mauer, "A 20-Year Maximum for Prison

Sentences," 39 *Democracy* (Winter 2016), https://democracyjournal.org/magazine/39/a-20-year-maximum-for-prison-sentences/.

190   **Research suggests that extremely high sentences create "upward pressure" on all sentences:** Marc Mauer, "A Proposal to Reduce Time Served in Federal Prison," *Testimony to Charles Colson Task Force on Federal Corrections* 2–3 (Mar. 11, 2015), sentencingproject.org/publications/a-proposal-to-reduce-time-served-in-federal-prison/ (citing American Law Institute, *Model Penal Code—Sentencing, Tentative Draft No. 2* (2011) and Jonathan Simon, "How Should We Punish Murder?," 94 *Marquette Law Review* 1241, 1249 [2010–11]).

190   **one out of every seven people who are in prison is serving a life sentence:** Ashley Nellis, The Sentencing Project, *No End in Sight: America's Enduring Reliance on Life Imprisonment* (Feb. 17, 2021), sentencingproject.org/publications/no-end-in-sight-americas-enduring-reliance-on-life-imprisonment/.

190   **the number of people serving life sentences now exceeds the number of all people who were in prison in 1970:** The Sentencing Project, *People Serving Life Exceeds Entire Prison Population of 1970* (Feb. 2020), sentencingproject.org/wp-content/uploads/2020/02/People-Serving-Life-Exceeds-Entire-Prison-Population-of-1970.pdf.

193   **In a series of opinions that he wrote in 2017 and 2018:** *United States v. Stevenson*, 425 F. Supp. 3d 647 (S.D.W. Va. 2018); *United States v. Walker*, 423 F.Supp.3d 281, 295 (S.D.W. Va. 2017); *United States v. Wilmore*, 282 F. Supp. 3d 937 (S.D.W. Va. 2017).

193   **The rules that set the procedures for federal criminal cases say that a judge may either accept or reject a plea bargain:** Federal Rule of Criminal Procedure 11(c)(3), (4), (5); *In re* Morgan, 506 F.3d 705, 708 (9th Cir. 2007) (noting "the broad discretion that district courts enjoy when choosing to accept or reject plea agreements").

194   **the notes from the committee that wrote the rule make clear that the judge is free to choose his own criteria:** Federal Rules of Criminal Procedure 11 advisory committee's note to 1974 amendments ("The plea agreement procedure does not attempt to define criteria for the acceptance or rejection of a plea agreement. Such a decision is left to the discretion of the individual trial judge.").

195   **By 2016 that number plummeted to 0.29 trials per federal prosecutor employee and 2.79 trials per federal judge:** *United States v. Walker*, 423 F. Supp. 3d 281, 295 (S.D.W. Va. 2017).

195   **Neither was, as he put it in one of his opinions, "overburdened by trials.":** *United States v. Walker*, 423 F. Supp. 3d 281, 296 (S.D.W. Va. 2017).

195   **(As a constitutional matter, courtrooms have to be open to the public except in rare circumstances.):** *Globe Newspaper Co. v. Superior Court for Norfolk County*, 457 U.S. 596 (1982); *Richmond Newspapers, Inc. v. Virginia*, 448 U.S. 555 (1980).

196   **judge and jury are merely stage props to convince the general public that the criminal justice system they see nightly on television is being busily played out in the big courtroom downtown.":** *United States v. Stevenson*, 425 F. Supp. 3d 647, 658 (S.D.W. Va. 2018).

197   **in order to make sure that he can punish any prosecutor who fails to turn over this evidence:** Hon. Emmet G. Sullivan, "Enforcing Compliance with Constitutionally-Required Disclosures: A Proposed Rule," *Cardozo Law Review de novo* 138, 141 (2016).

197   **prosecutors from the Department of Justice had failed to disclose exculpatory evidence to Stevens's defense attorneys:** Neil A. Lewis, "Tables Turned on Prosecution in Stevens Case," *New York Times* (Apr. 7, 2009).

197   **found that prosecutors had violated Stevens's constitutional rights to have that material turned over before trial:** Del Quentin Wilber and Sari Horwitz, "Prosecutors concealed evidence in Ted Stevens case, report finds," *Washington Post* (Mar. 15, 2012).

198   **Unfortunately, Ted Stevens didn't live to see Judge Sullivan's response to Department of Justice's misconduct: he died before the investigation was concluded:** William Yardley and Liz Robbins, "Former Senator Ted Stevens Killed in Plane Crash," *New York Times* (Aug. 10, 2010).

198   **"that is favorable to defendant":** A copy of Judge Sullivan's standing order can be found at https://www.dcd.uscourts.gov/sites/dcd/files/StandingBradyOrder _November2017.pdf.

201   **more than a dozen states allow judges to reject plea bargains that they think are inappropriate:** Andrew Manuel Crespo, "The Hidden Law of Plea Bargaining," 118 *Columbia Law Review* 1303, 1363–1364 (2018).

201   **These rules could help to regulate the plea bargaining process and make it fairer for everyone:** Andrew Manuel Crespo, 1368–1379.

201   **She ran on a platform that included ending cash bail and refusing to prosecute low-level marijuana cases:** Rachel Weiner, "In Arlington, veteran prosecutor under fire from the left," *Washington Post* (Jun. 5, 2019).

201   **She was one of several reform prosecutors elected in Northern Virginia that year:** Justin Jouvenal, "'A sea change' for prosecutors in Northern Virginia as liberal democratic candidates sweep races," *Washington Post* (Nov. 5, 2019).

201   **and since her election, Dehghani-Tafti has captured headlines by filing a lawsuit against the judges in her jurisdiction:** Tom Jackman, "Arlington prosecutor goes to Va. Supreme Court against judges who challenge her new policies," *Washington Post* (Aug. 28, 2020).

202   **a demand that Dehghani-Tafti says exceeds the judges' authority:** Parisa Dehghani-Tafti, "Opinion: Why I am fighting for prosecutorial discretion in Arlington," *Washington Post* (Aug. 21, 2020).

204   **The decision of prosecutors not to prosecute certain crimes has drawn a lot of criticism:** Carissa Byrne Hessick and F. Andrew Hessick, "The National Police Association Is Throwing a Fit Over Prosecutorial Discretion," *Slate* (Jan. 4, 2019); Maria Cramer, "DA candidate Rachael Rollins hailed nationally, but locally her plan not to prosecute petty crimes alarms some," *Boston Globe* (Sept. 12, 2018).

204   **"One of the original Freedom Riders, Joan Trumpauer Mulholland:** Loki Mullholland, *She Stood for Freedom: The Untold Story of a Civil Rights Hero, Joan Trumpauer Mulholland* (2016).

205   **Some academics have attributed the initial decisions to criminalize marijuana to racism:** Doris Marie Provine, *Unequal Under Law: Race in the War on Drugs* 81–86 (Chicago: University of Chicago Press, 2007).

205   **pointing to a higher correlation between alcohol and violence than for marijuana:** Studies appear to confirm this. E.B. De Sousa Fernandes Perna, et al., "Subjective aggression during alcohol and cannabis intoxication before and after aggression exposure," 233 *Psychopharmacology* 3331 (2016); Peter N.S. Hoaken and Sherry H. Stewart, "Drugs of abuse and the elicitation of human aggressive behavior," 28 *Addictive Behaviors* 1533 (2003).

206   **an open letter to Stamos, criticizing her for securing 98 percent of her convictions from plea bargains rather than trials—a rate that was much higher than neighboring counties:** Rachel Weiner, "In Arlington, veteran prosecutor under fire from the left," *Washington Post* (Jun. 5, 2019).

207   **wrote an op-ed in the *Washington Post* defending her power:** Parisa Dehghani-Tafti, "Opinion: Why I am fighting for prosecutorial discretion in Arlington," *Washington Post* (Aug. 21, 2020).

207   **and inspired lawmakers to introduce a bill in the state legislature that would guarantee prosecutors the power even if judges object:** Margaret Matray, "Prosecutors will be able to drop marijuana cases — and others — under new law inspired by Norfolk," *Virginian-Pilot* (Oct. 22, 2020).

207   **Under Massachusetts law, Rollins had the authority to decide not to pursue the case:** *Commonwealth v. Webber,* No. SJ-2019–0366, 2019 WL 4263308, at *1 (Mass. Sept. 9, 2019) ("The prosecutor's sole authority to determine which cases to prosecute, and when not to pursue a prosecution, has been affirmed repeatedly by this court since the beginning of the nineteenth century."); Joey Garrison, "Straight Pride Parade fallout: Boston DA wins fight over counter protester arrests," *USA Today* (Sept. 9, 2019).

208   **Rollins has said that she wants to have her office turn over more evidence before defendants plea bargain:** law.nyu.edu/centers/admin ofcriminallaw/events/plea-bargaining "Whither the Prosecutor" panel at 1:10:00.

213   **A report that the groups released explained that, because plea bargaining is all done verbally, and because there are no records kept of those negotiations, the report could not include any statistical information about it:** Reclaim Chicago, the People's Lobby, Chicago Council of Lawyers, and Chicago Appleseed Fund for Justice, *Creating a Culture of Fairness and Accountability: Defense attorneys report on Kim Foxx's progress towards transforming the priorities of her office* 4 (Oct. 2019), chicagoappleseed.org/wp -content/uploads/2019/10/2019–10-Report-Kim-Foxx_ForPrint_FINAL .pdf.

213   **more likely to either immediately divert the case to a program that only required defendants to take a low-cost or free education class on drug use or just dismiss the case entirely:** Reclaim Chicago, the People's Lobby, Chicago Council of Lawyers, and Chicago Appleseed Fund for Justice, *Creating a Culture of Fairness and Accountability: Defense attorneys report on Kim Foxx's*

progress towards transforming the priorities of her office 5–6 (October 2019), chicagoappleseed.org/wp-content/uploads/2019/10/2019-10-Report-Kim -Foxx_ForPrint_FINAL.pdf.

Chapter 10

217 **Hundreds of people who were found guilty at trial have since been exonerated by DNA evidence.** Daniel S. Medwed, "Talking about a Revolution: A Quarter Century of DNA Exonerations," in *Wrongful Convictions and the DNA Revolution: Twenty-Five Years of Freeing the Innocent,* ed. Daniel S. Medwed, 1, 4 (Cambridge, UK: Cambridge University Press, 2017).

217 **he was able to identify a number of problems contributed to those false convictions:** Brandon L. Garrett, *Convicting the Innocent: Where Criminal Prosecutions Go Wrong* (Cambridge, Massachusetts: Harvard University Press, 2012).

217 **But not much has been done to change those law enforcement tactics:** Carissa Byrne Hessick, "DNA Exonerations and the Elusive Promise of Criminal Justice Reform," 15 *Ohio State Journal of Criminal Law* 271, 275 (2017).

217 **But only ten states have made reforms:** Stephanie Roberts Hartung, "Post-Conviction Procedure: The Next Frontier in Innocence Reform," in *Wrongful Convictions and the DNA Revolution: Twenty-Five Years of Freeing the Innocent,* 247, 248.

217 **Most states don't even require police to videotape their interrogations:** Stephanie Roberts Hartung, 247, 249–250.

219 **Initially, the number of trials increased and bargaining appeared to be mostly limited to a small number of cases that were specifically approved by the attorney general or his top staff:** Alaska Judicial Council, *Alaska's Plea Bargaining Ban Re-evaluated* 3–4 (Jan. 1991), ojp.gov/pdffiles1/ Digitization/128812NCJRS.pdf; Teresa White Carns & Dr. John Kruse, *A Re-evaluation of Alaska's Plea Bargaining Ban,* 8 *Alaska Law Review* 27, 32–33 (1991).

219 **Some attorneys who were interviewed for the study didn't even realize that a plea bargaining ban was even in effect!:** Alaska Judicial Council, *Alaska's Plea Bargaining Ban Re-evaluated* 7 (Jan. 1991), ojp.gov/pdffiles1/ Digitization/128812NCJRS.pdf.

219 **A study of Alaska's criminal cases during the years 2005 to 2012 found that 97 percent of defendants who were convicted of a felony had pleaded guilty:** Brad A. Myrstol, Alaska Justice Statistical Analysis Center, "Alaska Superior CourtFelony Case Processing, 2005–2012 at 2 (May 2013), https://scholarworks.alaska.edu/bitstream/handle/11122/2595/ajsac.13–05 .superior_courts_felonies.pdf?sequence=4&isAllowed=y.

219 **there have been a few instances of local bans:** Robert A. Weninger, "The Abolition of Plea Bargaining: A Case Study of El Paso County, Texas," 35 *UCLA Law Review* 265, 294 n.115 (1987) (collecting examples).

219 **The trial rate jumped from 21 percent to more than 40 percent:** Robert A. Weninger, 292 tbl. 1.

219   **Even under the official ban, the district attorney permitted plea bargaining in death penalty cases, sexual assault cases, and cases in which defendants agreed to cooperate against others:** Robert A. Weninger, 296.

219   **individual prosecutors routinely defied office policy and plea bargained other cases, sometimes with a judge's approval:** Robert A. Weninger, 307–308.

220   **the district attorney had threatened to fire any prosecutors who negotiated a plea in violation of office policy:** Robert A. Weninger, 309.

220   **The bans in Alaska and El Paso were eventually lifted:** "A deal you can't refuse," *The Economist* (Nov. 11, 2017), economist.com/interna tional/2017/11/09/the-troubling-spread-of-plea-bargaining-from-america -to-the-world. Although the state's 1975 ban was lifted in the 1990s, the Alaska Attorney General reinstituted a ban of plea bargaining in some cases in 2013. Jill Burke, "Will Alaska's plea bargain plan serve justice, or cause it to grind to a halt?," *Anchorage Daily* (Aug. 13, 2013).

220   **This change not only resulted in weaker cases never being filed but also required police to perform better investigations than before:** Alaska Judicial Council, *Alaska's Plea Bargaining Ban Re-evaluated* 12–13 (Jan. 1991), ojp.gov/pdffiles1/Digitization/128812NCJRS.pdf.

221   **If a case was overcharged, then a jury was more likely to acquit, which would be embarrassing for the office:** Robert A. Weninger, 299.

INDEX